JavaScript and JQuery

Carson King

ISBN-13: 978-1984075420

Contents

iii

3 STRING SCANNING   37

4 CHARACTERS, CSETS, AND STRINGS   47

Contents

Contents

Appendixes

Contents

1

Getting Started

This chapter introduces a few basic concepts of Icon — enough to get started. Subsequent chapters discuss these concepts in greater detail.

PROGRAM STRUCTURE

A good way to learn a programming language is to write programs. There is a fine tradition for beginning to learn a new programming language by writing a program that produces a greeting. In Icon this takes the form:

```
procedure main()
    write("Hello world")
end
```

This program writes Hello world.

The reserved words procedure and end bracket a procedure declaration. The procedure name is main. Every program must have a procedure with the name main; this is where program execution begins. Most programs, except the simplest ones, consist of several procedures.

Procedure declarations contain expressions that are evaluated when the procedure is called. The call of the function write simply writes its argument, a string that is given literally in enclosing quotation marks. When execution of a procedure reaches its end, it returns. When the main procedure returns, program execution stops.

To illustrate the use of procedures, the preceding program can be divided into two procedures as follows:

```
procedure main()
   hello()
end

procedure hello()
   write("Hello world")
end
```

Note that **main** and **hello** are procedures, while **write** is a function that is built into the Icon language. Procedures and functions are used in the same way. The only distinction between the two is that functions are built into Icon, while procedures are declared in programs. The procedure **hello** writes the greeting and returns to **main**. The procedure **main** then returns, terminating program execution.

Expressions in the body of a procedure are evaluated in the order in which they appear. Therefore, the program

```
procedure main()
   write("Hello world")
   write("  this is a new beginning")
end
```

writes two lines:

```
Hello world
  this is a new beginning
```

Procedures may have parameters, which are given in a list enclosed in the parenthe-ses that follow the procedure name in the declaration. For example, the program

```
procedure main()
   greet("Hello", "world")
end

procedure greet(what, who)
   write(what)
```

```
        write(who)

    end
```

writes

```
    Hello
    world
```

Like most programming languages, Icon has both values and variables that have values. This is illustrated by

```
procedure main()

    line := "Hello world"
    write(line)

end
```

The operation

```
    line := "Hello world"
```

assigns the value "Hello world" to the identifier line, which is a variable. The value of line is then passed to the function write.

All 256 ASCII characters may occur in strings. Strings may be written literally as in the example above, and they can be computed in a variety of ways. There is no limit on the length of a string except the amount of memory available. The empty string, given literally by "", contains no characters; its length is 0.

Identifiers must begin with a letter or underscore, which may be followed by other letters, digits, and underscores. Upper- and lowercase letters are distinct. Examples of identifiers are comp, Label, test10, and entry_value. There are other kinds of variables besides identifiers; these are described in later chapters.

Note that there is no declaration for the identifier line. Scope declarations, which are described in Chapter 8, are optional for local identifiers. In the absence of a scope declaration, an identifier is assumed to be local to the procedure in which it occurs, as is the case with line. Local identifiers are created when a procedure is called and are destroyed when the procedure returns. A local identifier can only be accessed in the procedure call in which it is created.

Most identifiers are local. The default to local is an example of a design philosophy of Icon: Common usages usually default automatically without the need for the programmer to write them out.

Icon has no type or storage declarations. Any variable can have any type of value. The correctness of types is checked when operations are performed. Storage for values is provided automatically. The programmer need not be concerned about it.

The character # in a program signals the beginning of a comment. The # and the remaining characters on the line are ignored when the program is compiled. An example of the use of comments is

```
# This procedure illustrates the use of parameters. The
# first parameter provides the message, while the second
# parameter specifies the recipient.
#
procedure greet(what, who)

   write(what)              # message
   write(who)               # recipient

end
```

Note that the end of a line terminates a comment. Each line of a multi-line comment must have a #.

If a # occurs in a quoted literal, it stands for itself and does not signal the beginning of a comment. Therefore,

```
write("#======#")
```

writes

```
#======#
```

SUCCESS AND FAILURE

The function read() reads a line. For example,

```
write(read())
```

reads a line and writes it out. Note that the value produced by read() is the argument of write().

The function read() is one of a number of expressions in Icon that may either *succeed* or *fail*. If an expression succeeds, it produces a value, such as a line of input. If an expression fails, it produces no value. In the case of read(), failure occurs when the end of the input file is reached. The term *outcome* is used to describe the result of evaluating an expression, whether it is success or failure.

Expressions that may succeed or fail are called *conditional expressions*. Comparison operations, for example, are conditional expressions. The expression

```
count > 0
```

succeeds if the value of count is greater than 0 but fails if the value of count is not greater than 0.

As a general rule, failure occurs if a relation does not hold or if an operation cannot be performed but is not actually erroneous. For example, failure occurs when an attempt is made to read but when there are no more lines. Failure is an important part of the design philosophy of Icon. It accounts for the fact that there are situations in which operations cannot be performed. It corresponds to many real-world situations and allows programs to be formulated in terms of attempts to perform computations, the recognition of failure, and the possibility of alternatives.

Two other conditional expressions are find(s1, s2) and match(s1, s2). These functions succeed if s1 is a *substring* of s2 but fail otherwise. A substring is a string that occurs in another string. The function find(s1, s2) succeeds if s1 occurs anywhere in s2, while match(s1, s2) succeeds only if s1 is an *initial* substring that occurs at the beginning of s2. For example,

        find("on", "slow motion")

succeeds, since "on" is contained in "slow motion", but

        find("on", "radio noise")

fails, since "on" is not a *substring* of "radio noise" because of the intervening blank between the "o" and the "n". Similarly,

        match("on", "slow motion")

fails, since "on" does not occur at the beginning of "slow motion". On the other hand,

        match("slo", "slow motion")

succeeds.

If an expression that fails is an argument in another expression, the other expression fails also, since there is no value for its argument. For example, in

        write(read())

if read() fails, there is nothing to write. The function write() is not called and the whole expression fails.

The context in which failure occurs is important. Consider

        line := read()
        write(line)

If read() succeeds, the value it produces is assigned to line. If read() fails, however, no new value is assigned to line, because read() is an argument of the assignment operation. There is no value to assign to line if read() fails, no assignment is performed, and the value of line is not changed. The assignment is *conditional* on the success of read(). Since

```
line := read()
```

and

```
write(line)
```

are separate expressions, the failure of read() does not affect write(line); it just writes whatever value line had previously.

CONTROL STRUCTURES

Control structures use the success or failure of an expression to govern the evalua-tion of other expressions. For example,

```
while line := read() do
   write(line)
```

repeatedly evaluates read() in a loop. Each time read() succeeds, the value it produces is assigned to line and write(line) is evaluated to write that value. When read() fails, however, the assignment operation fails and the loop terminates. In other words, the success or failure of the expression that follows while controls evaluation of the expression that follows do.

Note that assignment is an expression. It can be used anywhere that any expression is allowed.

Words like while and do, which distinguish control structures, are reserved and cannot be used as identifiers. A complete list of reserved words is given in Appendix A.

Another frequently used control structure is if-then-else, which selects one of two expressions to evaluate, depending on the success or failure of a conditional expression. For example,

```
if count > 0 then sign := 1 else sign := –1
```

assigns 1 to sign if the value of count is greater than 0, but assigns –1 to sign otherwise. The else clause is optional, as in if count > 0 then sign := 1

which assigns a value to sign only if count is greater than 0.

PROCEDURES

Procedures are the major units of a program. Each procedure in a program typically performs a separate logical task. Some examples follow.

The following procedure prints only the lines that contain the string s:

```
procedure locate(s)

   while line := read() do
      if find(s, line) then write(line)

end
```

For example,

```
procedure main()

   locate("fancy")

end
```

writes all the lines of the input file that contain an occurrence of the string "fancy".

This procedure is more useful if it also writes the numbers of the lines that contain s. To do this, it is necessary to count each line as it is read:

```
procedure locate(s)

   lineno := 0

   while line := read() do
      { lineno := lineno + 1
      if find(s, line) then write(lineno, ": ", line)
      }
end
```

The braces in this procedure enclose a *compound expression*, which in this case consists of two expressions. One expression increments the line number and the other writes the line if it contains the desired substring. Compound expressions must be used wherever one expression is expected by Icon's syntax but several are needed.

Note that write() has three arguments in this procedure. The function write() can be called with many arguments; the values of the arguments are written one after another, all on the same line. In this case there is a line number, followed by a colon and a blank, followed by the line itself.

To illustrate the use of this procedure, consider an input file that consists of the following song from Shakespeare's play *The Merchant of Venice*:

>Tell me, where is fancy bred,
>Or in the heart or in the head?
>How begot, how nourished?
>   Reply, reply.
>It is engender'd in the eyes,
>With gazing fed; and fancy dies
>In the cradle where it lies:
> Let us all ring fancy's knell;
>I'll begin it, – Ding, dong, bell.

The lines written by locate("fancy") are:

>1: Tell me, where is fancy bred, 6:
>With gazing fed; and fancy dies 8:
>Let us all ring fancy's knell;

This example illustrates one of the more important features of Icon: the automatic conversion of values from one type to another. The first argument of write() in this example is an integer. Since write() expects to write strings, this integer is converted to a string; it is not necessary to specify conversion. This is another example of a default, which makes programs shorter and saves the need to explicitly specify routine actions where they clearly are the natural thing to do.

Like other expressions, procedure calls may produce values. The reserved word return is used to indicate a value to be returned from a procedure call. For example,

```
procedure countm(s)

   count := 0

   while line := read() do
      if match(s, line) then count := count + 1

   return count

end
```

produces a count of the number of input lines that begin with s.

A procedure call also can fail. This is indicated by the reserved word fail, which causes the procedure call to terminate but fail instead of producing a value. For example, the procedure

```
    procedure countm(s)
        count := 0
        while line := read() do
            if match(s, line) then count := count + 1
        if count > 0 then return count else fail
    end
```

produces a count of the number of lines that begin with **s**, provided that the count is greater than 0. The procedure fails, however, if no line begins with the string **s**.

EXPRESSION SYNTAX

Icon has several types of expressions, as illustrated in the preceding sections. Literals such as "Hello world" and 0 are expressions that designate values literally. Identifiers, such as line, are also expressions.

Function and procedure calls, such as

```
    write(line)
```

and

```
    greet("Hello", "world")
```

are expressions in which parentheses enclose arguments.

Operators are used to provide a concise, easily recognizable syntax for common operations. For example, $-i$ produces the negative of i, while $i + j$ produces the sum of i and j. The term argument is used for both operators and functions to describe the expressions on which they operate.

Infix operations, such as $i + j$ and $i * j$, have precedences that determine which operations apply to which arguments when they are used in combination. For example,

```
    i + j * k
```

groups as

```
    i + (j * k)
```

since multiplication has higher precedence than addition, as is conventional in numerical computation.

Associativity determines how expressions group when there are several occurrences of the same operation in combination. For example, subtraction associ-ates from left to right so that

i − j − k

groups as

(i − j) − k

On the other hand, exponentiation associates from right to left so that

i ^ j ^ k

groups as

i ^ (j ^ k)

Assignment also associates from right to left.

The precedences and associativities of various operations are mentioned as the operations are introduced in subsequent chapters. Appendix A summarizes the precedences and associativities of all operations.

Parentheses can be used to group expressions in desired ways, as in

(i + j) * k

Since there are many operations in Icon with various precedences and associativi-ties, it is safest to use parentheses to assure that operations group in the desired way, especially for operations that are not used frequently.

Where the expressions in a compound expression appear on the same line, they must be separated by semicolons. For example,

```
while line := read() do {
  count := count + 1
  if find(s, line) then write(line)
  }
```

also can be written as

```
while line := read() do
  {count := count + 1; if find(s, line) then write(line)}
```

Programs usually are easier to read if the expressions in a compound expression are written on separate lines, in which case semicolons are not needed.

Unlike many programming languages, Icon has no statements; it just has expressions. Even control structures, such as

if *expr1* then *expr2* else *expr3*

are expressions. The outcome of such a control structure is the outcome of *expr2* or *expr3*, whichever is selected. Even though control structures are expressions, they usually are not used in ways that the values they produce are important. They usually stand alone as if they were statements, as illustrated by the examples in this chapter.

Keywords, consisting of the character & followed by one of a number of specific words, are used to designate special operations that require no arguments. For example, the value of &time is the number of milliseconds of processing time since the beginning of program execution.

Any argument of a function, procedure, operator, or control structure may be any expression, however complicated that expression is. There are no distinctions among the kinds of expressions; any kind of expression can be used in any context where an expression is legal.

PREPROCESSING

Icon programs are preprocessed before they are compiled. During preprocessing, constants can be defined, other files inserted, code can be included or excluded, depending on the definition of constants, and so on.

Preprocessor directives are indicated by a $ at the beginning of a line, as in

$define Limit 100

which defines the symbol Limit and gives it the value 100. Subsequently, whenever Limit appears, it is replaced by 100 prior to compilation. Thus,

if count > Limit then write("limit reached")

becomes

if count > 100 then write("limit reached")

The text of a definition need not be a number. For example,

$define suits "SHDC"

defines suits to be a four-character string.

Another useful preprocessor directive allows a file to be included in a pro-gram. For example,

> $include "disclaim.icn"

inserts the contents of the file "disclaim.icn" in place of the $include directive.

Other preprocessor directives and matters related to preprocessing are de-scribed in Appendix C.

NOTES

Notation and Terminology

In describing what operators and functions do, the fact that their arguments may be syntactically complicated is not significant. It is the values produced by these expressions that are important.

Icon has several types of data: strings, integers, real numbers, and so forth. Many functions and operations require specific types of data for their arguments. Single letters are used in this book to indicate the types of arguments. The letters are chosen to indicate the types that operations and functions expect. These letters usually are taken from the first character of the type name. For example, i indicates an argument that is expected to be an integer, while s indicates an argument that is expected to be a string. For example, –i indicates the operation of computing the negative of the integer i, while i1 + i2 indicates the operation of adding the integers i1 and i2. This notation is extended following usual mathematical conventions, so that j and k also are used to indicate integers. Other types are indicated in a similar fashion. Finally, x and y are used for arguments that are of unknown type or that may have one of several types. Chapter 10 discusses types in more detail.

This notation does not mean that arguments must be written as identifiers. As mentioned previously, any argument can be an expression, no matter how compli-cated that expression is. The use of letters to stand for expressions is just a device that is used in this book for conciseness and to emphasize the expected data types of arguments. These are only conventions. The letters in identifiers have no meaning to Icon. For example, the value of s in a program could be an integer. In situations where the type produced by an expression is not important, the notation *expr*, *expr1*, *expr2*, and so on is used. Therefore,

> while *expr1* do *expr2*

emphasizes that the control structure is concerned with the evaluation of its arguments, not with their values or their types.

In describing functions, phrases such as "the function match(s1, s2) ... " are used to indicate the name of a function and the number and types of its arguments.

Strictly speaking, match(s1, s2) is not a function but rather a *call* of the function match. The shorter phraseology is used when there can be no confusion about its meaning. In describing function calls in places where the specific arguments are not relevant, the arguments are omitted, as in write(). Similarly, other readily under-stood abbreviations are used. For example, "an integer between 1 and i" sometimes is used in place of "an integer between 1 and the value of i".

As illustrated by examples in this chapter, different typefaces are used to distinguish program material and terminology. The sans serif typeface denotes literal program text, such as procedure and read(). Italics are used for expressions such as *expr*.

Running an Icon Program

The best way to learn a new programming language is to write programs in it. Just entering the simple examples in this chapter and then extending them will teach you a lot.

Chapter 14 describes how to run Icon programs. All you need to get started is to know how to name Icon files and how to compile and execute them. Although this varies somewhat from platform to platform, in command-line environments like MS-DOS and UNIX, it's this simple:

- Enter an Icon program in a file with the suffix .icn. An example is hello.icn.

- At the command-line prompt, enter

   icont hello.icn

- The result is an executable file that starts with hello and may end with .exe or have no suffix at all. In any event, from the command-line prompt, enter

   hello

   to run the program.

If you are using a visual environment rather than a command-line one, the steps will be somewhat different. Consult the Icon user manual for your platform. See Appendix J for sources of Icon and documentation about it.

The Icon Program Library

The Icon program library contains a large collection of programs and proce-dures (Griswold and Townsend, 1996). The programs range from games to utilities. The procedures contain reusable code that extends Icon's built-in repertoire.

Library procedures are organized into modules. A module may contain one or many procedures. A module can be added to a program using the link declaration, as in

```
link strings

procedure main()
    ...
```

which adds the module strings to a program.

Useful material in the program library is mentioned at appropriate places in this book. The use of library procedures and ways of creating new library proce-dures are described in Chapter 15.

See Appendix J for information on how to get the Icon program library.

Testing Icon Expressions Interactively

Although Icon itself does not provide a way to enter and evaluate individual expressions interactively, there is a program in the Icon program library that does. This program, named qei, allows a user to type an expression and see the result of its evaluation. Successive expressions accumulate and results are assigned to variables so that previous results can be used in subsequent computations.

At the > prompt, an expression can be entered, followed by a semicolon and a return. (If a semicolon is not provided, subsequent lines are included until there is a semicolon.) The computation is then performed and the result is shown as an assignment to a variable, starting with r1_ and continuing with r2_, r3_, and so on. Here is an example of a simple interaction.

```
>    1 + 3;
     r1_ := 4
>    r1_ * 10;
     r2_ := 40
```

If an expression fails, qei responds with Failure, as in

```
>    1 < 0;
     Failure
```

The program qei has several other useful features, such as optionally showing the types of results. To get a brief summary of qei's features and how to use them, enter :help followed by a return.

Syntactic Considerations

The value of a constant defined by preprocessing can be any string. The string simply is substituted for subsequent uses of the defined symbol. For example,

```
$define Sum i + j
```

defines Sum to be i + j and i + j is substituted wherever sum appears subsequently. In such uses, expressions should be parenthesized to assure proper grouping. For example, in

    k * Sum

the result of substitution is

    k * i + j

which groups as

    (k * i) + j

which presumably is not what is wanted and certainly does not produce the result suggested by

    k * Sum

On the other hand

    $define Sum (i + j)

produces the expected result:

    k * (i + j)

2

Expressions

The evaluation of expressions causes the computations that are performed during program execution. Icon has a large repertoire of functions and operations, each of which performs a different kind of computation.

The most important aspect of expression evaluation in Icon is that the outcome of evaluating an expression may be a single result, no result at all (failure), or a sequence of results (generation). The possibilities of failure and generation distin-guish Icon from most other programming languages and give it its unusual expressive capability. These possibilities also make expression evaluation a more important topic than it is in most other programming languages.

Several control structures in Icon are specifically concerned with failure and generation. This chapter introduces the basic concepts of expression evaluation in Icon. Chapter 7 contains additional information about expression evaluation.

SEQUENTIAL EVALUATION

In the absence of control structures, expressions in an Icon procedure are evaluated in the order in which they appear; this is called sequential evaluation. Where expressions are nested, inner expressions are evaluated first to provide values for outer ones. For example, in

```
i := k + j
write(i)
```

the values of k and j are added to provide the value assigned to i. Next, the value of i is written. The two lines also could be combined into one, as

        write(i := k + j)

although the former version is more readable and generally better style.

The sequential nature of expression evaluation is familiar and natural. It is mentioned here because of the possibilities of failure and generation. Consider, for example

        i := find(s1, s2)
        write(i)

As shown in Chapter 1, find(s1, s2) may produce a single result or it may fail. It may also generate a sequence of results.

The single-result case is easy — it is just like

        i := k + j

in which addition always produces a single result.

Suppose that find(s1, s2) fails. There is no value to assign to i and the assignment is not performed. The effect is as if the assignment failed because one of its arguments failed. Consequently, in

        i := find(s1, s2)
        write(i)

if find(s1, s2) fails, i is not changed, and execution continues with write(i), which writes the value i had prior to the evaluation of these two lines. It generally is not good programming practice to let possible failure go undetected. This subject is discussed in more detail later.

Since a substring can occur in a string at more than one place, find(s1, s2) can have more than one possible result. The results are generated, as needed, in order from left to right. In the example above, assignment needs only one result, so the first result is assigned to i and sequential execution continues (writing the newly assigned value of i). The other possible results of find(s1, s2) are not produced.

The next section illustrates situations in which a generator may produce more than one result.

GOAL-DIRECTED EVALUATION

Failure during the evaluation of an expression causes previously evaluated genera-tors to produce additional values. This is called *goal-directed evaluation*, since failure of a part of an expression does not necessarily cause the entire expression to fail; instead other possibilities are tried in an attempt to find a combination of values that makes the entire expression succeed.

Goal-directed evaluation is illustrated by the following expression

if find(s1, s2) > 10 then write("good location")

Suppose s1 occurs in s2 at positions 2, 8, 12, 20, and 30. The first value produced by find(s1, s2) is 2, and the comparison is:

2 > 10

This comparison fails, which causes find(s1, s2) to produce its next value, 8. The comparison again fails, and find(s1, s2) produces 12. The comparison now succeeds and good location is written. Note that find(s1, s2) does not produce the values 20 or 30. As in assignment, once the comparison succeeds, no more values are needed.

Observe how natural the formulation

find(s1, s2) > 10

is. It embodies in a concise way a conceptually simple computation. Try formulating this computation in Pascal or C for comparison. This method of expression evalu-ation is used very frequently in Icon programs. It is a large part of what makes Icon programs short and easy to write. It is not necessary to think about all the details of what is going on.

Failure may cause expression evaluation to go back to a previously evaluated expression. For example, in the preceding example, failure of a comparison opera-tion caused evaluation to return to a function that had already produced a value. This is called *control backtracking*. Control backtracking only happens in the presence of generators. An expression that produces a value and may be capable of producing another one *suspends*. Instead of just producing a value and "going away", it keeps track of what it was doing and remains "in the background" in case it is needed again. Failure causes a suspended generator to be *resumed* so that it may produce another value. If a generator is resumed but has no more values, its resumption fails. While the term *failure* is used to describe an expression that produces no value at all, a resumed generator that does not produce a value (*failed resumption*) has the same effect on expression evaluation — there is no value to use in an outer expression.

Note that when an outer computation succeeds there may be suspended generators. They are discarded when there is no longer any need for them.

ITERATION

It is not necessary to rely on failure and goal-directed evaluation to produce several values from a generator. In fact, there are many situations in which all (or most) of the values of a generator are needed, but without any concept of failure. The *iteration* control structure

       every *expr1* do *expr2*

is provided for these situations. In this control structure, *expr1* is first evaluated and then repeatedly resumed to produce all its values. *expr2* is evaluated for every value that is produced by *expr1*.

For example,

```
every i := find(s1, s2) do
   write(i)
```

writes all the values produced by find(s1, s2). Note that the repeated resumption of find(s1, s2) provides a sequence of values for assignment. Thus, as many assign-ments are performed as there are values for find(s1, s2).

The do clause is optional. This expression can be written more compactly as

```
every write(find(s1, s2))
```

INTEGER SEQUENCES

Icon has several expressions that generate sequences of values. One of the most useful is

       i to j by k

which generates the integers from i to j in increments of k. The by clause is optional; if it is omitted, the increment is 1. For example,

```
$define Limit 10

every i := 1 to Limit do
   write(i ^ 2)
```

writes the squares 1, 4, 9, 16, 25, 36, 49, 64, 81, and 100.

Note that iteration in combination with integer generation corresponds to the for control structure found in many programming languages. There are, however, many other ways iteration and integer generation can be used in combination. For example, the expression above can be written more compactly as

```
every write((1 to Limit) ^ 2)
```

The function **seq**(i, j) generates a sequence of integers starting at i with increments of j, but with no upper bound.

ALTERNATION

Since a generator may produce a sequence of values and those values may be used in goal-directed evaluation and iteration, it is natural to extend the concept of a sequence of values to apply to more than one expression. The *alternation* control structure,

expr1 | *expr2*

does this by first producing the values for *expr1* and then the values for *expr2*. For example,

```
0 | 1
```

generates 0 and 1. Thus, in

```
if i = (0 | 1) then write("okay")
```

okay is written if the value of i is either 0 or 1. The arguments in an alternation expression may themselves be generators. For example,

```
(1 to 3) | (3 to 1 by −1)
```

generates 1, 2, 3, 3, 2, 1.

When alternation is used in goal-directed evaluation, such as

```
if i = (0 | 1) then write(i)
```

it reads naturally as "if i is equal to 0 *or* 1, then …". On the other hand, if alternation is used in iteration, as in

```
every i := (0 | 1)
    do write(i)
```

it reads more naturally as "i is assigned 0 *then* 1".

The *or/then* distinction reflects the usual purpose of alternation in the two different contexts and suggests how to use alternation to formulate computations.

CONJUNCTION

As explained earlier, an expression succeeds only if all of its component subexpressions succeed. For example, in

      find(s1, s2) = find(s1, s3)

the comparison expression fails if either of its argument expressions fails. The same is true of

      find(s1, s2) + find(s1, s3)

and, in fact, of all operations and functions. It often is useful to know if two or more expressions succeed, although their values may be irrelevant. This operation is provided by *conjunction*,

      expr1 & *expr2*

which succeeds (and produces the value of *expr2*) only if both *expr1* and *expr2* succeed. For example,

      if find(s1, s2) & find(s1, s3) then write ("okay")

writes okay only if s1 is a substring of both s2 and s3.

Note that conjunction is just an operation that performs no computation (other than returning the value of its second argument). It simply binds two expressions together into a single expression in which the components are mutually involved in goal-directed evaluation. Conjunction normally is read as "*and*". For example,

      if (i > 100) & (i = j) then write(i)

might be read as "if i is greater than 100 *and* i equals j ..."

Note also that in goal-directed contexts,

      expr1 | *expr2* | ... | *exprn*

and

      expr1 & *expr2* & ... & *exprn*

correspond closely to logical disjunction and conjunction, respectively. Thus, *and/ or* conditions can be easily composed using conjunction and alternation.

LOOPS

There are two control structures that evaluate an expression repeatedly, depending on the success or failure of a control expression:

> while *expr1* do *expr2*

described earlier, and

> until *expr1* do *expr2*

which repeatedly evaluates *expr2* until *expr1* succeeds. In both cases *expr1* is evaluated before *expr2*. The do clauses are optional. For example,

> while write(read())

copies the input file to the output file.

A related control structure is

> not (*expr*)

which fails if *expr* succeeds, but succeeds if *expr* fails. Therefore,

> until *expr1* do *expr2*

and

> while not (*expr1*) do *expr2*

are equivalent. The form that is used should be the one that is most natural to the situation in which it occurs.

The while and until control structures are loops. Loops normally are terminated only by the failure or success of their control expressions. Sometimes it is necessary to terminate a loop, independent of the evaluation of its control expression.

The break expression causes termination of the loop in which it occurs. The following program illustrates the use of the break expression:

```
procedure main()
  count := 0
  while line := read() do
    if match("stop", line) then break
    else count := count + 1
  write(count)
end
```

This program counts the number of lines in the input file up to a line beginning with the substring "stop".

Sometimes it is useful to skip to the beginning of the control expression of a loop. This can be accomplished by the next expression. Although the next expression is rarely needed in simple cases, the following example illustrates its use:

```
procedure main()

    while line := read() do
        if match("comment", line) then next
        else write(line)

end
```

This program copies the input file to the output file, omitting lines that begin with the substring "comment".

The break and next expressions may appear anywhere in a loop, but they apply only to the innermost loop in which they occur. For example, if loops are nested, a break expression only terminates the loop in which it appears, not any outer loops. The use of a break expression to terminate an inner loop is illustrated by the following program, which copies the input file to the output file, omitting lines between those that begin with "skip" and "end", inclusive.

```
procedure main()

    while line := read() do
        if match("skip", line) then {          # check for lines to skip
            while line := read() do             # skip loop
                if match("end", line) then break
            }
        else write(line)                        # write line in main loop

end
```

There is one other looping control structure:

```
repeat expr
```

This control structure evaluates *expr* repeatedly, regardless of whether it succeeds or fails. It is useful when the controlling expression cannot be placed conveniently at the beginning of a loop. A repeat loop can be terminated by a break expression.

Consider an input file that is organized into several sections, each of which is terminated by a line beginning with "end". The following program writes the number of lines in each section and then the number of sections.

```
procedure main()

  setcount := 0

  repeat {
    setcount := setcount +
    1 linecount := 0
    while line := read() do {
      linecount := linecount + 1
      if match("end", line) then {
        write(linecount)
        break
        }
      }
    if linecount = 0 then break        # end of file
    }

  write(setcount, " sections")

end
```

The outcome of a loop, once it is complete, is failure. That is, a loop itself produces no value. In most cases, this failure is not important, since loops usually are not used in ways in which their outcome is important.

SELECTION EXPRESSIONS

The most common form of selection occurs when one or another expression is evaluated, depending on the success or failure of a control expression. As described in Chapter 1, this is performed by

> if *expr1* then *expr2* else *expr3*

which evaluates *expr2* if *expr1* succeeds but evaluates *expr3* if *expr1* fails.

If there are several possibilities, if-then-else expressions can be chained to-gether, as in

```
if match("begin", line) then depth := depth + 1
else if match("end", line) then depth := depth − 1
else other := other + 1
```

The else portion of this control structure is optional:

> if *expr1* then *expr2*

evaluates *expr2* only if *expr1* succeeds. The not expression is useful in this abbrevi-ated if-then form:

> if not (*expr1*) then *expr2*

which evaluates *expr2* only if *expr1* fails. In this situation, parentheses are often needed around *expr1* because not has high precedence.

While if-then-else selects an expression to evaluate, depending on the success or failure of the control expression, it is often useful to select an expression to evaluate, depending on the *value* of a control expression. The case control structure provides selection based on value and has the form

> case *expr* of {
>   *case-clause*
>   *case-clause*
>   .
>   .
>   .
> }

The expression *expr* after case is a control expression whose value controls the selection. There may be several case clauses. Each case clause has the form

> *expr1* : *expr2*

The value of the control expression *expr* is compared with the value of *expr1* in each case clause in the order in which the case clauses appear. If the values are the same, the corresponding *expr2* is evaluated, and its outcome becomes the outcome of the entire case expression. If the values of *expr* and *expr1* are different, or if *expr1* fails, the next case clause is tried.

There is also an optional default clause that has the form

> default : *expr2*

If no comparison of the value of the control expression with *expr1* is successful, *expr2* in the default clause is evaluated, and its outcome becomes the outcome of the case expression. The default clause may appear anywhere in the list of case clauses, but it is evaluated last. It is good programming style to place it last in the list of case clauses.

Once an expression is selected, its outcome becomes the value of the case expression. Subsequent case clauses are not processed, even if the selected expres-sion fails. A case expression itself fails if (1) its control expression fails, (2) if the selected expression fails, or (3) if no expression is selected.

Any kind of value can be used in the control expression. For example,

```
case s of {
  "begin" : depth := depth + 1
  "end" : depth := depth − 1
  }
```

increments depth if the value of s is the string "begin" but decrements depth if the value of s is the string "end". Since there is no default clause, this case expression fails if the value of s is neither "begin" nor "end". In this case, the value of depth is not changed.

The expression in a case clause does not have to be a constant. For example,

```
case i of {
  j + 1 : write("high") j − 1
  : write("low")
  j : write("equal") default :
  write("out of range")
  }
```

writes one of four strings, depending on the relative values of i and j.

The expression in a case clause can be a generator. If the first value it produces is not the same as the value of the control expression, it is resumed for other possible values. Consequently, alternation provides a useful way of combining case clauses. An example is:

```
case i of {
  0           : write("at origin")
  1 | −1 : write("near origin") default
  : write("not near origin")
  }
```

Since the outcome of a case expression is the outcome of the selected expres-sion, it sometimes is possible to "factor out" common components in case clauses. For example, the case expression above can be written as

```
write(
  case i of {
    0           : "at origin"
    1 | −1 : "near origin"
    default : "not near origin"
    }
  )
```

Such constructions can be difficult to read and should be used with restraint.

Note that each case clause allows just a single expression to be executed. If multiple expressions are needed, they must be grouped using braces.

COMPARISON OPERATIONS

A comparison operation such as

i = j

produces the value of its right operand if it succeeds. For example

write(find(s1, s2) = find(s3, s4))

writes the first common position if there is one.

Comparison operations are left associative, so an expression such as

i < j < k

groups as

(i < j) < k

Since a comparison operation produces the value of its right operand if it succeeds, the expression above succeeds if and only if the value j is between the values of i and k.

ASSIGNMENT

One of the most commonly used operations is assignment, which has the form

x := y

and assigns the value of y to the variable x.

Assignment associates to the right, so that

x := y := z

groups as

x := (y := z)

Consequently, the value of z is assigned to both y and x.

Augmented Assignment

One of the most common operations in programming is incrementing the numerical value of a variable, as in

    i := i + 1

In order to make such operations more concise and to avoid two references to the same variable, Icon provides *augmented assignment* operations that combine assignment with the computation to be performed. For example,

    i +:= 1

adds one to the value of i.

There are augmented assignment operations corresponding to all infix opera-tions (except assignment operations themselves); the := is simply appended to the operator symbol. For example,

    i *:= 10

is equivalent to

    i := i *10

Similarly,

    i >:= j

assigns the value of j to i if the value of i is greater than the value of j. This may seem a bit strange at first sight, since most programming languages do not treat compari-son operations as numerical computations, but this feature of Icon sometimes can be used to advantage.

Exchanging Values

The operation

    x :=: y

exchanges the values of x and y. For example, after evaluating

    s1 := "begin"
    s2 := "end"
    s1 :=: s2

the value of s1 is "end" and the value of s2 is "begin".

The exchange operation associates from right to left and returns its left argument as a variable. Consequently,

> x :=: y :=: z

groups as

> x :=: (y :=: z)

VALUES, VARIABLES, AND RESULTS

Some expressions produce values, while others (such as assignment) produce variables, which in turn have values. For example, the string literal "hello" is a value, while the identifier line is a variable. It is always possible to get the value of a variable. This is done automatically by operations such as i + j, in which the values of i and j are used in the computation.

On the other hand, values are not obtained from variables unless they are needed. For example, the expression x | y generates the variables x and y, so that

> every (x | y) := 0

assigns 0 to both x and y. The if-then-else and case control expressions also produce variables if the selected expression does.

The term *result* is used collectively to include both values and variables. Consequently, it is best to describe

> *expr1 | expr2*

as generating the results of *expr1* followed by the results of *expr2*.

Note that the term outcome includes results (values and variables) as well as failure.

The keyword &fail does not produce a result. It can be used to indicate failure explicitly.

ARGUMENT EVALUATION

The arguments of function and procedure calls are evaluated from left to right. If the evaluation of an argument fails, the function or procedure is not called. If more arguments are given in a call than are expected, the extra arguments are evaluated, but their values are not used. If the evaluation of an extra argument fails, the function or procedure is not called, just as in the case of the evaluation of any other argument.

If an argument is omitted, as in write(), the value of that argument is *null*. Many functions have defaults that are used if an argument is null. For example, in write(), the null value defaults to an empty string and an empty (blank) line is written. Another example is the function seq(i, j), which was described earlier. If its arguments are omitted, and hence null, they default to 1. Consequently, seq() generates 1, 2, 3, ... and seq(7) generates 7, 8, 9 ... .

The keyword &null produces the null value. Consequently, write() and write(&null) are equivalent. The null value is described in more detail in Chapter 10.

PROCEDURE RETURNS

As shown in Chapter 1, a procedure call may return a value, as in

```
return count
```

or it may fail and not return a value by using fail. A procedure call also may fail by flowing off the end of the procedure body without an explicit return.

A procedure also may generate a sequence of values by using suspend, as in the following example:

```
procedure To(i, j)
  while i <= j do {
    suspend i
    i +:= 1
    }
  fail
end
```

The suspend expression produces a value from the procedure call in the same manner as return, but the call is suspended and can be resumed. If it is resumed, evaluation continues following the point of suspension. In the example above, the first result produced is the value of i, provided it is less than or equal to j. If the call is resumed, i is incremented. If i is still less than or equal to j, the call suspends again with the new value of i. If i is greater than j, the loop terminates and fail is evaluated, which causes the resumption of the call to fail. The fail expression is not necessary, since flowing off the end of the procedure body has the same effect. Consequently,

```
every write(To(1, 10))
```

is equivalent to

```
every write(1 to 10)
```

The **suspend** expression is like the **every** expression; if its argument is a generator, the generator is resumed when the procedure call is resumed. Thus,

suspend (1 | 3 | 5 | 7 | 11)

suspends with the values 1, 3, 5, 7, 11 as the call in which it appears is successively resumed.

NOTES

Testing Icon Expressions Interactively

Success, failure, and generation in expression evaluation are powerful programming tools, but they may be unfamiliar. Testing various expressions interac-tively (or in a simple program) can help with understanding expression evaluation in Icon and dispel potential misconceptions.

The program qei, mentioned in the **Notes** section of Chapter 1, is particularly useful in this context. The command :every at the beginning of a line instructs qei to show every result of a generator. For example

>   :every 1 to 5;

produces

                1
                2
                3
                4
                5

Care should be taken not to specify a generator that has a large number of results.

Syntactic Considerations

The way that expressions are grouped in the absence of braces or parentheses is determined by the precedence and associativity of the syntactic tokens that comprise expressions. Appendix A contains detailed information on these matters.

Ideally, precedence and associativity lead to natural groupings of expressions and produces the expected results. In some cases, however, what is natural in one context is not natural in another, and precedence and associativity rules may cause expressions to group differently than expected. Such potential problems are noted at the ends of subsequent chapters.

The grouping of conjunction and alternation with other operations is a frequent source of problems. Conjunction has the lowest precedence of all opera-tions. Alternation, on the other hand, has a medium precedence. Consequently,

expr1 & *expr2* | *expr3*

groups as

expr1 & (*expr2* | *expr3*)

Since, in the absence of parentheses, such expressions are easily misinterpreted, it is good practice to use parentheses even if they are not necessary. There are many other cases where this rule applies. For example,

1 to 10 | 20

groups as

1 to (10 | 20)

The moral is clear: Parenthesize for readability as well as correctness.

When control structures are nested, braces can be used for grouping as shown in examples earlier in this chapter. Even if braces are not necessary, using them helps avoid errors that may result from unexpected groupings in complicated expres-sions. Using braces to delimit expressions also can make programs easier to read — it is difficult for human beings to parse nested expressions.

Consistent and appropriate indentation ("paragraphing") also makes pro-grams easier to read. There are several styles of indentation. The one to use is largely a matter of taste, but it should be consistent and should accurately reflect the grouping of expressions.

There are a few common syntactic problems that arise in control structures. One is that the do clause in every, which, and until is optional. If a do clause is intended but omitted by accident, the results can be unexpected. Consider for example,

```
while line := read()
   process(line)
```

This is syntactically correct, but since there is no do, all input lines are read and then process(line) is evaluated once. Because of the omitted do, only the last input line is processed.

The precedence of not is higher than that of any infix operation. For example,

    not find(s1, s2) = 10

groups as

    (not find(s1, s2)) = 10

As a general rule, it is advisable to use parentheses for grouping in expressions containing not to avoid such unexpected results, as shown in earlier examples.

If there is a "dangling" else in nested if-then-else expressions, the else clause is grouped with the nearest preceding if. Consider, for example, the following section of a program for analyzing mailing lists:

    if find("Mr.", line)
    then if find("Mrs.",
    line) then mm := mm
    + 1 else mr := mr + 1

These lines group as

    if find("Mr.", line) then {
        if find("Mrs.", line) then mm := mm + 1
        else mr := mr + 1
        }

The precedence of then and else is lower than the precedence of any infix operation, so

    if i > j then k := i else k := j

groups as

    if i > j then (k := i) else (k := j)

which usually is what is intended.

In Icon, unlike many other programming languages, control structures are expressions. For example, the outcome of

    if *expr1* then *expr2* else *expr3*

is the outcome of *expr2* or *expr3* depending on whether *expr1* succeeds or fails. Consequently, it is possible to write expressions such as

    (if i > j then i else j) := 0

to assign 0 to either i or j, depending on the relative magnitudes of their values. Although Icon allows such constructions, they tend to make programs difficult to read. It usually is better style to write such an expression as

   if i > j then i := 0 else j := 0

The assignment and numerical comparison operators are easily confused. Thus,

   i = (1 | 2)

compares the value of i to 1 and then 2, while

   i := (1 | 2)

assigns 1 to i. (The second argument of alternation is not used, since assignment only needs one value.)

3

String Scanning

Icon has many facilities for manipulating strings of characters (text). Its most powerful facility is high-level scanning for analyzing and synthesizing strings in a general way. This chapter is devoted to string scanning. Other string-processing facilities are described in Chapter 4.

THE CONCEPT OF SCANNING

Icon's string scanning facility is based on the observation that many operations on strings can be cast in terms of a succession of operations on one string at a time. By making this string, called the *subject*, the focus of attention of this succession of operations, it need not be mentioned in each operation. Furthermore, operations on a string often involve finding a position of interest in the string and working from there. Thus, the position serves as a focus of attention within the subject. The term *scanning* refers to changing the position in the subject. String scanning therefore involves operations that examine a subject string at a specific position and possibly change the position.

The form of a string-scanning expression is

expr1 ? *expr2*

where *expr1* provides the subject to be scanned and *expr2* does the scanning. The outcome of the scanning expression is the outcome of *expr2*. String scanning is illustrated by the function move(i), which increments the position by i characters if that is possible but fails if it is not. This function also produces the portion of the subject between the old and new positions. A function that produces a substring of the subject while changing the position is called a *matching function*.

Scanning starts at the beginning of the subject, so that

```
text ? {
    while move(1) do
        write(move(1))
    }
```

writes the even-numbered characters of text on separate lines.

STRING POSITIONS

In Icon, positions in strings are between characters and are numbered starting with 1, which is the position to the left of the first character:

```
    d    r    a    g    o    n
    _    _    _    _    _    _    _
    1    2    3    4    5    6    7
```

For convenience in referring to characters with respect to the right end of the string, there are corresponding nonpositive position specifications:

```
    d      r    a      g      o    n
    _    _    _    _    _    _    _
   −6      −5   −4     −3     −2        −10
```

The matching function tab(i) sets the position in the subject to i. For example,

```
text ? {
    if tab(3) then
        while move(1) do
            write(move(1))
    }
```

writes the even-numbered characters of text starting with the fourth one, provided text is that long. The argument of tab() can be given by a nonpositive specification, and a negative argument to move() decreases the position in the subject. Conse-quently,

```
text ? {
    tab(0)
    while write(move(−1))
    }
```

writes the characters of text from right to left. Notice that it is not necessary to know how long text is.

The function pos(i) succeeds if the position in the subject is i but fails otherwise. For example,

> *expr* & pos(0)

succeeds if the position is at the right end of the string after *expr* is evaluated.

STRING ANALYSIS

String analysis often involves finding a particular substring. The string-analysis function find(s1, s2), used earlier to illustrate failure and generation, performs this operation. When find() is used in string scanning, its second argument is omitted, and the subject is used in its place. For example,

> write(text ? find("the"))

writes the position of the first occurrence of "the" in text, provided there is one. Similarly,

> every write(text ? find("the"))

writes all the positions of "the" in text. Note that the scanning expression generates all the values generated by find("the").

In string analysis, the actual value of the position of a substring usually is not as interesting as the context in which the substring occurs — for example, what precedes or follows it. Since a string-analysis function produces a position and the matching function tab() moves to a position and produces the matched substring, the two can be used in combination. For example,

> write(text ? tab(find(",")))

writes the initial portion of text prior to the first comma in it (if any). Similarly,

```
text ? {
  if tab(find(",") + 1) then
    write(tab(0))
  }
```

writes the portion of text after the first comma in it (if any).

Alternation may be used in the argument of find() to look for any one of several strings. For example,

```
text ? {
   if tab(find("a" | "e" | "i" | "o" | "u") + 1)
      then write(tab(0))
   }
```

writes the portion of text after a lowercase vowel. Since alternatives are tried only if they
are needed, if there is an "a" in text, the string after it is written, even if there is another
vowel before the "a".

CSETS

In the example above, what happens depends on the order in which the alternatives are
written. On the other hand, in string analysis, order often is not important or even
appropriate. For example, the scanning expression at the end of the preceding section
does not write the first lowercase vowel.

Csets (character sets) are provided for such purposes. A cset is just what it sounds
like — a set of characters. There is no concept of order in a cset; all the characters in it
are on a par. A cset is therefore very different from a string, which is a sequence of
characters in which order is very important.

A cset can be given literally by using single quotes to enclose the characters (as
opposed to double quotes for string literals). Thus,

```
vowel := 'aeiou'
```

is a cset that contains the five lowercase "vowels". There also are built-in csets. For
example, the value of the keyword &letters is a cset containing the upper- and lowercase
letters.

Icon has several string-analysis functions that use csets instead of strings. One of
these is upto(c), which generates the positions in the subject in which any character in
the cset c occurs. For example,

```
every write(text ? upto(vowel))
```

writes the positions of every vowel in text, and

```
text ? {
   if tab(upto(vowel) + 1) then
      write(tab(0))
   }
```

writes the portion of text after the first instance of a lowercase vowel (if any).

Another string-analysis function that uses csets is many(c), which produces the
position after a sequence of characters in c. For example,

```
text ? {
  while write(tab(upto(' ')))
    do tab(many(' '))
  write(tab(0))
  }
```

writes the strings of characters between strings of blanks. Strings of blanks are matched by the expression tab(many(' ')), skipping over them in scanning. Note that tab(0) is used to match the remainder of the subject after the last blank (if any).

Similarly, the following scanning expression writes all the "words" in text:

```
text ? {
  while tab(upto(&letters)) do
    write(tab(many(&letters)))
  }
```

Treating a "word" as simply a string of letters is, of course, naive. In fact, there is no simple definition of "word" that is satisfactory in all situations. However, this naive one is easy to express and suffices in many situations.

STRING-ANALYSIS FUNCTIONS

There are three string-analysis functions in addition to find(), many(), and upto().

Matching Substrings

If s occurs at the current position in the subject, the function match(s) produces the position in the subject at the end of s. It fails if s does not occur at the current position in the subject. For example,

"The theory is fallacious" ? match("The")

produces 4, while

"The theory is fallacious" ? match(" theory")

fails, since string scanning starts at the beginning of the subject.

The operation =s is equivalent to tab(match(s)). For example, if line begins with the substring "checkpoint", then

```
line ? {
  if ="checkpoint" then
    base := tab(0)
  }
```

assigns the remainder of line to base.

Matching a Character

If the character at the current position in the subject is in the cset c, any(c) produces the position after that character. It fails otherwise. For example,

write("Our conjecture has support" ? tab(any('aeiouAEIOU')))

writes O, while

write("Our conjecture has support" ? tab(any('aeiou')))

fails and does not write anything.

Note that any() resembles match(), except that any() depends on the character at the current position, not a substring, and any one of several of characters may be specified. It also resembles many(), but any() matches one character instead of several.

Matching Balanced Strings

The function bal(c1, c2, c3) generates the positions of characters in c1, pro-vided the preceding substring is "balanced" with respect to characters in c2 and c3. This function is useful in applications that involve the analysis of formulas, expres-sions, and other strings that have balanced bracketing characters.

The function bal() is like upto(), except that c2 and c3 specify sets of characters that must be balanced in the usual algebraic sense up to a character in c1. If c2 and c3 are omitted, '(' and ')' are assumed. For example,

"−35" ? bal('−')

produces 1 (the string preceding the minus is empty) but

write("((2∗x)+3)+(5∗y)" ? tab(bal('+')))

writes ((2∗x)+3). Note that the position of the first "+" is not preceded by a string that is balanced with respect to parentheses.

Bracketing characters other than parentheses can be specified. The expression

write("[+, [2, 3]], [∗, [5, 10]]" ? tab(bal(',', '[', ']')))

writes [+, [2, 3]].

In determining whether or not a string is balanced, a count is kept starting at zero as characters in the subject are examined. If a character in c1 is encountered and the count is zero, bal() produces that position. Otherwise, if a character in c2 is encountered, the count is incremented, while the count is decremented if a character in c3 is encountered. Other characters leave the count unchanged.

If the counter ever becomes negative, or if the count is positive after examining the last character of the subject, bal() fails.

All characters in c2 and c3 have equal status; bal() cannot be used to determine proper nesting of different bracketing characters. For example, the value produced by

```
"([a+b))+c]" ? bal('+', '([', ')]')
```

is 8.

If c2 and c3 both contain the same character, its presence in c2 counts; it has no effect as a character in c3.

Since bal() is a generator, it may produce more than one result. For example,

```
every write(formula ? bal('*'))
```

writes the positions of all asterisks in formula that are preceded by parenthesis-balanced substrings.

SCANNING ENVIRONMENTS

The subject and position in string scanning, taken together, constitute an "environ-ment" in which matching and string-analysis functions operate.

A scanning expression,

expr1 ? *expr2*

starts a new scanning environment. It first saves the current scanning environment, then starts a new environment with the subject set to the string produced by *expr1* and the position set to 1 (the beginning of the subject). Next, *expr2* is evaluated. When the evaluation of *expr2* is complete (whether it produces a result or fails), the former scanning environment is restored.

Since scanning environments are saved and restored in this fashion, string-scanning expressions can be nested. An example is:

```
text ? {
  while  tab(upto(&letters))  do  {
    word  :=  tab(many(&letters))
    word ? {
```

```
        if upto('aeiou') then write(move(1))
        }
    }
}
```

This expression writes the first letter of those words that contain a lowercase vowel.

SCANNING KEYWORDS

The subject and position in scanning environments are maintained automatically by scanning expressions and matching functions. There usually is no need to refer to the subject and position explicitly — in fact, the whole purpose of string scanning is to treat these values implicitly so that they do not have to be mentioned during string scanning.

In some situations, however, it may be useful, or even necessary, to refer to the subject or position explicitly. Two keywords are provided for this purpose: &subject and &pos.

For example, the following line writes the subject and position:

```
write("subject=", &subject, ", position =", &pos)
```

If a value is assigned to &subject, it becomes the subject in the current scanning environment and the position is automatically set to 1. If a value is assigned to &pos, the position in the current scanning environment is changed accordingly, provided the value is in the range of the subject. If it is not in range, the assignment to &pos fails.

AUGMENTED STRING SCANNING

Augmented assignment,

```
s ?:= expr
```

can be used to scan s and assign a new value to it. The value assigned is the value produced by *expr*. For example,

```
line ?:= {
    tab(many(' ')) & tab(0)
    }
```

removes any initial blanks from line. If line does not begin with a blank, the scanning expression fails and the value of line is not changed.

NOTES

Testing Expressions Interactively

String scanning is one of the most powerful features of Icon. Its apparent simplicity masks a wealth of uses. String scanning also may be difficult to under-stand initially, and it may be hard to see how to use it to perform string analysis.

Again, testing expressions interactively (or writing small programs) can be very helpful in learning to use string scanning.

In qei (available in the Icon program library and described in the **Notes** section of Chapter 1) a helpful approach is to set up a string for subsequent tests. An example from this chapter is:

```
>    text := "The theory is fallacious";
     r1_ := text := "The theory is fallacious"
```

Note that the string is assigned to both text and r1_ (or some other variable qei creates if r1_ already has been created). Now various scanning expressions can be tried, as in

```
>    text ? match("The");
     r2_ := 4
>    text ? match("theory");
>    Failure
```

As in examples shown earlier, scanning may involve several expressions. This is easily handled in qei by opening a compound expression with a left brace without a terminating semicolon and writing the remaining expressions on separate lines without semicolons, finally ending with a right brace and semicolon, as in

```
>    text ? {
>       tab(5)
>       move(1)
>       };
>    r3_ := "t"
```

Library Resources

The library module scan contains several procedures that supplement Icon's built-in scanning functions.

In addition, this module contains a procedure snapshot() that shows the subject and the current position in scanning.

Syntactic Considerations

The second argument of ? often is fairly complicated, since it contains the expressions that perform scanning. Consequently, the precedence of ? is low, and

```
text ? i := find(s)
```

groups as

```
text ? (i := find(s))
```

However, the precedence of ? is greater than & (conjunction), so that

```
text ? i := find(s1) & j := find(s2)
```

groups as

```
(text ? i := find(s1)) & (j := find(s2))
```

This probably is not what is intended, and the source of the problem may be hard to locate. The difficulty is that j := find(s2) is not evaluated with text as the subject, since the completion of the scanning expression at the left of the conjunction restores the subject and position to their former values. Consequently, find(s2) does not operate on text but on some other subject. (In the absence of any scanning expression, the subject is a zero-length, empty string.) Whether find(s2) succeeds or fails, its outcome has nothing to do with text. However, it looks like it does, which may make debugging difficult.

Because of the likelihood of conjunction in scanning expressions, it is good practice to clearly delimit the second argument of the scanning expression. One such form, which is used in most of the examples of string scanning in this book, is

```
s ? {
   ...
   }
```

Since scanning expressions can be complicated, it is important to be careful that the outcome of scanning is the intended one. Consider the following expression:

```
line ?:= {
   while tab(upto(&letters))
     do tab(many(&letters))
   }
```

The scanning expression eventually fails, regardless of the value of line, since the while loop itself fails. Consequently, no value is assigned to line.

4

Characters, Csets,
and Strings

Icon has no character data type, but it has two data types that are composed of characters: *strings*, which are sequences of characters, and *csets*, which are sets of characters. These two organizations of characters, described briefly in previous chapters, are useful for representing various kinds of information and for operating on textual data in different ways.

CHARACTERS

Since strings are of major importance in Icon, and csets only somewhat less so, it is important to understand the significance of the characters from which they are composed.

Icon uses eight-bit characters and allows all 256 of them to be used; no characters are excluded from use. Although most computer systems do not allow all 256 characters to be entered from input devices, they all can be represented in Icon programs by escape sequences in string and cset literals, and any character can be computed directly during program execution.

Most files are composed of characters, and most input and output consists of characters. Some characters are "printable" and have graphics ("glyphs") associ-ated with them. Other characters are used for control purposes, such as for indicat-ing the end of a line on a display device or printer. The printable characters, control characters, and their uses vary from one computer system to another. The associa-tion between the numeric value of the pattern of bits (code) for a character and its graphic also depend on the "character set" the system uses. For example, the letter A is associated with the bit pattern 01000001 (decimal code 65) in the ASCII character set, but with the bit pattern 11000001 (decimal code 193) in the EBCDIC character set. Most computer systems use ASCII. The exceptions are IBM mainframes, which use EBCDIC.

Most text processing involves printable characters that have graphics and, for the most part, it does not matter which codes correspond to which characters. For example, programs that analyze text files usually work the same way, regardless of whether the character set is ASCII or EBCDIC. Such programs usually are written in terms of the graphics for the characters (such as A) and the associated codes are irrelevant.

There are exceptions, however. Comparison of characters and sorting depend on the numeric codes associated with graphics. In ASCII, the digits are associated with codes near the beginning of the character set, while in EBCDIC they are near the end. In both cases, the digits are in the order of their character codes, so strings of digits compare the same way in both ASCII and EBCDIC. However, the digits occur before the letters in ASCII but after the letters in EBCDIC, so strings containing both letters and digits may compare differently in ASCII and EBCDIC. While these differences cannot be helped, they usually do not cause problems because an Icon program running on an ASCII system produces the results that the user of an ASCII system expects, and similarly on an EBCDIC system. And, as mentioned earlier, almost all computers use ASCII.

See Appendix B for more information about character sets, the glyphs used in different situations, and listings for several platforms.

STRINGS

Strings are used more frequently than csets because the sequential organization of strings allows the representation of complex relationships among characters. Writ-ten text, such as this book, is just a sequence of characters. Most of the information processed by computers consists of sequences of characters, especially when it is read in, written out, and stored in files.

String Literals

As described earlier, strings are represented literally with surrounding double quotation marks. For example,

vowel := "aeiou"

assigns the string "aeiou" to vowel.

A single string literal can be continued from one line to the next by ending each line that is incomplete with an underscore and continuing on the next line. White space (blanks and tabs) are discarded at the beginning of the next line and the parts are joined. An example is

```
sentence := "This string literal is too _
   long to be written comfortably _
   on a single line."
```

Note that blanks to separate words are put before underscores at the ends of lines.

The escape sequences can be used in string literals for characters that cannot be keyboarded directly. Escape sequences start with the character \ (backslash). For example, " \t" is a string consisting of a tab and "\n" is a string consisting of a newline character. Similarly, "\"" is a string representing a double quote and " \\" is a string consisting of a single backslash. Therefore,

```
write("What I want to say is\n\"Hello world\"")
```

writes

```
What I want to say
is "Hello world"
```

A complete listing of escape sequences is given in Appendix A.

Character Codes

The function char(i) produces the one-character string corresponding to the integer i. For example, the internal integer representation for A is 65 in ASCII, so char(65) produces the one-character string "A" in ASCII.

The inverse function ord(s) produces the integer (ordinal) corresponding to the one-character string s.

String Length

The length of a string is the number of characters in it. The operation *s produces the length of s. For example,

```
*"Hello world"
```

produces the integer 11.

There is no practical limit to the length of a string, although very long strings are awkward and expensive to manipulate. The smallest string is the *empty string*, which contains no characters and has zero length. The empty string is represented literally by "".

LEXICAL COMPARISON

Strings can be compared for their relative magnitude in a manner similar to the comparison of numbers. The comparison of strings is based on lexical (alphabetical) order rather than numerical value. Lexical order is based on the codes for the characters. The character c1 is lexically less than c2 if the code for c1 is less than the code for c2. For example, in ASCII the code for "B" is 66, while the code for "R" is 82, so "B" is lexically less than "R".

Although the relative values of letters and digits are the same in ASCII and EBCDIC and produce the expected results in lexical comparisons, there are important differences between the ordering in the two character sets. As mentioned earlier, the ASCII codes for the digits are smaller than the codes for letters, while the opposite is true in EBCDIC. In addition, uppercase letters in ASCII have smaller codes than lowercase letters, while the opposite is true in EBCDIC. Furthermore, there is relatively little relationship between the codes for other characters, such as punctuation, in the two character sets.

For longer strings, lexical order is determined by the lexical order of their characters, from left to right. Therefore, in ASCII "AB" is less than "aA" and "aB" is less than "ab". If one string is an initial substring of another, the shorter string is lexically less than the longer. For example, "Aba" is lexically less than "Abaa" in both ASCII and EBCDIC. The empty string is lexically less than any other string. Two strings are lexically equal if and only if they have the same length and are identical, character by character. There are six lexical comparison operations:

s1 << s2	lexically less than
s1 <<= s2	lexically less than or equal
s1 >> s2	lexically greater than
s1 >>= s2	lexically greater than or equal
s1 == s2	lexically equal
s1 ~== s2	lexically not equal

The use of lexical comparison is illustrated by the following program, which determines the lexically largest and smallest lines in the input file.

```
procedure main()

  min := max := read()              # initial min and max

  while line := read() do
    if line >> max then max := line else
    if line << min then min := line

  write("lexically largest line is: ", max)
  write("lexically smallest line is: ", min)

end
```

This program can be rephrased in a way that is more idiomatic to Icon by using augmented assignment operations:

```
procedure main()
   min := max := read()                 # initial min and max
   while line := read() do
     (max <<:= line) | (min >>:= line)
   write("lexically largest line is: ", max)
   write("lexically smallest line is: ", min)
 end
```

STRING CONSTRUCTION

Concatenation

One of the more commonly used operations on strings is *concatenation*,

```
s1 || s2
```

which produces a string consisting of the characters in s1 followed by those in s2. For example,

```
"Hello " || "world"
```

produces the string "Hello world".

The empty string is the identity with respect to concatenation; concatenating the empty string with another string just produces the other string. The empty string therefore is a natural initial value for building up a string by successive concatena-tions. For example, suppose that the input file consists of a number of lines, each of which contains a single word. Then the following procedure produces a list of these words with each followed by a comma.

```
procedure wordlist()
   wlist := ""                          # initialize
   while word := read() do
     wlist := wlist || word || ","
   return wlist
 end
```

The augmented assignment operation for concatenation is particularly useful for appending strings onto an evolving value. For example,

    wlist ||:= word || ","

is equivalent to

    wlist := wlist || word || ","

The do clause in the while loop above is not necessary; the expression can be written more compactly as

    while wlist ||:= read() || ","

STRING-VALUED FUNCTIONS

When producing formatted output, it often is useful to have "fields" of a specific width that line up in columns. There are three functions that position a string in a field of a specified width, aligning the string in the field at the right, left, or in the center.

Positioning Strings

The function right(s1, i, s2) produces a string of length i in which s1 is positioned at the right and s2 is used to pad out the remaining characters to the left. For example,

    right("Detroit", 10, "+")

produces "+++Detroit". Enough copies of s2 are concatenated on the left to make up the specified length. If s2 is omitted, blanks are used for padding.

If the length of s1 is greater than i, it is truncated at the left so that the value has length i. Therefore,

    right("Detroit", 6)

produces "etroit".

The value of s2 usually is a one-character string, but it may be of any length. The resulting string is always of size i; however, any extra characters that might result from prepending copies of s2 are discarded. For example,

    right("Detroit", 10, "+*")

produces "+*+Detroit". Note that the padding string is truncated at the right.

A common use of right() is to position data in columns. The following program, which prints out a table of the first four powers of the integers from 1 to 10, illustrates such an application:

```
$define Limit 10

procedure main()
  every i := 1 to Limit do {
    write(right(i, 5), right(i ^ 2, 8), right(i ^ 3, 8), right(i ^ 4, 8))
    }
end
```

The output of this program is:

```
 1    1     1      1
 2    4     8     16
 3    9    27     81
 4   16    64    256
 5   25   125    625
 6   36   216   1296
 7   49   343   2401
 8   64   512   4096
 9   81   729   6561
10  100  1000  10000
```

The function left(s1, i, s2) is similar to right(s1, i, s2) except that the position is reversed: s1 is placed at the left, padding is done on the right, and truncation (if necessary) is done at the right. Therefore,

```
left("Detroit", 10, "+")
```

produces "Detroit+++" and

```
left("Detroit", 6)
```

produces "Detroi". The padding string is truncated at the left if necessary.

The function center(s1, i, s2) centers s1 in a string of length i, padding on the left and right, if necessary, with s2. If s1 cannot be centered exactly, it is placed to the left of center. Truncation is then done at the left and right if necessary. Therefore,

```
center("Detroit", 10, "+")
```

produces "+Detroit++", while

```
center("Detroit", 6)
```

produces "etroit" and

>   center("Detroit", 9, "+ –")

produces "+Detroit–".

Tabular Data

Tab characters are useful for separating fields and displaying them in an aligned fashion on devices such as computer terminals.

The function entab(s, i1, i2, ..., in) produces a string obtained by replacing runs of consecutive blanks in s by tab characters. There is an implicit tab stop at 1 to establish the interval between tab stops. The remaining tab stops are at i1, i2, ..., in. Additional tab stops, if necessary, are obtained by repeating the last interval. If no tab stops are specified, the interval is 8 with the first tab stop at 9.

For the purposes of determining positions, printable characters have a width of 1, the backspace character has a width of –1, and a newline or return character restarts the counting of positions. Other nonprintable characters have zero width.

A lone blank is never replaced by a tab character, but a tab character may replace a single blank that is part of longer run.

The function detab(s, i1, i2, ..., in) produces a string obtained by replacing each tab character in s by one or more blanks. Tab stops are specified in the same way as for entab().

Replicating Strings

When several copies of the same string are to be concatenated, it is more repl(s, convenient and efficient to use i), which produces the concatenation of i copies of s. For example,

>   repl("+∗+", 3)

produces "+∗++∗++∗+". The expression repl(s, 0) produces the empty string.

Reversing Strings

The function reverse(s) produces a string consisting of the characters of s in reverse order. For example,

>   reverse("string")

produces "gnirts".

Mapping Characters

The function map(s1, s2, s3) produces a string resulting from a character mapping of s1 in which each character of s1 that appears in s2 is replaced by the corresponding character in s3. Characters of s1 that do not appear in s2 are not changed. For example,

map("mad hatter", "a", "+")

produces "m+d h+tter" and

map("mad hatter", "aeiou", "12345")

produces "m1d h1tt2r".

Several characters in s2 may have the same corresponding character in s3. For example,

map("mad hatter", "aeiou", "+++++")

produces "m+d h+tt+r".

If a character appears more than once in s2, the rightmost correspondence with s3 applies. Duplicate characters in s2 provide a way to mask out unwanted characters. For example, marking the positions of vowels in a string can be accom-plished by mapping every vowel into an asterisk and mapping all other letters into blanks. An easy way to do this is to set up a correspondence between every letter and a blank and then append the correspondences for the vowels:

```
s2 := &letters || "AEIOUaeiou"
s3 := repl(" ", *&letters) || "**********"
```

In this correspondence, s2 is a string consisting of all letters followed by the vowels, 62 characters in all, since each vowel appears twice. The value of s3 is 52 blanks followed by 10 asterisks. The last 10 characters in s2 and s3 override the previous correspondences between the vowels and blanks. Consequently,

map(line, s2, s3)

produces a string with asterisks in the positions of the vowels and blanks for all the other letters.

Trimming Strings

The function trim(s, c) produces a string consisting of the initial substring of s with the omission of any trailing characters contained in c. That is, it trims off characters in c. If c is omitted, blanks are trimmed. For example, trim("Betelgeuse ")

produces "Betelgeuse", while

trim("Betelgeuse", 'aeiou')

produces just "Betelgeus".

SUBSTRINGS

Since a string is a sequence of characters, any subsequence or *substring* is also a string. A substring is simply a portion of another string. For example, "Cl" is a substring of "Cleo", as are "leo" and "e". "Co", however, is not a substring of "Cleo", since "C" and "o" do not occur consecutively in "Cleo". Any string is a substring of itself. The empty string is a substring of every string.

Subscripting Strings

A substring is produced by a subscripting expression, in which a *range specification* enclosed in brackets gives the positions that bound the desired substring. One form of range specification is i:j, where i and j are the bounding positions. For example,

"Cleo"[1:3]

produces "Cl". Note that this is a substring of two characters, not three, because the characters are between the specified positions. Range specifications usually are applied to strings that are the values of identifiers, as in

text[1:4]

which produces the first three characters of text, those between positions 1 and 4. If the value of text is less than three characters long, the subscripting expression fails. This is another example of the design philosophy of Icon: If an operation cannot be performed, it does not produce a result. In this case the failure occurs because the specified substring does not exist.

Expressions can be used to provide the bounds in range specifications. For example,

text[2:*s]

produces the substring of text between 2 and the size of s. Similarly, any expression whose value is a string can be subscripted, as in

s := read()[2:10]

which assigns a substring of a line of input to **s**. Note that this expression may fail for two reasons: if **read()** fails because there is no more input, or if **read()** produces a line that is not long enough. Expressions containing such *ambiguous failure* should be avoided, since they can be the source of subtle programming errors.

The following program illustrates the use of substrings to copy the input file to the output file, truncating long output lines to 60 characters.

```
procedure main()

  while line := read() do {
    line := line[1:61] # truncate write(line)

  }

end
```

Note that

```
write(line[1:61])
```

does not work properly in place of the two lines in the previous procedure, since this subscripting expression fails if a line is less than 60 characters long. There would be no output for such lines.

Nonpositive position specifications, described in Chapter 3, also can be used in range specifications. For example, line[−1:0] is the last character of line. Positive and nonpositive specifications can be mixed.

The two positions in a range specification can be given in either order. The leftmost position need not be given first; only the bounding positions are significant. Therefore, line[1:4] and line[4:1] are equivalent.

Range specifications also can be given by a position and an offset from that position. The range specification i+:j specifies a substring starting at i of length j. The offset can be negative: i −:j specifies a substring starting at i but consisting of the j characters to the left of i, rather than to the right. For example,

```
write(line[1+:60])
```

writes the first 60 characters of line, as does

```
write(line[61−:60])
```

If a substring consists of only a single character, it can be specified by the position before it. Therefore,

```
write(line[2])
```

writes the second character of line and is equivalent to

    write(line[2+:1])

Similarly,

    last := line[−1]

assigns the last character of line to last.

Assignment can be made to a subscripted variable to change the substring corresponding to the range specification. For example, if the value of word is "two",

    word[2] := "o"

changes the value of word to "too". Similarly,

    word[−1] := ""

deletes the last character of word so that its value becomes "to". Note that an assignment that changes a substring may change the length of a string. Assignment to change a substring is a just shorthand notation for concatenation. For example,

    word[2] := "o"

is shorthand for

    word := word[1] || "o" || word[3:0]

If two variables have the same string value, changing a substring in one does not change the value of the other. Therefore, in

    line := read()
    old := line
    line[2+:3] := ""

the value of old is not changed by the assignment to line[2+:3]. A new value is assigned to line, but not to old.

Assignment can be made to a subscripting expression to change the value of a string only if the range specification is applied to a variable. For example,

    "Cleo"[1] := "K"

is erroneous, since a literal value cannot be changed.

Randomly Selected Characters

The operation ?s produces a randomly selected one-character substring of s provided that s is not empty. If s is empty, ?s fails. For example,

    ?"HT"

produces the string "H" or "T" with approximately equal probability.

If s is a string-valued variable, assignment can be made to ?s to replace a randomly selected character of s. For example,

    ?s := ""

deletes a randomly selected character of s.

Character Generation

The expression !s generates the one-character substrings of s in order from first to last, left to right. For example,

    every write(!s)

writes the characters of s, one per line. This expression is equivalent to

    every write(s[1 to *s])

If s is a string-valued variable, the expression !s produces a variable, just as s[i] does. For example,

    !s := ""

is equivalent to

    s[1] := ""

and deletes the first character in the value of s.

In an expression such as

    every !s := *expr*

the value of s is changed with each assignment, but the position in s is incremented repeatedly until the end of the string is reached. If the assignment changes the length of s, the result can be confusing.

CSETS

Cset Literals

A cset can be written literally by using single quotes to enclose the characters.

The order of the characters in a cset literal is not important, and duplicate characters are ignored. Consequently, 'aeiou', 'uoiea', and 'aeiouaeiou' all produce the same cset.

Built-in Csets

Icon provides keywords for commonly needed csets, such as the uppercase letters, lowercase letters, all the letters, and digits: &ucase, &lcase, &letters, and &digits, respectively.

For example,

```
text ? {
  while tab(upto(&digits))
    do write(move(1))
}
```

writes out all the digits in text, one per line.

Other built-in csets are &cset, the set of all 256 characters, and &ascii, the set of the first 128 characters in ASCII.

Operations on Csets

Icon has four operations on csets:

c1 ++ c2	union
c1 ** c2	intersection
c1 – – c2	difference
~c	complement

The union of two csets is a cset that contains all the characters in either of the two. For example, &letters ++ &digits contains all the letters and digits. The intersection of two csets is a cset that contains all the characters that appear in both csets. The difference of two csets is a cset that contains all the characters in the first that are not in the second. For example, &cset – – &digits contains all the characters that are not digits. The complement of a cset contains all the characters that are not in it. For example, ~&digits is equivalent to &cset – – &digits. The operation *c produces the number of characters in c.

STRING ANALYSIS

As illustrated earlier, string analysis functions are not restricted to string scanning. The analysis functions can be applied to a specific string by adding that string as an additional argument. For example, find(s1, s2) generates the positions where s1 occurs as a substring of s2, and upto(c, s) generates the position at which characters in c occur in s. In such usages, the subject and the position in it are irrelevant.

All the string analysis functions also may have two additional arguments that restrict the range in which the analysis is done. For example, upto(c, s, i, j) restricts the value to positions between i and j in s. Therefore,

upto('aeiou', "The theory is fallacious", 5, 11)

produces 7. Note that this is a position in s; the value produced by

upto('aeiou', "The theory is fallacious"[5:11])

is 3.

An omitted value of i defaults to 1, the beginning of s. An omitted value of j defaults to 0 and restricts the value to positions between i and the end of the string.

Like range specifications, the range-restriction arguments can be given either as positive or nonpositive position specifications and can be given in either order. For example,

find(s1, s2, 0, −10)

restricts the range in s2 to the last 10 characters. Substrings are always found from left to right, regardless of the form of the specification.

CONVERSION BETWEEN CSETS AND STRINGS

As described in Chapter 1, Icon automatically converts values from one type to another according to context. This conversion applies to csets and strings. For example, the following procedure produces a cset of all the characters that occur in the input file.

```
procedure inset()
  chars := ''                      # empty cset to start
  while line := read() do
    chars := chars ++ line
  return chars
end
```

The cset chars initially starts out empty, given literally by enclosing no characters in single quotes. Then the characters in each line of input are added to chars. In the union operation, the value of line is a string that is automatically converted to a cset.

This procedure can be written more compactly using augmented assignment:

```
procedure inset()
    chars := ' '                          # empty cset to start
    while chars ++:= read()
    return chars
end
```

NOTES

Library Resources

The module strings contains many procedures for manipulating strings. Some of the most useful procedures in this module are:

cat(s1, s2, ...)	concatenate an arbitrary number of strings
deletec(s, c)	delete all occurrences of characters in c from s
deletes(s1, s2)	delete all occurrences of s2 in s1
replace(s1, s2, s3)	replace all occurrences of s2 in s1 by s3
rotate(s, i)	rotate s by i characters

Syntactic Considerations

Concatenation associates from left to right. Its precedence is higher than that of the numerical comparison operations, but lower than that of addition. If concat-enation is used in combination with numerical computation, it is advisable to use parentheses to specify desired grouping.

All the lexical comparison operations associate from left to right and have the same precedence as the numerical comparison operations. A lexical comparison operation produces the value of its right argument, provided that the comparison succeeds. Therefore, the expression

```
s1 << s2 << s3
```

succeeds and produces s3, provided s2 is strictly between s1 and s3 in lexical order.

5

Numerical Computation and Bit Operations

Numerical computation in Icon is similar to that in most programming languages. The usual operations on integers and real numbers are provided. Integers are converted to real numbers automatically in mixed-mode operations that involve both integers and real numbers. There are also bit operations on integers.

Integers in Icon can be arbitrarily large; they are not restricted to the size of machine integers. Real (floating-point) numbers vary in range and precision from platform to platform. They normally are represented by the double-precision floating-point values native to the computer on which Icon runs.

NUMERIC LITERALS

Integers are represented literally in the usual way. For example, 36 represents the integer 36 and 1024 represents the integer 1,024. Real numbers can be represented literally using either decimal or exponent notation. For example, 27e2 and 2700.0 are equivalent and represent the real number 2,700.0.

Bases other than 10 can be used for integer literals. Such *radix literals* have the form $i\,r\,j$, where i is a base-10 integer that specifies the base for j. For example, 2r11 represents the integer 3, while 8r10 represents 8. The base can be any value from 2 through 36; the letters a, b, ..., z are used to specify "digits" in j that are larger than 9. For example, 16ra represents 10, while 36rcat represents 15,941. See Appendix A for additional details of the syntax of numeric literals.

ARITHMETIC

Icon has two prefix (unary) operations for numerical computation. The operation +N produces the numeric value of N, while −N produces the negative of N. The infix (binary) operations for numerical computation are as follows:

expression	operation	relative precedence	associativity
N1 ^ N2	exponentiation	3	right to left
N1 % N2	remaindering	2	left to right
N1 / N2	division	2	left to right
N1 * N2	multiplication	2	left to right
N1 − N2	subtraction	1	left to right
N1 + N2	addition	1	left to right

In integer division the remainder is discarded; that is, the value is truncated toward 0. For example,

−7 / 2

produces −3.

The operation

N1 % N2

produces the remainder of N1 divided by N2 with the sign of N1. For example,

−10 % 3

produces −1, but

10 % −3

produces 1.

Division by zero and raising a negative real number to a real power are erroneous. Such errors cause program execution to terminate with a diagnostic message.

The function abs(N) produces the absolute value of N. For example,

abs(−7 / 2)

produces 3.

Any numerical computation that involves a real number is performed using floating-point arithmetic and produces a real number. For example, the result of

$$10 + 3.14159$$

is 13.14159 and the result of

$$-7 / 2.0$$

is −3.5.

NUMERICAL COMPARISON

Icon's numerical comparison operations are

N1 < N2	less than
N1 <= N2	less than or equal to
N1 = N2	equal to
N1 >= N2	greater than or equal to
N1 > N2	greater than
N1 ~= N2	not equal to

MATHEMATICAL COMPUTATIONS

Icon provides the standard trigonometric functions:

sin(r)	sine of r
cos(r)	cosine of r
tan(r)	tangent of r
asin(r)	arc sine of r
acos(r)	arc cosine of r
atan(r1, r2)	arc tangent of r1 / r2

In all cases, angles are given in radians. The default for r2 in atan() is 1.0.

The following functions convert between radians and degrees:

dtor(r)	the radian equivalent of r given in degrees
rtod(r)	the degree equivalent of r given in radians

Icon also provides the following functions for mathematical calculations:

sqrt(r)	square root of r
exp(r)	*e* raised to the power r
log(r1, r2)	logarithm of r1 to the base r2

The default for r2 is *e*.

Keywords provide values of frequently used mathematical constants:

&e	base of the natural logarithms, 2.71828…
&phi	golden ratio, 1.61803…
&pi	ratio of circumference to diameter of a circle, 3.14159…

RANDOM NUMBERS

The operation ?i produces a pseudo-random number. If the value of i is a positive integer i, the value produced by ?i is an integer j in the range $1 \leq j \leq$ of i is i. If the value 0, the value produced by ?i is a real number r in the range 0.0 $\leq r < 1.0$.

For example, the expression

if ?2 = 1 then "H" else "T"

produces the string "H" or "T" with approximately equal probability.

Pseudo-random numbers are produced by a linear congruence relation start-ing with an initial seed of 0. This sequence is the same from one program execution to another, allowing programs to be tested in a reproducible environment. The seed can be changed by assigning an integer value to &random. For example,

&random := 0

resets the seed to its initial value.

The same pseudo-random sequence is used for all random operations. For example, the operation ?s described in Chapter 4 uses the same sequence as ?i.

BIT OPERATIONS

Icon has five functions that operate on integers at the bit level. All these operations produce integers.

The function iand(i, j) produces the bitwise *and* of i and j. For example,

iand(4, 5)

produces 4.

The functions ior(i, j) and ixor(i, j) produce the bitwise inclusive and exclusive *or* of i and j, respectively. For example,

ior(4, 6)

produces 6, while

ixor(4, 6)

produces 2.

The function icom(i) produces the bitwise complement of i. For example,

icom(1)

produces −2.

The function ishift(i, j) shifts i by j positions. If j is positive, the shift is to the left, and vacated bit positions are filled with zeros. If j is negative, i is shifted to the right with sign extension. For example,

ishift(2, 3)

produces 16, while

ishift(2, −3)

produces 0.

NOTES

Library Resources

The library module numbers contains a large collection of procedures for formatting numbers and performing simple numeric computations.

Large Integers

As mentioned in the beginning of this chapter, there is no limitation on the magnitude of integers in Icon.

Internally, Icon uses integers native to the platform on which it runs. These native integers are at least 32 bits long and may be longer. Integers that are larger than native integers are represented by blocks of data that Icon manages in a way that is transparent in writing and running Icon programs.

Large integers are supported in all arithmetic computations, but there are a few places where only integers that are small enough to be represented as native integers can be used:

```
i to j by k
seq(i, j)
integer-valued keywords
```

It is also worth knowing that large integer literals in a program such as

174359213645100235

are converted to actual large integers when evaluated during program execution. Consequently, such literals should not be placed in loops or other places in which they are evaluated frequently.

Syntactic Considerations

All infix arithmetic operations have precedence higher than that of assign-ment. Consequently,

N := N + 1

groups as

N := (N + 1)

Prefix operations have higher precedence than infix operations. For example,

−N + 3

groups as

(−N) + 3

The comparison operations all have the same precedence, which is lower than that of any numerical computation operation, but higher than that of assignment. Therefore,

N1 > N2 + 1

groups as

N1 > (N2 + 1)

while
N1 := N2 > 10

groups as

N1 := (N2 > 10)

Note that this expression assigns the value 10 to N1 if the comparison succeeds.

Comparison operations associate from left to right, which allows compound comparisons to be written in a natural way. For example,

1 <= N <= 10

groups as

(1 <= N) <= 10

and succeeds if the value of N is between 1 and 10, inclusive.

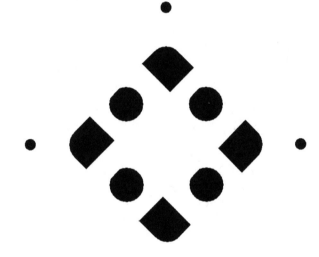

6

Structures

Structures are collections of values. Icon has four kinds of structures: records, lists, sets, and tables. Different kinds of structures have different access methods and organizations.

RECORDS

Records are fixed in size and their values are referenced by field names. Records, like procedures, are declared and are global to the entire program. (A record declaration cannot appear within a procedure declaration.) The declaration for a record with *n* fields has the form

> record *name*(*field1*, *field2*, ..., *fieldn*)

where *name* is the name of the record and *field1*, *field2*, ..., *fieldn* are the field names associated with the record. The syntax of record names and field names is the same as the syntax for identifiers (see Appendix A). An example of a record declaration is

> record complex(rpart, ipart)

Such a record declaration might be used to represent complex numbers with real and imaginary parts. Similarly, the record declaration

> record employee(name, age, ssn, salary)

might be used to represent an employee whose name, age, social security number, and salary are attributes of interest.

An instance of a record is created by a *record constructor* function correspond-ing to the record name and with values in positions corresponding to the field names. For example,

origin := complex(0.0, 0.0)

assigns a complex record with zero real and imaginary parts to origin, while

clerk := employee("John Doe", 36, "123–45–6789", 35000.00)

assigns an employee record to clerk.

Fields of records are referenced by expressions of the form *name . field.* For example, the value of

origin.rpart

is 0.0. Field references are variables, and values can be assigned to the corresponding fields. Therefore,

origin.ipart +:= 6.0

increments the imaginary part of origin by 6.0.

Records can be referenced (subscripted) by field number or field name, as in

origin[2] +:= 2.5

which adds 2.5 to the ipart field of origin, and

origin["rpart"] := 1.0

which sets the rpart of origin to 1.0. The operation ?R produces a randomly selected reference to a field of R. The size of a record is produced by the same operation that is used to get the size of a string. For example, *origin produces 2. The operation !R generates the fields of R from first to last. For example,

every !R := 0

assigns 0 to every field of R.

LISTS

Lists in Icon have two roles. In one role, they are one-dimensional arrays (vectors) that can be subscripted by position. In the other role, they can be manipulated by stack and queue access functions and hence grow and shrink.

List Creation

A list can be created by placing brackets around a list of values. For example,

oracles := ["Delphi", "Heracles", "Claros"]

assigns a list of three strings to oracles. The values can be given by expressions, as in

powers := [i, i ^ 2, i ^ 3, i ^ 4]

which assigns a list of four integers to powers.

The values in a list do not have to be of the same type. For example,

city := ["Tucson", 700000, "Arizona", "Pima"]

assigns a list containing three strings and one integer to city.

The values in a list may be of any type. For example,

expression := ["+", ["a"], ["/", ["c"], ["d"]]]

assigns a list of three values to expression. The first value is a string, while the second and third values are other lists, and so on. Such a list can be used to represent a tree in which the first value in the list is associated with the contents of a node and subsequent values represent subtrees. The tree corresponding to expression can be visualized as:

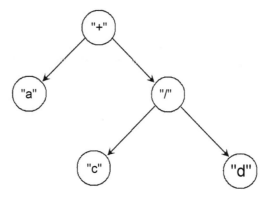

Lists also can be created by the function

list(i, x)

which creates a list of i values, each of which has the value of x. For example,

    vector := list(100, 0.0)

assigns to vector a list of 100 values, each of which is 0.0.

An *empty list*, which contains no values, is created by [ ] or list(0). The size of a list is produced by the same operation that is used for strings and records. For example, *vector produces 100, while *[ ] produces 0.

List Referencing

The values in a list can be referenced (subscripted) by position. For example,

    write(oracles[2])

writes Heracles. Note that positions are numbered starting at 1. Similarly,

    every i := 1 to *vector do
       write(vector[i])

writes all the values in the list vector. Since positions can be computed in the subscripting expressions, this loop can be written more compactly as

    every write(vector[1 to *vector])

A list reference is a variable. It can be changed by assignment to its position, which may be specified positively or nonpositively. For example,

    oracles[−1] := "Branchidae"

changes the last value of oracles, so that the list becomes

    ["Delphi", "Heracles", "Branchidae"]

Similarly,

    city[2] +:= 1000

changes the second value in city to 701,000.

List subscripting fails if the position specified does not correspond to a value in the list; that is, if the subscript is out of range.

The operation !L generates the elements of L. Consequently, the values in a list can be written without specific reference to positions:

    every write(!vector)

Assignment can be made to !L to change the values of the elements. For example

```
every !vector := 1.0
```

assigns 1.0 to every element of vector.

The following program, which tabulates word lengths, illustrates a typical use of lists.

```
$define MaxLen 20

procedure main()
  wordlen := list(MaxLen, 0)      # initial zero counts
  while line := read()
    do line ? {
      while tab(upto(&letters)) do {
        word := tab(many(&letters))
        wordlen[*word] +:= 1
        }
      }
  every i := 1 to *wordlen do
    write(right(i, 2), right(wordlen[i], 5))
end
```

The values in wordlen accumulate counts of word lengths from 1 to 20. After the input has been processed, the results are written out. Note that any word that is longer than 20 characters is not tabulated; the expression

```
wordlen[*word] +:= 1
```

fails, since the subscript is out of range for word lengths greater than 20.

Lists are one dimensional, but a list of lists can be used to simulate a multi-dimensional array. The following procedure constructs an i-by-j array in which each value is x:

```
procedure array(i, j, x)
  L := list(i)
  every !L := list(j, x)
  return L
end
```

For example,

```
board := array(8, 8, 0)
```

assigns to **board** an 8-by-8 array in which each value is 0. A list reference can itself be subscripted so that

```
board[2][4]
```

references the value in "column" 4 of "row" 2 of **board**. This expression also can be written as

```
board[2, 4]
```

The operation ?L produces a randomly selected reference to the list L. If L is empty, ?L fails. Assignment can be made to ?L to change the subscripted value. For example,

```
?vector := 2.0
```

assigns 2.0 to a randomly selected element of **vector**.

List Concatenation

Lists can be concatenated in a manner similar to the concatenation of strings. The list concatenation operation has three vertical bars to distinguish it from string concatenation. An example is

```
city := city ||| [1883]
```

which assigns a new list

```
["Tucson", 550000, "Arizona", "Pima", 1883]
```

to **city**. An empty list is an identity with respect to list concatenation.

As for other infix operations, there is an augmented assignment operation for list concatenation operation, as in

```
city |||:= [1883]
```

Note that both arguments in list concatenation must be lists;

```
city |||:= 1883
```

is erroneous.

List Sections

A list section is a list composed of a sequence of values from another list. List sections are like substrings, except that they are new lists that are distinct from the list from which they are obtained, instead of being a part of it. List sections are produced by range specifications applied to lists, much as substrings are produced by range specifications applied to strings. For the value of city given in the preceding section, the value of

city[3:5]

is the list

["Arizona", "Pima"]

There is one other important distinction between subscripting lists and strings: If L is a list, L[i] refers to the ith *value* in the list, while L[i : j] is a *list* consisting of the values between positions i and j in L. In particular, L[i : j] is a list that is distinct from L, and assignment cannot be made to it to change L.

Queue and Stack Access to Lists

Queue and stack access functions provide ways to add and remove values from the ends of lists. When the elements of a list are viewed from left to right, L[1] is the left end of a list and L[*L] or L[−1] is the right end of a list.

The function put(L, x) adds the value of x to the right end of the list L, increasing the size of L by 1. One use of put() is to build a list whose size cannot be determined when the list is created. For example, the following procedure produces a list of all words in input:

```
procedure words()

  wordlist := [ ]

  while line := read()
    do line ? {
      while tab(upto(&letters)) do
        put(wordlist, tab(many(&letters)))
      }

  return wordlist

end
```

Since put() adds values at the right end, the words in the list are in the order that they appear in input. That is, the first value in the list is the first word, the second value is the second word, and so on.

Values are removed from a list by the operation, get(L). Each time get(L) is evaluated, it removes a value from the left end of L and produces this value. If L is empty, get(L) fails.

For example, the following program uses the procedure words() to produce a list of words and then writes out only those words that begin with an uppercase letter:

```
procedure main()
  wlist := words()
  while word := get(wlist) do
    word ? {
      if any(&ucase) then write(word)
      }
end
```

When the execution of this program is complete, the list wlist is empty, since each call of get() removes a value from it.

The functions put() and get() provide a queue access method for lists; put(L, x) adds x to the right end of L, and get(L) removes a value from the left end of L.

Two functions provide a corresponding stack access method for lists. The function push(L, x) adds x to the left end of L and pop(L) removes a value from the left end of L. For example, if the expression

```
put(wordlist, tab(many(&letters)))
```

in the procedure words() given previously is replaced by

```
push(wordlist, tab(many(&letters)))
```

the list that is produced has the words in the opposite order from their order in input: the first word in the list is the last one in input, and so on.

Note that get(L) and pop(L) both remove a value from the left end of L. The two names for the same function are provided to accommodate the usual terminology for queue and stack access methods. The function pull(L) removes a value from the right end of L, so push() and pull() also provide a queue access method. The four functions together provide an access method for double-ended queues, or *deques*.

The functions put(L, x) and push(L, x) produce L.

The functions put() and push() can have additional trailing arguments to add several values to a list in one call. For example,

```
put(wordlist, "the", "a", "an")
```

appends these values to wordlist.

When push() is used to add values to the left end of a list, the values are pushed in the order they are given. For example, as a result of

push(wordlist, "source", "many", "any")

"any" is the first element of wordlist.

Since the queue and stack access functions add and remove elements from lists, they affect subsequent subscripting. For example, after push(L, x), the former element L[1] is L[2]. The effects of the queue and stack access function on subscripting generally are not a problem, since queue and stack access usually are not used in combination with positional access.

SETS

A set is an unordered collection of values. Sets in Icon have many of the properties normally associated with sets in the mathematical sense. The function

set(L)

creates a set that contains the distinct elements of the list L. For example,

set(["abc", 3])

creates a set with two members, "abc" and 3. If the argument to set() is omitted, an empty set is created.

Any specific value can occur only once in a set. For example,

set([1, 2, 3, 3, 1])

creates a set with only three members: 1, 2, and 3.

There are several operations on sets. The function

member(S, x)

succeeds and produces x if x is a member of the set S, but fails otherwise. For example,

member(S1, member(S2, x))

succeeds if x is a member of both S1 and S2.

The function

        insert(S, x)

inserts x into the set S and returns S. For example, the following procedure produces a set containing all the different words in the input file:

```
procedure diffwords()
  wordset := set() while
  line := read() do
    line ? {
      while tab(upto(&letters)) do
        insert(wordset, tab(many(&letters)))
    }
  return wordset
end
```

The function

        delete(S, x)

deletes the member x from the set S and produces S.

The functions insert(S, x) and delete(S, x) succeed, whether or not x is in S. This allows their use in loops in which failure may occur for other reasons. For example,

```
S := set()
while insert(S, read())
```

builds a set that consists of the (distinct) lines from the input file.

The operations

```
S1 ++ S2
S1 ** S2
S1 −− S2
```

create the union, intersection, and difference of S1 and S2, respectively. In each case, the result is a new set.

Note that these operations apply both to sets and csets. There is no automatic type conversion between csets and sets; the result of the operation depends on the types of the arguments. For example,

        'aeiou' ++ 'abcde'

produces the cset 'abcdeiou', while

> set([1, 2, 3]) ++ set([2, 3, 4])

produces a set that contains 1, 2, 3, and 4.

Several operations that apply to lists also apply to sets. *S produces the size of S, and ?S produces a randomly selected member of S. The operation !S generates the members of S but in no predictable order.

TABLES

A table is a collection of pairs, where a pair consists of a key and a corresponding value. These pairs are called *elements*. Tables resemble lists, except that the keys, or "subscripts", need not be integers but can be values of any type. Tables are much like the symbol tables used in compilers and similar software, but lookup and insertion are taken care of automatically.

Table Creation and Referencing

A table is created by the function

> table(x)

where x is the default value for new elements in the table. Table references are variables and are similar to list references in appearance. For example, if words is a table created by

> words := table(0)

then

> words["The"] := 1

assigns the value 1 to the key "The" in words. Subsequently,

> write(words["The"])

writes 1.

The value associated with a key can be changed, as in

> words["The"] := 2

Augmented assignment is particularly useful for tables. The expression

> words["The"] +:= 1

increments the value associated with "The".

When a table is first created, it is empty and has a size of zero. Every time a value is assigned to a new key, the size of the table increases by 1. The operation *T produces the size of T (the number of elements in it).

An element is added to a table only when an assignment is made to a new key. Therefore, if "way" has not been assigned a value in words, the expression

        words["way"]

produces the default value of 0, but "way" is not added to the table and the size of the table does not change. On the other hand,

        words["way"] +:= 1

adds "way" to words and increases the size of words by 1.

As illustrated above, if a table is used to count values, a useful default value is 0. For example, the following procedure produces a table of the number of times each different word occurs in the input file.

```
procedure countwords()

  wordcount := table(0)

  while line := read()
    do line ? {
      while tab(upto(&letters)) do
        wordcount[tab(many(&letters))] +:= 1
      }

  return wordcount

end
```

The operation ?T produces a randomly selected reference to the table T. If T is empty, ?T fails. Assignment can be made to ?T to change the value of the element. For example,

        ?T +:= 1

increments the value of a randomly selected element in T.

The operation !T generates the values of elements in T, while key(T) generates the keys in T. The order of generation is not predictable. For example, the following expression writes all the keys and their corresponding values in the table T:

```
every x := key(T) do
  write(x, ":", T[x])
```

Note that it is always possible to get from a key to its corresponding value.

Testing and Changing Table Elements

The functions member(), insert(), and delete() apply to tables as well as sets. The function member(T, x) succeeds if x is a key in the table T but fails otherwise.

The function insert(T, x, y), which is equivalent to T[x] := y, inserts an element with key x and value y into table T. If there already is a key x in T, its corresponding value is changed. An omitted third argument defaults to the null value. Note that insert() has three arguments when used with tables but only two when used with sets.

The function delete(T, x) removes the element with key value x from T. If x is not a key in T, no operation is performed; delete() succeeds in either case.

PROPERTIES OF STRUCTURES

Structures are created during program execution as illustrated by previous ex-amples. A structure value is a reference (pointer) to a collection of values. Assign-ment copies the reference (pointer) but not the collection of values to which it points. There are several consequences of these properties of structures that may not be immediately obvious. Consider

```
index := list(50,
0) temp := index
temp[1] := 1
```

The assignment of the value of index to temp does not copy the 50 values pointed to by the value of index. Instead, index and temp both reference the *same* collection of values. Therefore, the assignment of 1 to temp[1] changes the contents of the list that temp and index share as their value. The effect is as if

```
index[1] := 1
```

had been evaluated. Consider also

```
cycle := ["x"]
put(cycle, cycle)
```

These expressions construct a loop in which cycle contains its own value. This can be visualized as follows:

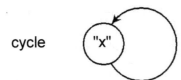

Since assignment does not copy structures, the result of an expression such as

L1 := L2 := list(i, 0)

is to assign the *same* list to both L1 and L2. Subsequently, assignment to a position in L2 changes the value of that position in L1, and conversely. Similarly, the effect of

L := list(3, list(5, 0))

is to assign the *same* list of five values to each of the three values in L. Compare this to the procedure for constructing two-dimensional arrays that is given earlier in this chapter.

The remarks above apply to all types of structures. For example, a set can be a member of (reference) itself, as in

S := set()
insert(S, S)

NOTES

Library Resources

The Icon program library contains three modules specifically related to structures: lists, sets, and tables.

The lists module contains many procedures that operate on lists in a fashion similar to the built-in repertoire of string operations. Some examples are

lmap(L1, L2, L3)	map elements of L1 in the style of map(s1, s2, s3)
lrep(L, i)	replicate L in the style of repl(s, i)
lreverse(L)	reverse L in the style of reverse(s)

The sets module extends the built-in repertoire with procedures such as

seteq(S1, S2)	test equivalence of S1 and S2
setl(S1, S2)	test inclusion of S1 in S2

The **tables** module provides a variety of procedures such as

keylist(T)	list of keys in T
tbldflt(T)	default value for T
vallist(T)	list of values in T

Syntactic Considerations

A subscripting expression can be subscripted as in

expression[3][2]

As noted earlier, subscripted subscripts can be abbreviated by placing a list of subscripts in one pair of brackets, as in

expression[3, 2]

which is equivalent to the example above. Subscripted subscripts can be used to any level as in

expression[3, 2, 4, 1]

The field references associate from left to right. Consequently,

x.y.z

groups as

(x.y).z

where y and z are field names.

The field reference operation has higher precedence than any other operation, including the prefix operations. This is an exception to the general rule that prefix operations have higher precedence than infix operations. As a result,

−x.y

groups as

−(x.y)

7

Expression Evaluation

The way that Icon evaluates expressions is one of the most important aspects of the language. It gives Icon much of its power and provides many interesting ways of programming that are not available in most other programming languages.

Most aspects of expression evaluation are described in Chapter 2 and are illustrated by examples in subsequent chapters. This chapter describes a few more advanced aspects of expression evaluation and explores in more depth the interac-tion between generators and goal-directed evaluation.

BACKTRACKING

Control Backtracking

In function calls and operations (as opposed to control structures), arguments are evaluated from left to right. For example, in

expr1 < *expr2*

the order of evaluation is *expr1* then *expr2*. If these expressions produce results, the comparison operation is performed. It is easier to follow the order of evaluation if such expressions are written in postfix form with the operator following its argu-ments:

      (expr1, expr2) <

This is not proper Icon syntax and is used here only to help explain the order of evaluation.

      In this form, evaluation is strictly left to right: *expr1*, *expr2*, and then the comparison operation. Consider the following example:

      !x < !y

written in postfix form, this becomes

      (x!, y!) <

Suppose both expressions produce results and suspend. This can be depicted as follows:

      g1 ← *g2* ← last suspended generator

      (x!,   y!) <

The arrow from the suspended generator for !y, *g2*, back to the suspended generator for !x, *g1*, shows the order for resumption. If the comparison operation fails, *g2* is resumed. If *g2* produces another result, the situation is as it was before and the comparison is performed again. However, if *g2* does not produce a result, it is removed from the chain of suspended generators and *g1* is resumed:

      g1 ← last suspended generator

      (x!,   y!) <

If *g1* produces another result, !y is evaluated again, just as it was when !x produced its first result. On the other hand, if *g1* does not produce another result, the entire expression fails.

      The left-to-right expression evaluation and last-in/first-out resumption of suspended generators results in what is called "cross-product evaluation with depth-first search". Note that it may be advisable to compose expressions in ways that take advantage of this form of search. For example, since find() produces values in order of increasing magnitude, it is better to use

      if find(s1) < find(s2) then write("condition satisfied")

than to use

      if find(s2) > find(s1) then write("condition satisfied")

since if a value for find(s1) is less than a value for find(s2), any subsequent values for find(s2) are also.

Cross-product evaluation of several generators potentially tries all possible combinations of values from the generators. This allows complex searches to be expressed very simply. Of course it is possible for such searches to be very time consuming. Three things diminish this potential problem: (1) the search is done internally and hence more efficiently than if it had to be written at the source-language level with loops and local variables, (2) most situations in which cross-product evaluation is used do not involve large "search spaces" (the problem is rarely seen in practice), and (3) generation can be limited as shown later.

Data Backtracking

Although the matching functions tab() and move() are not generators, they suspend when they produce a result. If they are resumed because of subsequent failure, they restore the former position in the subject before themselves failing. That is, they undo the change they made to the position. This is called *data backtracking*.

Only a few Icon expressions perform data backtracking. Most changes in values caused by expression evaluation are not undone during control backtrack-ing. For example, in

```
text ? {
  (i := 10) &
  (j := (i < find(s)))
  }
```

the assignment of 10 to i is not undone even if i < find(s) fails, despite the conjunction and resulting control backtracking.

The reason that matching functions perform data backtracking for the position in the subject is so that alternative matches can be specified without the failure of one interfering with another. For example, in

```
text ? {
  (tab(upto(',') +1) & write(move(1))) | write(tab(upto('.')))
  }
```

if text contains a comma, the character after it is written, while otherwise the initial position of text up to a period is written (if any). If text contains only one comma as its last character, the move(1) fails, and nothing is written. Since

```
tab(upto(',') + 1)
```

is evaluated in conjunction with write(move(1)), the suspension from tab() is resumed and it restores the position to the beginning of the resumption. Consequently the alternative tab(upto('.')) starts at the beginning of the subject. If tab() had not performed data backtracking, the position would have been left at the end of the subject, so the alternative tab(upto('.')) would have inevitably failed.

As mentioned earlier, an assignment expression such as i := 10 does not perform data backtracking; its effect is irreversible. There is, however, a reversible form of assignment, indicated by <– instead of := . For example, in

```
text ? {
  (i <– 10) &
  (j := (i < find(s)))
  }
```

the assignment of 10 to i is reversed if i < find(s) fails, and it is restored to the value it had prior to the scanning expression.

There is also a reversible exchange operation, <–>, which is like :=: except that the assignments are reversed if it is resumed.

BOUNDED EXPRESSIONS

Failure within an expression causes the resumption of suspended generators, resulting in backtracking to previously evaluated portions of the expression. If there were no limits on backtracking, failure would cause control to backtrack further and further toward the first expression in a program.

Such unlimited backtracking has several undesirable effects. The most serious is that there usually are places in a program beyond which backtracking is inappro-priate. For example, in

if find(s) then *expr1* else *expr2*

if find(s) produces a result, *expr1 is* evaluated. However, if *expr1* fails, find(s) should not be resumed. While there might be a use for such behavior, it would not be what is meant by if-then-else.

Another problem with unlimited backtracking is that suspended generators must be kept until program execution terminates. This obviously requires space that in most cases is unneeded.

Icon handles the problem of limiting backtracking by using *bounded expres-sions*. If an expression is bounded and produces a result, all suspended generators in it are discarded.

It is therefore impossible to backtrack into a bounded expression. Put another way, a bounded expression cannot generate a sequence of results.

Expressions are bounded in specific syntactic contexts. For example, the control expression in if-then-else is bounded. Consequently, in

    if find(s) then *expr*1 else *expr*2

if find(s) produces a result but *expr1* fails, find(s) is not resumed. The places that bounded expressions occur are the natural ones for control flow. These are shown below, underlined:

    case <u>*expr*</u> of {
     <u>*expr1*</u> : <u>*expr2*</u>
     <u>*expr3*</u> : <u>*expr4*</u>
          ...
     }

    every *expr1* do <u>*expr2*</u>

    if <u>*expr1*</u> then *expr2* else *expr3*

    not <u>*expr*</u>

    repeat <u>*expr*</u>

    return <u>*expr*</u>

    suspend *expr1* do <u>*expr2*</u>

    until <u>*expr1*</u> do <u>*expr2*</u>

    while <u>*expr1*</u> do <u>*expr2*</u>

    { <u>*expr1*</u>; <u>*expr2*</u>; ...; *exprn* }

A few consequences of bounding (and the lack of it) deserve attention. Since *expr2* and *expr3* in if-then-else are not bounded, they can generate sequences of results. An example of the usefulness of this is

    if i < j then (i to j) else (j to i)

In most cases of sequential execution, when an expression is evaluated it is logically complete and backtracking into it is neither intended nor desired. Since all expressions in a compound expression except the last one are bounded, compound expressions provide the primary means of avoiding backtracking in sequential execution.

When backtracking is not desired, the composition of sequential portions of a program is facilitated by the fact that semicolons are added at the ends of lines, provided the expression on the line is complete and a new expression begins on the next line. Consequently,

    i := find(s1)
    write(i)
    j := find(s2)

is equivalent to

```
i := find(s1);
write(i);
j := find(s2);
```

Thus, it is natural to write separate (bounded) expressions on separate lines. As execution goes from one line to the next, suspended generators are discarded and backtracking to preceding lines is impossible.

On the other hand, conjunction can be used to bind several lines together without bounding the expressions. For example, in

```
i := find(s1)
& write(i) &
j := find(s2)
```

semicolons are not added at the ends of the first two lines, since the expressions on those lines are not complete. Consequently, if find(s1) produces a result but find(s2) fails, find(s1) is resumed.

Note that bounded expressions prevent data backtracking in string scanning by preventing control backtracking.

For example, in

```
if tab(upto(',') + 1) then write(move(1))
```

the tab() expression is bounded, so that if move() fails, tab() is not resumed and the former position is not restored.

MUTUAL EVALUATION

If the mutual success of several expressions is needed, conjunction can be com-pounded, as in

expr1 & *expr2* & ...   & *exprn*

This notation is cumbersome, especially if the expressions are themselves complex. An alternative is *mutual evaluation,* denoted by

(*expr1, expr2, ..., exprn*)

which evaluates *expr1, expr2, ..., exprn* just like the evaluation of the arguments in a function call. If all the expressions produce results, the result of mutual evaluation is the result of the last expression, *exprn*. Otherwise, the mutual-evaluation expres-sion fails. The effect is exactly the same as in a compound conjunction. For example,

$$i := (upto(' ', line1), upto(' ', line2))$$

assigns to i the position of the first blank in line2, provided both line1 and line2 contain a blank.

Sometimes a number of expressions need to be mutually evaluated, but a result other than the last one is desired. The expression

$$expr\ (expr1,\ expr2,\ ...,\ exprn)$$

produces the result of *expri*, where the value of *expr* is the integer *i*, provided that all the expressions produce a result. If any of the expressions fails, however, the mutual evaluation expression fails. For example, the value of

$$i := 1(upto(' ', line1), upto(' ', line2))$$

assigns to i the position of the first space in line1, provided both line1 and line2 contain a space.

The value of *expr* can be negative, in which case the result is selected from right to left in the manner of nonpositive position specifications.

If the value of *expr* is out of range, the mutual-evaluation expression fails. For example,

$$3(expr1,\ expr2)$$

always fails, regardless of whether or not *expr1* and *expr2* produce results.

Although mutual evaluation has the same syntax as a function call, there is no ambiguity. If the value of *expr* is an integer *i*, the result is the result of *expri*. If the value of *expr* is a function or procedure, however, the function or procedure is called with the arguments, and the outcome of the expression is the outcome of the call.

LIMITING GENERATION

While a bounded expression is limited to at most one result, it sometimes is useful to explicitly limit an expression to a specific number of results. This can be done by the *limitation* control structure,

$$expr \setminus i$$

which limits *expr* to at most *i* results (the value of *i* is computed before *expr* is evaluated, an exception to the otherwise left-to-right evaluation of expressions). For example,

```
every write(upto(&lcase, line) \ 3)
```

writes at most the first three positions at which lowercase letters occur in line.

Note that limitation to one result corresponds to a bounded expression. This form of limitation is particularly useful in preventing unwanted backtracking. Consider the following procedure, which is intended to generate the words in its argument

```
procedure words(text)

  text ? {
    while tab(upto(&letters)) do
      suspend tab(many(&letters))
    }

  end
```

The problem in this formulation is that when the procedure is resumed after generating one word, suspend resumes its argument. Since tab() suspended to allow for data backtracking, it is resumed and restores the scanning position to its former value. The while loop continues, but since the position is now back to where it was (at a letter), upto() produces this same position again. This procedure just generates the first word in text endlessly!

In order to prevent the unwanted data backtracking, the suspend expression can be limited as follows:

```
suspend tab(many(&letters)) \ 1
```

In this case, tab() is not resumed, and the while loop continues to the next word.

REPEATED ALTERNATION

It sometimes is useful to generate a sequence of results repeatedly. The *repeated alternation* control structure,

```
|expr
```

repeatedly generates the sequence of results for *expr*. A simple example is

```
|1
```

which generates the sequence 1, 1, ... Another example is

```
|(1 to 3)
```

which generates the endless sequence 1, 2, 3, 1, 2, 3, ...

Such sequences never terminate of their own accord and normally are used in situations where they are not resumed endlessly. For example,

every write(|(0 to 7) \ 128)

writes the octal digits 16 times.

An exception to endless generation for repeated alternation occurs if *expr* fails. If the sequence for *expr* is empty, then the sequence for |*expr* is empty; it fails. Furthermore, if *expr* has a non-empty sequence initially, but its sequence subse-quently becomes empty during the evaluation of |*expr*, the sequence for |*expr* terminates at that point. For example, the sequence for

|read()

consists of the lines of the input file, terminating when the end of the input file is reached.

NOTES

Testing Expressions Interactively

As mentioned in the **Notes** section of Chapter 2, Icon's expression evaluation mechanism is powerful but may be difficult to understand initially. That is espe-cially true of material in this chapter. Running qei (or writing small programs) can provide insight and dispel misconceptions.

Syntactic Considerations

In using mutual evaluation to select an expression, care needs to be taken to avoid unexpected grouping. For example

$-1(expr1, expr2, ... , exprn)$

groups as

$-(1(expr1, expr2, ... , exprn))$

which probably is not the intention. This problem can be avoided by using paren-theses:

$(-1)(expr1, expr2, ... , exprn)$

8

Procedures

Procedures contain expressions that are evaluated when the program is run. The arrangement of the expressions in a program into procedures specifies the organi-zation of the program. Icon has no block structure; procedures cannot be placed inside procedures.

Functions and procedures are very similar in Icon. Functions are essentially procedures that are built into the Icon system. Both procedures and functions are "first-class" values that can be assigned to variables, passed as arguments in procedure calls, and so forth.

Most values are accessed via identifiers. Scope determines the identifiers a procedure can access. Icon uses lexical scoping.

PROCEDURE DECLARATIONS

A procedure declaration has the form

> procedure *name* (*parameter-list*)
> *local-declarations initial-clause*
>
> *procedure-*
> *body* end

The parameter list, which is optional, consists of identifiers separated by commas:

identifier, identifier, ...

These identifiers are local to the procedure and are not accessible elsewhere in the program. Different procedure declarations can have parameters with the same names, but parameters with the same names in different procedures have no connection with each other.

Other identifiers can be declared to be local to a procedure in optional local declarations at the beginning of the procedure declaration. Local declarations have the form

local *identifier-list*

The initial clause, which also is optional, has the form

initial *expr*

where *expr* is an expression that is evaluated the first time the procedure is called. Uses of the initial clause are mentioned later.

The body of the procedure consists of a sequence of expressions. These expressions are evaluated when the procedure is called.

Representative procedure declarations appear in preceding chapters but without declarations for local identifiers. A typical procedure with local declara-tions is

```
procedure exor(s1,
  s2) local count, line

  count := 0

  while line := read()
    do line ? {
      if find(s1) then {
        if not find(s2) then count +:= 1
        }
      else if find(s2) then count +:= 1
      }

  return count

end
```

A procedure can be declared to have a variable number of arguments by appending [ ] to the last (or only) parameter in the parameter list. In this form of declaration, the arguments are passed to the last parameter in a list. An example is:

```
procedure cat(s1, s2, rest[ ])

    result := s1 || s2
    every result ||:= !rest

    return result

end
```

If called as cat("a", "b", "c", "d", "e"), the parameters have the following values:

s1	"a"
s2	"b"
rest	["c", "d", "e"]

and the result returned is "abcde".

In this form of declaration, the last parameter always is a list. This list consists of the arguments not assigned to previous parameters. If the previous parameters consume all the arguments, the list is empty. If there are not enough arguments for the previous parameters, the null value is used for the remaining ones, but the last parameter still is an empty list.

SCOPE

The identifiers in the parameter list and the identifiers in the local declarations of a procedure are local to calls of that procedure and are accessible only to expressions in the body of that procedure. Such identifiers are called *dynamic local identifiers*.

Identifiers can be made global and accessible to all procedures in a program by global declarations, which have the form

   global *identifier-list*

Global declarations are on a par with procedure declarations, and they may not appear inside procedure declarations. If an identifier that is declared global also appears in a parameter list or local declaration, it is local to the procedure, not global. A declaration of a global identifier need not appear before the appearance of the identifier in a procedure.

Global identifiers can be used to share values among procedures. Suppose, for example, procedures p1() and p2() both must increment the same counter. Then the following format could be used:

```
global counter

procedure p1()
        ...
    counter +:= 1
        ...
end
```

```
procedure p2()
        ...
    counter +:= 1
        ...
end
```

A procedure name is a global identifier. The procedure itself is a value. It is the value of the identifier that names the procedure.

The names of record types also are global. Record field names are not identifiers; they apply to the entire program and are not affected by scope declara-tions.

Identifiers that are not declared to be global are local to the procedure in which they occur, whether or not they are explicitly declared to be local in that procedure. This default scope interpretation saves writing but may lead to errors. For example, a global declaration, perhaps unrelated to the procedure containing an undeclared local identifier, can cause an undeclared identifier that otherwise would be local to be interpreted as global. It is good practice to declare all local identifiers explicitly.

Variables for dynamic local identifiers come into existence when a procedure is called and cease to exist when the procedure returns; they are only accessible during the duration of the procedure call. Local identifiers can be made *static* by using the declaration

static *identifier-list*

A static local identifier does not cease to exist when the procedure in which it is declared returns. Such an identifier retains its value for subsequent calls of that procedure. Therefore, a static identifier can provide memory for a procedure.

Static identifiers are useful when a procedure that is called many times uses a value that must be computed but is always the same. Consider a program that writes the first string of letters and digits of each line of the input file. This program can be adapted to other uses more easily if it is divided into two procedures: one that generates the strings and another that writes them. An example is:

```
procedure main()
    every write(alphan())
end

procedure alphan()
    local line, chars
    chars := &letters ++ &digits
```

```
        while line := read()
          do line ? {
             if tab(upto(chars)) then suspend tab(many(chars))
             }
    end
```

Note that the value assigned to chars is computed every time alphan() is called. This unnecessary computation can be avoided by making chars a static identifier and computing its value only once the first time that alphan() is called:

```
    procedure alphan()
      local line
      static chars

      initial chars := &letters ++ &digits

      while line := read()
        do line ? {
           if tab(upto(chars)) then suspend tab(many(chars))
           }
    end
```

Keywords have global scope and their values are not affected by procedure calls.

PROCEDURE INVOCATION

Procedure Calls

Procedures are invoked by procedure calls, which have the form

   expr (*expr1*, *expr2*, ... , *exprn*)

where the value of *expr* is the procedure to be called and *expr1*, *expr2*, ..., *exprn* are expressions that provide the arguments.

Normally, there are as many arguments as there are parameters in the procedure declaration. For example,

   exor("Mr.", "Mrs.")

is a call of the procedure exor() given previously. The values of the expressions are assigned to the identifiers in the parameter list (s1 and s2 in this case). Evaluation then starts at the beginning of the body of the procedure for exor().

Arguments are transmitted by value; there is no call-by-reference or other method of argument transmission. Notice, however, that since structures in Icon are pointers to aggregates of values, structures are effectively passed by reference.

A procedure or function also can be called with a list or record that contains its arguments. This form of call is

> *expr1* ! *expr2*

where the value of *expr1* is the procedure or function to be called and *expr2* is a list or record containing the arguments. For example,

> select ! ["a", "b", "c", "d", "e"]

is equivalent to

> select("a", "b", "c", "d", "e")

Returning from a Procedure

Evaluation of the expression

> return *expr*

returns from the procedure call in which it occurs. The outcome of *expr* becomes the outcome of the procedure call, and evaluation continues at the place where the call was made. A return expression always returns. If *expr* fails, the procedure call fails. If *expr* is omitted, the null value is returned.

The fail expression, which is equivalent to return &fail, causes a procedure to return and fail explicitly, as illustrated in previous examples. An implicit fail expression is provided at the end of the procedure body. Consequently, a procedure call that returns by flowing off the end of the procedure body fails. It is important to provide an explicit return expression at the end of such a procedure body unless failure is intended.

The return and fail expressions cause return from a procedure call and destruction of all dynamic local identifiers for that call. On the other hand,

> suspend *expr1* do *expr2*

returns from the procedure call and produces the value of *expr1* but leaves the call in suspension with the values of dynamic local variables intact. In this case, the procedure call can be resumed to continue evaluation.

The do clause is optional. If it is present, *expr2* is evaluated when the suspend-ing procedure is resumed. Next, *expr1* is resumed. If it produces another result, the procedure suspends again. In this sense, suspend is very similar to every; the difference is that **suspend** causes the procedure in which it occurs to generate a value for each value generated by *expr1*.

Procedures as Values

As mentioned earlier, functions are built-in procedures. The term procedure is used here for both declared procedures and built-in procedures. Procedures are the initial values of global identifiers. Procedures are known and accessed by these global identifiers — their "names". For example, the value of the global identifier write is the function that writes strings. Consequently, in write(s), the value of write is the function that is applied to s.

Since procedures are values, they may be assigned to variables, passed as arguments, and so forth. Therefore,

    print := write

assigns the procedure for write to print, and print(s) subsequently performs the same operation as write(s).

Similarly, if a procedure is declared with the name write, the declared proce-dure value replaces the built-in one, which is then inaccessible. It is good practice to avoid using names for declared procedures that have the same names as built-in ones.

Although the procedure that is applied in a procedure call usually is produced by an identifier, it can be the value of an expression. Therefore,

    plist := [upto, any, many]

constructs a list of procedures and

    plist[2](c, s)

is equivalent to

    any(c, s)

The procedure that is applied in a call is just the "zeroth" argument; it is evaluated before the other arguments.

VARIABLES AND DEREFERENCING

Roughly speaking, a variable is anything to which a value can be assigned. There are several kinds of variables: identifiers (global, local, and static), the elements of lists and tables, the fields of records, subscripted string-valued variables, and some keywords.

When an expression produces a variable and its value is needed, the value of the variable is obtained automatically. This process is called *dereferencing*. Derefer-encing, like type conversion, occurs implicitly. For example, in

```
write(line)
```

the variable line is dereferenced to produce its value, which then is written.

Variables are dereferenced only when a value is needed. For example, in

```
(if i > j then i else j) := 0
```

the variable in the selected clause is not dereferenced and 0 is assigned to i or j, depending on which has the larger prior value.

If the argument of a return expression is a local variable, it is dereferenced and the value is returned, since local variables are accessible only to the procedure in which they are declared. For example, in

```
procedure max(i, j)
   return (if i > j then i else j)
end
```

the result returned is the value of i or j, not the variable.

When a variable is returned from a procedure, it is dereferenced only if it is local or static. Other variables — global variables, keywords that are variables, subscripted structures, and subscripted global strings — are returned as variables and may be assigned a value. Consider the following procedure, which produces the largest value in the list L:

```
procedure maxel(L)
   local i, j, max
   j := 1
   max := L[1]

   every i := 2 to *L do
      if max <:= L[i] then j := i

   return L[j]
end
```

Since the result that is returned is a list element, it is not dereferenced and a value can be assigned to it. For example, maxel(L) := 0

replaces the maximum value in L by 0.

The possibility of such an assignment can be prevented by use of the explicit dereferencing operation .*expr*, which produces the value of *expr*. For example, if the return expression in the previous procedure is changed to

return .L[j]

the result returned is the value of the list element and an attempt to assign to it is erroneous.

The dereferencing operation can be applied to any expression, not just one that produces a variable. Consequently, it is not necessary to know whether or not an expression produces a variable in order to apply the dereferencing operation to it.

In a function or procedure call, dereferencing is not done until all arguments have been evaluated. Consider

write(line, line := read())

In this expression a new value is assigned to line when the second argument,

line := read()

is evaluated. The first argument is not dereferenced until the value of line is changed by the evaluation of the second argument. At this time, both arguments have the same value, and two copies of the newly read line are written, not the former value of line followed by the newly read value.

Argument expressions with such side effects generally should be avoided, but explicit dereferencing can be used, if necessary, to prevent unexpected results from side effects, as in

write(.line, line := read())

NOTES

Recursive Calls

It is common in mathematics to define functions recursively in terms of themselves. The Fibonacci numbers provide a classic example:

$$
\begin{array}{ll}
f(i) = 1 & i = 1, 2 \\
f(i) = f(i-1) + f(i-2) & i > 2 \\
f(i) & \text{undefined otherwise}
\end{array}
$$

The sequence of Fibonacci numbers for $i = 1, 2, 3, \ldots$ is $1, 1, 2, 3, 5, 8, 13, \ldots$.

Since a procedure can call itself, this mathematical definition can be tran-scribed mechanically into a procedure that computes the Fibonacci numbers:

```
procedure fib(i)

    if i = (1 | 2) then return 1
    else return fib(i – 1) + fib(i – 2)

end
```

Recursive calls rely on the fact that the identifier for the procedure name is global. For example, within the procedure body for fib(), fib is a global identifier whose value is the procedure itself.

While a recursive definition may be elegant and concise, the use of recursion for computation can be very inefficient, especially when it depends on the compu-tation of previous values. For example, to compute fib(5), it is necessary to compute fib(4) and fib(3). The computation of fib(4) also requires the computation of fib(3), and so on. Redundant computations often can be avoided by finding an alternative iterative solution (see the exercises at the end of this chapter).

In some cases, iterative solutions can be difficult or impractical to formulate. The classic example is Ackermann's function (Manna, 1974):

$$
\begin{array}{ll}
a\,(\,i,j) = j + 1 & i = 0, j \geq 0 \\
a\,(\,i,j\,) = a\,(\,i-1,1\,) & i > 0, j = 0 \\
a\,(\,i,j) = a\,(\,i-1, a\,(i, j-1)) & i > 0, j > 0 \\
a\,(\,i,j\,) & \text{undefined otherwise}
\end{array}
$$

One method for avoiding redundant computation in recursive procedures is to provide a mechanism whereby the values of previous computations are remem-bered (Bird, 1980). These values then can be looked up instead of being recomputed. A static identifier can be used to provide the necessary memory. Consider the following reformulation of fib(i):

```
procedure fib(i)
    static fibmem
    local j

    initial {
        fibmem := table(0)
        fibmem[1] := fibmem[2] := 1
        }

    if (j := fibmem[i]) > 0 then return j
    else return fibmem[i] := fib(i – 1) + fib(i – 2)

end
```

A table with default value 0 is assigned to the static identifier fibmem when the procedure is called the first time. Note that 0 is not a possible value in the Fibonacci sequence. The values for 1 and 2 are placed in this table. In general, if the desired value has already been computed, fibmem[i] is greater than zero and is returned. Otherwise the desired value is computed and stored in the table before returning. Note that the computation still is recursive, but no value is computed recursively more than once.

Syntactic Considerations

The precedence of return is lower than that of any infix operation, so

```
return i + j
```

groups as

```
return (i + j)
```

The *expr* following return is optional; if *expr* is omitted, the null value is returned. This is useful in procedures that do not have any other value to return and corresponds to the initial null value of identifiers. Since *expr* is optional, if the value of an expression is to be returned, the expression must begin on the same line as the return. For example,

```
return
    expr
```

returns the null value and *expr* is never evaluated.

Static Variables and Initial Clauses

As shown in an example earlier in this chapter, static variables can be used in combination with an initial clause to perform a computation only once in order to provide a value needed in many calls of the same procedure, as in:

```
procedure alphan()
    local line
    static chars

    initial chars := &letters ++ digits
        ...
```

A common mistake is to forget the static declaration, as in

```
procedure alphan()
  local line

  initial chars := &letters ++ digits
         ...
```

In this case the procedure works correctly the first time it is called, but in subsequent calls the variable chars, not being static, is local by default and has the null value. Since the initial clause is only evaluated on the first call, chars is not assigned a value and an error results in most situations.

9

Co-Expressions

In normal expression evaluation, the results produced by an expression are limited to the place where that expression appears in the program. Furthermore, the results of an expression can be produced only by iteration or goal-directed evaluation; there is no mechanism for explicitly resuming an expression to get a result. Consequently, the results produced by an expression are strictly constrained, both in location and in the sequence of program evaluation.

Co-expressions overcome these limitations. A co-expression "captures" an expression so that it can be explicitly resumed at any time and place.

CO-EXPRESSION OPERATIONS

Co-Expression Creation

A co-expression is a data object that contains a reference to an expression and an environment for the evaluation of that expression. A co-expression is created by the control structure

> create *expr*

The create expression does not evaluate *expr*. Instead, it produces a co-expression that references *expr*. This co-expression can be assigned to a variable, passed as an

argument to a procedure, returned from a procedure, and in general handled like any
other first-class value. A co-expression contains not only a reference to its argument
expression, but also a copy of the dynamic local variables for the procedure in which the
create appears. These copied variables have the same values as the corresponding
dynamic local variables have at the time the **create** expression is evaluated. This frees
expr from the place in the program where it appears and provides it with an environment
of its own.

An example is

```
procedure writepos(s1, s2)

   locs1 := create find(s1)
   locs2 := create find(s2)
            ...
end
```

Here the values assigned to locs1 and locs2 are co-expressions corresponding to the
expressions find(s1) and find(s2), respectively.

Activating Co-Expressions

Control is transferred to a co-expression by *activating* it with the operation @C. At
this point, execution continues in the expression referenced by C. When this expression
produces a result, control is returned to the activating expression and the result that is
produced becomes the result of the activation expression. For example, if

```
articles := create("a" | "an" | "the")
```

then

```
write(@articles)
```

transfers control to the expression

```
"a" | "an" | "the"
```

which produces "a" and returns control to the activation expression, which then writes
that result.

If the co-expression is activated again, control is transferred to the place in its
expression where it last produced a result and execution continues there. Thus,
subsequent to the activation above,

```
second := @articles
```

assigns "an" to second and

third := @articles

assigns "the" to third. If article is activated again, the activation fails because there are no more results for the expression that is resumed.

The activation operation itself produces at most one result, but it fails when all results of the co-expression have been produced. Consequently,

while write(@locs1)

writes out all the positions at which s1 occurs in the subject and the loop terminates when find(s1) has no more results and @locs1 fails. Note that this expression produces the same results as

every write(find(s1))

In general, in the absence of side effects

|@C

generates the same results as the expression referenced by C. Activation may occur at any time and place, however, while producing results by iteration is confined to the site at which the expression occurs.

An important aspect of activation is that it produces at most one result. Therefore, the results of a generator can be produced one at a time, where and when they are needed. For example, the results of generators can be intermingled, as in

while write(@locs1, " ", @locs2)

which writes the locations of s1 and s2 in the subject, side-by-side in columns. Since activation fails when there are no more results, the loop terminates when one of the generators runs out of results.

The results produced by a co-expression are dereferenced according to the same rules that apply to procedures. Specifically, if the result is a local variable in the co-expression, it is dereferenced.

Refreshing Co-Expressions

Since activation produces a result for a co-expression, it has the side effect of changing the "state" of the co-expression, and effectively consumes a result, much in the way that reading a line of a file consumes that line. Sometimes it is useful to "start a co-expression over". Although there is no way to reset the state of a co-expression to its initial value at the time of its creation, the operation ^C produces a "refreshed" *copy* of a co-expression C. The term "refresh" is somewhat of a misnomer, since it sounds like C is refreshed; in fact, it does not change C, but instead produces a new co-expression. Typical usage is

    C := ^C

Number of Values Produced

The "size" of a co-expression, given by *C, is the number of results it has produced. Each successful activation of a co-expression increments its size (which starts at 0). For example,

    if *C = 0 then write(@C)

writes a result for C, provided it has not yet produced a result. Of course, @C fails if there are no results at all. Similarly,

    while @C
    write(*C)

writes the number of results for the expression referenced by C. Such usage obviously is risky, since an expression may have an infinite number of results.

Co-Expression Environments

As mentioned earlier, a co-expression is created with *copies* of the dynamic local identifiers for the procedure in which the **create** expression occurs. These copies have the values of the corresponding local variables at the time the **create** expression is evaluated. This aspect of co-expression creation has several implica-tions.

Since every co-expression has its own copies of dynamic local variables, two co-expressions can share a variable only if it is global or static. Failure to recognize that every co-expression has its own copy of its local variables can lead to program-ming mistakes, since the names of the variables in different co-expressions created in the same procedure are the same, making the variables appear to be the same.

When a new co-expression is created by ^C, new copies of the dynamic local variables are made, but with the values they had at the time that C was originally created. Consider, for example,

    local i

    i := 1
    seq1 := create |(i *:= 2)

    i := 3
    seq2 := create |(i *:= 2)

The results produced by successive activations of **seq1** are 2, 4, 8, ... , while the results produced by **seq2** are 6, 12, 24, ... Then, for

```
seq3 := ^seq1
```

the results produced by **seq3** are 2, 4, 8, ... , since the initial value of i in **seq1** is 1 and it is not affected by the assignment of 3 to i after **seq1** is created — the two variables are distinct.

USING CO-EXPRESSIONS

As mentioned earlier, co-expressions are useful in situations in which the produc-tion of the results of a generator needs to be controlled, instead of occurring automatically as the result of goal-directed evaluation or iteration. Since most of the utility of co-expressions comes from generators, most co-expression applications depend on the use of generators.

Labels and Tags

In some situations, a sequence of labels or tags is needed. For example, an assembler may need a source of unique labels for referencing the code it produces, while a procedure that traverses a graph may need tags to name nodes.

A generator, such as

```
"L" || seq()
```

is a convenient way of formulating a sequence of labels. However, the need for a new label may occur at different times and places in the program and a single generator such as the one above cannot be used. One solution to this problem is to avoid generators and use a procedure such as

```
procedure label()
   static i

   initial i := 0

   return "L" || (i +:= 1)
end
```

Consequently, every call of label() produces a new label.

The use of such a procedure gives up much of the power of expression evaluation in Icon, since it encodes, at the source level, the computation that a generator does internally and automatically. To use a generator, a co-expression such as

        label := create ("L" || seq())

suffices. Here, every evaluation of @label produces a new label.

Parallel Evaluation

One of the common paradigms that motivates co-expression usage is the generation of results from generators in parallel. Consider, for example, producing a tabulation showing the decimal, hexadecimal, and octal values for all characters, along with their images. The values for each column are easily produced by generators:

        0 to 255

        !"0123456789ABCDEF" || !"0123456789ABCDEF"

        (0 to 3) || (0 to 7) || (0 to 7)

        image(!&cset)

In order to produce a tabulation, however, the results of these generators are needed in parallel. This cannot be done by simple expression evaluation. The solution is to create a co-expression for each generator and to activate these co-expressions in parallel:

        decimal := create (0 to 255)
        hex := create (!"0123456789ABCDEF" || !"0123456789ABCDEF")
        octal := create ((0 to 3) || (0 to 7) || (0 to 7))
        character := create image(!&cset)

Then an expression such as

        while write(right(@decimal, 10), " \t ", right(@hex, 10), " \t
        ", right(@octal, 10), " \t ", right(@character, 12))

can be used to produce the tabulation:

0	00	000	"\x00"
1	01	001	"\x01"
2	02	002	"\x02"
3	03	003	"\x03"
4	04	004	"\x04"
	...		
97	61	141	"a"
98	62	142	"b"
99	63	143	"c"

100	64	144	"d"
		...	
251	FB	373	"\xfb"
252	FC	374	"\xfc"
253	FD	375	"\xfd"
254	FE	376	"\xfe"
255	FF	377	"\xff"

Another example of parallel evaluation occurs when the results produced by a generator are to be assigned to a sequence of variables. Suppose the first three results for find(s) are to be assigned to i, j, and k, respectively. This can be done as follows:

```
loc := create find(s)

every (i | j | k) := @loc
```

Of course, if find(s) has fewer than three results, not all of the assignments are made.

PROGRAMMER-DEFINED CONTROL STRUCTURES

Control structures are provided so that the flow of control during program execu-tion can be modified depending on the results produced by expressions. In Icon, most control structures depend on success or failure. For example, the outcome of

if *expr1* then *expr2* else *expr3*

depends on whether or not *expr1* succeeds or fails.

Icon's built-in control structures are designed to handle the situations that arise most often in programming. There are many possible control structures in addition to the ones that Icon provides (parallel evaluation is perhaps the most obvious).

Co-expressions make it possible to extend Icon's built-in repertoire of control structures. Consider a simple example of parallel evaluation:

```
procedure parallel(C1, C2)
   local x

   repeat {
     if x := @C1 then suspend x else fail if
     x := @C2 then suspend x else fail
     }

end
```

where C1 and C2 are co-expressions. For example, the results for

parallel(create !&lcase, create !&ucase)

are "a", "A", "b", "B", ... "z", and "Z". In this case, both co-expressions have the same number of results. In general, parallel(C1, C2) terminates when either C1 or C2 runs out of results.

This formulation of parallel evaluation is cumbersome, since the user must explicitly create co-expressions for each invocation of parallel(). Icon provides a form of procedure invocation in which arguments are passed as a list of co-expressions. This form of invocation is denoted by braces instead of parentheses, so that

p{*expr1*, *expr2*, ..., *exprn*}

is equivalent to

p([create *expr1*, create *expr2*, ..., create *exprn*])

Thus, p() is called with a single argument, so that an arbitrary number of co-expressions can be given.

Using this facility, parallel evaluation can be formulated as follows:

```
procedure Parallel(L) # called as Parallel{expr1, expr2} local
   x

   repeat {
     if x := @L[1] then suspend x else fail if
     x := @L[2] then suspend x else fail
     }

   end
```

For example, the results for Parallel{!&lcase, !&ucase} are "a", "A", "b", "B" ... "z", and "Z".

It is easy to extend parallel evaluation to an arbitrary number of arguments:

```
procedure Parallel(L) # called as Parallel{expr1, expr2, ..., exprn} local
   x, C

   repeat
     every C := !L do
       if x := @C then suspend x else fail

   end
```

Another example of the use of programmer-defined control structures is a procedure that generalizes alternation to an arbitrary number of expressions:

```
procedure Alt(L)              # called as Alt{expr1, expr2, ..., exprn}
   local C

   every C := !L do
      suspend |@C

end
```

Some operations on sequences of results are more useful if applied in parallel, rather than on the cross product of results. An example is

```
procedure Add(L)              # called as Add{expr1, expr2}

   suspend |(@L[1] + @L[2])

end
```

String invocation often is useful in programmer-defined control operations. An example is a procedure that "reduces" a sequence by applying a binary operation to successive results:

```
procedure Reduce(L)        # called as Reduce{op, expr}
   local op, opnds, result

   op := @L[1] | fail          # get the operator
   opnds := L[2]               # get the co–expression for the arguments

   result := @opnds | fail

   while result := op(result, @opnds)

   return result

end
```

For example, the result of **Reduce{"+", 1 to 10}** is 55.

Another application for programmer-defined control structures is in the production of a string representation of a sequence of results:

```
$define Limit 10

procedure Seqimage(L) # called as Seqimage{expr, i}
   local seq, result, i

   seq := ""

   i := @L[2] | Limit              # limit on number of results
```

```
while result := image(@L[1]) do
   { if *L[1] > i then {
       seq ||:= ", ..."
       break
       }
   else seq ||:= ", " || result
   }
return "{" || seq[3:0] || "}" | "{}"
end
```

For example, the result produced by Seqimage{1 to 8} is "{1, 2, 3, 4, 5, 6, 7, 8}".

OTHER FEATURES OF CO-EXPRESSIONS

Although co-expressions are motivated by the need to control the results produced by generators, they also can be used as coroutines. A general description of coroutine programming is beyond the scope of this book; see Knuth (1968); Marlin (1980); and Dahl, Dijkstra, and Hoare (1972).

Transfer of Control Among Co-Expressions

As illustrated earlier, a co-expression can transfer control to another co-expression by two means: activating it explicitly, as in @C, or returning control to it implicitly by producing a result. Despite the appearance of dissimilarity between these two methods for transferring control, they really are symmetric.

It is important to understand that transferring control from one co-expression to another co-expression by either method changes the place in the program where execution is taking place and changes the environment in which expressions are evaluated. Unlike procedure calls, however, transfer of control among co-expres-sions is not hierarchical.

This is illustrated by the use of co-expressions as coroutines. Consider, for example, the following program:

```
global C1, C2

procedure main()

   C1 := create note(C2, "co-expression C2")
   C2 := create note(C1, "co-expression C1")

   @C1

end

procedure note(C, tag)
```

```
      local i

      i := 0

      repeat {
        write("activation ", i +:= 1, " of ",
        tag) @C
        }

   end
```

When C1 is activated, the procedure note() is called with two arguments: the co-expression C2 and a string used for identification. Execution continues in note(). A line of output is produced, and C2 is activated. As a result, there is another call of note(). It writes a line of output and activates C1. At this point, control is transferred to the first call of note() at the point it activated C2. Control then transfers back and forth between the two procedure calls, and the output produced is

```
      activation 1 of co–expression C2
      activation 1 of co–expression C1
      activation 2 of co–expression C2
      activation 2 of co–expression C1
      activation 3 of co–expression C2
      activation 3 of co–expression C1
      activation 4 of co–expression C2
      activation 4 of co–expression C1
      activation 5 of co–expression C2
      activation 5 of co–expression C1
      activation 6 of co–expression C2
      activation 6 of co–expression C1
                    ...
```

This continues endlessly and neither procedure call ever returns.

Built-In Co-Expressions

There are three built-in co-expressions that facilitate transfer of control: &source, &current, and &main.

The value of &source is the co-expression that activated the currently active co-expression. Thus,

```
   @&source
```

"returns" to the activating co-expression.

The value of &current is the co-expression in which execution is currently taking place. For example, process(&current)

passes the current co-expression to the procedure process(). This co-expression could be used to assure return of control to the co-expression that was current when process() was called.

    The value of &main is the co-expression for the invocation of the main procedure. This co-expression corresponds to the invocation of the main procedure that initiates program execution, which can be viewed as

    @(create main())

The co-expression &main is the first co-expression that is created in every program.

    If program execution is taking place in any co-expression,

    @&main

returns control to the co-expression for the procedure main() at the point it activated a co-expression. Note that this location need not be in the procedure main() itself, since main() may have called another procedure from which the activation of a co-expression took place.

Transmission

    A result can be transmitted to a co-expression when it is activated. Transmis-sion is done by the operation

    expr @ C

where C is activated and the result of *expr* is transmitted to it. In fact, @C is just an abbreviation for

    &null @ C

so that every activation actually transmits a result to the co-expression that is being activated.

    On the first activation of a co-expression, the transmitted result is discarded, since there is nothing to receive it. On subsequent activations, the transmitted result becomes the result of the expression that activated the current co-expression.

    The use of transmission is illustrated by the following program, which reads in lines from standard input, breaks them up into words, and writes out these words on separate lines. Co-expressions are used to isolate the tasks: reading lines, producing the words from the lines, and writing out the words.

```
        global words, lines, writer

        procedure main()

          words := create word()
          lines := create reader()
          writer := create output()

          @writer

        end


        procedure word()

          while line := @lines do
            line ? while tab(upto(&letters)) do
              tab(many(&letters)) @ writer

        end


        procedure reader()

          while read() @ words

        end


        procedure output()

          while write(@words)

          @&main

        end
```

Note that output() activates main() to terminate program execution.

This example is designed to illustrate transmission, not as a recommended programming technique. The problem above can be solved more simply by using generators and procedure calls, since there is nothing in the problem that requires coroutine control flow or the generation of results at arbitrary times or places. Coroutine programming generally is appropriate only in large programs that benefit from the organization that coroutines allow. Knuth (1968) says "It is rather difficult to find short, simple examples of coroutines which illustrate the importance of the idea; the most useful coroutine applications generally are quite lengthy", and Marlin (1980) remarks " ... the choice of an example program is ... difficult ... . The programming methodology is intended for programming-in-the-large".

NOTES

Library Resources

The Icon program library has two modules that contain programmer-defined control operations:

pdco	procedures for various control operations
pdae	procedures for programmer-defined argument-evaluation methods

Multi-Thread Icon

There is a version of Icon, called MT-Icon, that supports the execution of several programs in the same execution space. Control is passed between programs using co-expression activation. See Jeffery (1993). This version of Icon also provides instrumentation that allows program activity to be monitored (Griswold and Jeffery, 1996).

Syntactic Considerations

The reserved word **create** has lower precedence than any operator symbol. For example,

        articles := create "a" | "an" | "the"

groups as

        articles := create ("a" | "an" | "the")

Although parentheses usually are unnecessary, they improve the readability of **create** expressions.

10

Data Types

As illustrated in the previous chapters, Icon has a large repertoire of types, twelve in all:

co–expression	list	set
cset	null	string
file	procedure	table
integer	real	window

Files and windows are described in Chapters 11 and 12.

In addition, record declarations add new "programmer-defined" types.

TYPE DETERMINATION

Sometimes it is useful, especially in program debugging, to be able to determine the type of a value. The function type(x) produces the string name of the type of x. For example, the value of

        type("Hello world")

is "string". Similarly,

        if type(i) == "integer" then write("okay")

writes okay if the value of i is an integer.

Functions, which are simply built-in procedures, have type procedure. For example, the value of

    type(write)

is "procedure".

A record declaration adds a type to the built-in repertoire of Icon. For example, the declaration

    record complex(rpart, ipart)

adds the type complex. If a complex record is assigned to origin, as in

    origin := complex(0.0, 0.0)

then the value of

    type(origin)

is "complex".

TYPE CONVERSION

Csets, integers, real numbers, and strings can be converted to values of other types. The possible type conversions are given in the following table.

type in	*type out*			
	cset	integer	real	string
cset	=	?	?	u
integer	u	=	?	u
real	u	u	=	u
string	u	?	?	=

The symbol u indicates a conversion that is always possible, while ? indicates a conversion that may or may not be possible, depending on the value. The = indicates that nothing needs to be done to convert a value to its own type.

A string can be converted to a numeric type only if it "looks like a number". For example, "1500" can be converted to the integer 1500, but "a1500" and "1,500" cannot be converted to integers. Signs and radix literals are allowed in conversion of strings to numeric types. For example, "−2.5" can be converted to −2.5 and "16ra" can be converted to 10. Leading and trailing blanks are ignored in strings that are converted to numeric types.

Since real numbers are limited in magnitude, the strings that can be converted to real numbers are correspondingly limited. When a real number is converted to an integer, any fractional part is discarded in the conversion; no rounding occurs.

When csets are converted to strings, the characters are put in lexical order. For example, conversion of &lcase to a string produces "abcdefghijklmnopqrstuvwxyz".

When a cset is converted to a numeric type, it is first converted to a string, and then string-to-numeric conversion is performed.

Type conversions take two forms: *implicit* and *explicit*.

Implicit Type Conversion

Implicit type conversion occurs in contexts where the type of a value is different from the type expected by an operation. For example, in

    write(*line)

the integer produced by *line is converted to a string in order to be written. Similarly, in

    i := upto("aeiou", line)

the string "aeiou" is automatically converted to a cset.

In some situations, implicit conversion can be used to convert a value to a desired type. For example,

    N := +s

is a way of converting a string that looks like a number to an actual number. Note that the converted value is assigned to N, but the value of s remains unchanged.

Implicit type conversion sometimes can have unexpected effects. For example, a comparison operation produces the value of its right argument, converted to the type expected by the comparison. Therefore,

    i := (j > "20")

assigns the integer 20, not the string "20" to i, provided the comparison succeeds.

Unnecessary type conversion can be a source of inefficiency. Since there is no direct evidence of implicit type conversion, this problem can go unnoticed. For example, in an expression such as

upto("aeiou")

the argument is converted from a string to a cset every time the expression is evaluated. If this expression occurs in a loop that is evaluated frequently, program execution speed may suffer. Where a cset is expected, it is important to use a cset literal or some other cset-valued expression that does not require conversion.

An implicit type conversion that cannot be performed is an error and causes program execution to terminate with a diagnostic message. For example,

N +:= "a"

is erroneous.

Implicit type conversion is not performed for comparing values in case clauses or for the keys in tables. For example, T[1] and T["1"] reference different elements in T.

Explicit Type Conversion

Explicit conversion is performed by functions whose names correspond to the desired types. For example,

s := string(x)

converts x to a string and assigns that string value to s. The other explicit type-conversion functions are cset(x), integer(x), and real(x). The function numeric(x) converts strings to their corresponding numeric values if possible. This function is useful for converting a value that may represent either an integer or a real number. For example,

numeric("10.5")

produces 10.5, but

integer("10.5")

produces 10.

Explicit conversion sometimes can be used as a way of performing a compu-tation that otherwise would be difficult. For example,

s := string(cset(s))

eliminates duplicate characters of s and puts the remaining characters in lexical order.

If an explicit type conversion cannot be performed, the type conversion function fails. For example,

numeric("a")

fails. Explicit type conversion therefore can be used to test the convertibility of a value without risking program termination.

THE NULL VALUE

The null value is a single, unique value of type null. Identifiers, except for those for functions and procedures, have the null value initially.

The null value, usually provided as the result of an omitted argument, is also used to specify default values in many functions. Most other uses of the null value are erroneous. This prevents the accidental use of an uninitialized identifier in a computation. For example, if no value has been assigned to i, evaluation of the expression

j := i + 10

causes program termination with a diagnostic message.

Since the null value cannot be used in most computations, care should be taken to specify appropriate initial values for structures. Similarly,

words := table()

creates a table in which the default value is null. Consequently,

words["The"] +:= 1

is erroneous, since this expression attempts to add 1 to the null value.

Assignment is indifferent to the null value. Therefore,

x := &null

assigns the null value to x.

There are two operations that succeed or fail, depending on whether or not an expression has the null value. The operation

/x

succeeds and produces the null value if x has the null value, but it fails if x has any other value.

The operation

\x

succeeds and produces the value of x if that value is not the null value, but it fails if x produces the null value. This operation is useful for determining if a variable has been initialized.

If the argument of one of these operations is a variable and the operation succeeds, the operation produces the variable. Therefore, assignment can be made to the result of such an operation, so that

/x := 0

assigns 0 to x if x has the null value, while

\x := 0

assigns 0 to x if x does not have the null value.

As in all operations, the arguments of these operations can be expressions. For example, if a table is created with the null default value, as in

T := table()

then

\T["the"]

succeeds if the key "the" in T has been assigned a nonnull value; otherwise, this expression fails.

The control structure not *expr* produces the null value if *expr* fails.

COMPARING VALUES

Five of the twelve built-in data types in Icon — csets, integers, real numbers, strings, and the null value — have the property of having "unique" values. This means that equivalent values of these types are indistinguishable, regardless of how they are computed. For example, there is just one distinguishable integer 0. This value is the same, regardless of how it is computed.

Whether or not two numbers are the same can be determined by a numerical comparison operation. Therefore,

$$(1 - 1) = (2 - 2)$$

succeeds, because the two arguments have the same value.

The property of uniqueness is natural for numbers and is essential for numeri-cal computation. The uniqueness of csets and strings is not a necessary consequence of their inherent properties, but it plays an important role in Icon. For example,

$$("ab" \parallel "cd") == ("a" \parallel "bcd")$$

succeeds because both arguments have the same value, even though the value is computed in different ways.

Numerical and string comparisons are restricted to specific data types, al-though type conversions are performed automatically.

There is also a general value-comparison operation

$$x === y$$

which compares arbitrary values x and y, as well as the converse operation

$$x \sim=== y$$

Unlike string comparison, value comparison fails if x and y do not have the same type: No implicit type conversion is performed. For the types that have unique values, value comparison succeeds if the values are the same, regardless of how they are computed. For other types, value comparison succeeds only if the values are *identical*.

Lists can be equivalent without being identical. For example,

$$list(10, 0) === list(10, 0)$$

fails because the two lists are not identical, even though they are equivalent in size and contents. However, in

```
vector := list(10, 0)
vector1 := vector
vector === vector1
```

the comparison succeeds because assignment does not copy structures and the two arguments have identical values.

Value comparison is used implicitly in case expressions and table references. For example, if the value of x is the integer 1, in

```
case x of {
  "1": expr
    ...
}
```

the first case clause is not selected, since the types of the values compared are different. Similarly,

> T["abcdefghijklmnopqrstuvwxyz"]

and

> T[&lcase]

reference different values in the table T, but

> T["abcdefghijklmnopqrstuvwxyz"]

and

> T[string(&lcase)]

reference the same value, since string values are unique.

COPYING VALUES

Any value can be copied by copy(x). For lists, sets, tables, and records, a new copy of x is made. This copy is distinct from x. For example, in

```
vector := list(10, 0)
vector === copy(vector)
```

the comparison fails. Only the list itself is copied; values in the copy are the same as in the original list (copying is "one level"). For example, in

```
L1 := [ ]
L2 := [L1]
L3 := copy(L2)
L3[1] === L2[1]
```

the comparison succeeds, since both L2[1] and L3[1] are the same list, L1.

For values other than lists, sets, tables, and records, copy(x) simply produces the value of x; no actual copy is made. Therefore,

    "Hello" === copy("Hello")

succeeds. Copying a co-expression does not produce a refreshed copy of it.

NOTES

Large Integers

Conversion between integers and strings and csets is supported for both native integers and integers too large to represented as native integers. (See **Notes** in Chapter 5.) However, the time required to convert a large integer to a string (and hence cset) and the time to convert a string to a large integer are proportional to the square of the number of digits. For very large integers, this can be an important consideration.

For example, as of this writing the largest known prime is $2^{1257787} - 1$, which has 378,632 digits. It takes about 123 times as long to convert this number to a string as it does to compute it.

Since writing a large integer requires its conversion to a string, care should be taken not do this unnecessarily.

11

Input and Output

FILES

All reading and writing in earlier examples use *standard input* and *standard output*. In an interactive system, standard input usually comes from the user's console and standard output usually is written to this console. These standard files are implicit in reading and writing operations; they are the default in case no specific files are given.

On most systems standard input and standard output can be connected to specific files when the Icon program is run. This allows a program to use any input and output files without having to incorporate the names of the files in the text of the program. By convention, *standard error output* is used for error messages, so that such messages are not mixed up with normal output.

Values of type file are used to reference actual files of data that are external to the program. There are three predefined values of type file:

&input standard input &output standard output &errout standard error output

The values of these keywords cannot be changed.

While many programs can be written using just standard input and output, sometimes it is necessary to use other files. For example, some programs must read from specific files or write to specific files.

The name of a file is specified when it is opened for reading or writing; at this time a value of type file is created in the program and connected with the actual file that is to be read or written. The function open(s1, s2) opens the file named s1 according to options given in s2 and produces a value of type file that can be used to reference the named file. How files are named is a property of the operating system under which Icon runs, not a property of Icon itself.

The options given in s2 specify how the file is to be used. Some options can be used in combination. These options inherently are somewhat dependent on the operating system, although some options are common to all operating systems. The two basic options for opening files are:

"r"	open for reading
"w"	open for writing

Other options are:

"b"	open for reading and writing (bidirectional)
"a"	open for writing in append mode
"c"	create and open for writing
"t"	open in translated mode
"u"	open in untranslated mode
"p"	open pipe

The "b" option usually applies to interactive input and output at a terminal that behaves like a file that is both written and read. With the "p" option, the first argument is passed to an operating-system shell for execution. Not all operating systems support pipes. If a file is opened for writing but not for reading, "c" is implied. The "c" and "a" options have no effect on pipes. Upper- and lowercase letters are equivalent in option specifications. The translated and untranslated modes and pipes are described later in this chapter.

If the option is omitted, "r" is assumed. For example,

    intext := open("shaw.txt")

opens the file shaw.txt for reading and assigns the resulting file to intext. The omission of the second argument with the subsequent default to "r" is common practice in Icon programming.

A file that is opened for reading must already exist; if it does not, open() fails. A file that is opened for writing may or may not already exist. If it does not exist, a new file with the name s1 is created. If this is not possible (there may be various reasons, depending on the environment), open() fails. If the file does exist, the previous contents of the file are destroyed unless the "a" option is used, in which case new output is appended to the end of the old data. Some files may be protected to prevent them from being modified; open() fails if an attempt is made to open such a file for writing.

Since open() may fail for a variety of reasons, it is good practice to check for possible failure, even if it is not expected. An example is

if not(intext := open("shaw.txt")) then stop("cannot open shaw.txt")

This also can be formulated as

intext := open("shaw.txt") | stop("cannot open shaw.txt")

The function close(f) closes the file f. This has the effect of physically complet-ing output for f, such as flushing output buffers, and making the file inaccessible for further input or output. A file that has been closed can be opened again, however. The function flush(f) flushes any accumulated output for f.

If several files are used, it is good practice to close files when they are no longer needed, since most operating systems allow only a limited number of files to be open at the same time. All open files are closed automatically when program execution terminates.

INPUT

The function read(f) reads the next line from the file referenced by f. If f is omitted, standard input is assumed, as is illustrated in earlier examples. For example, the following program copies shaw.txt to standard output:

```
procedure main()

    intext := open("shaw.txt") | stop("cannot open
    shaw.txt") while write(read(intext))

end
```

In text files, line terminators separate the lines. These line terminators are discarded by read(f) and are not included in the strings it produces.

When there is no more data in a file, read() fails. This end-of-file condition can be used to terminate a loop in which the read occurs, as illustrated in earlier examples.

The operation !f generates the lines from the file f, terminating when an end of file is reached. As with read(), line terminators are discarded. For example,

```
every line := !&input do ...
```

is equivalent to

```
while line := read() do ...
```

Sometimes it is useful to be able to read a fixed number of characters instead of lines. This is done by

```
reads(f, i)
```

where f is the file that is read and i specifies how many characters are to be read. If f is omitted, standard input is assumed. If i is omitted, 1 is assumed. The function reads(f, i) reads a string of i characters; line terminators are not discarded and they appear in the string that is read. If there are not i characters remaining, only the remaining characters are read. In this case the value produced is shorter than i. The function reads() fails if there are no characters remaining in the file.

There is no limit to the length of a string that can be produced by read() or reads() except for the amount of memory needed to store it.

OUTPUT

The function

```
write(x1, x2, ..., xn)
```

writes a line. What write() does depends on the types of its arguments. The simplest case is

```
write(s)
```

which simply writes a line consisting of the string s to standard output. The function write() automatically appends a line terminator, so s becomes a new line at the end of the file.

If there are several string arguments, as in

```
write(s1, s2, ..., sn)
```

then s1, s2, ..., sn are written in sequence and a line terminator is appended to the end. Therefore, the line consists of the concatenation of s1, s2, ..., sn, although the concatenation is done on the file, not in the Icon program. When several strings are written in succession to form a single line, it is more efficient to use write() with several arguments than to actually concatenate the strings in the program.

The most general case is

write(x1, x2, ..., xn)

where x1, x2, ..., xn may have various types. If the ith argument, xi, is not a string, it is converted to a string if possible and then written. If xi is a file, subsequent output is directed to that file. The following program, for example, copies shaw.txt to standard output and also copies it to shaw.cpy:

```
procedure main()

    intext := open("shaw.txt") | stop("cannot open shaw.txt")
    outtext := open("shaw.cpy", "w") | stop("cannot open shaw.cpy")

    while line := read(intext) do
      { write(line)
      write(outtext, line)
      }
end
```

The output file can be changed in midstream. Therefore,

write(&errout, s1, &output, s2)

writes s1 to standard error output and s2 to standard output. A separate line is written to each file; a line terminator is appended whenever the file is changed.

If the ith argument, xi, is not a file and is not convertible to a string, program execution terminates with a diagnostic message. There is one exception; the null value is treated like an empty string. Therefore,

write()

writes an empty line (a line terminator) to standard output.

The function

writes(x1, x2, ..., xn)

is like write(), except that a line terminator is not appended to the end. One line of a file can be built up using writes() several times. Similarly, prompting messages to users of interactive programs can be produced with writes() to allow the user at a computer terminal to enter input on the same visual line as the prompt. For example, the following program prompts the user for the names of the input and output files for a file copy:

```
procedure main()

  writes("specify input file: ")

  while not(intext := open(read())) do
    writes("cannot open input file, respecify: ")

  writes("specify output file: ")
  while not(outtext := open(read(), "w")) do
    writes("cannot open output file, respecify: ")

  while write(outtext, read(intext))

end
```

In addition to writing, write() and writes() produce the value of their last argument. For example,

```
last := write("The final value is ", count)
```

assigns the value of count to last.

There is no limit to the length of a string that can be written by write() or writes() except for the amount of file space needed for it.

TEXT FILES AND BINARY FILES

Text files are usually thought of as files composed of lines that contain printable characters, while binary files (such as executable programs) have no line structure and may contain nonprintable characters. While this view of text and binary files fits most situations well, in reality the distinction is not that clear.

Some computer systems, notably UNIX, do not differentiate at all between text and binary files. On these systems, a file is simply a sequence of characters. Other computer systems distinguish between text and binary files, and a file can be opened in either text or binary mode. How a file is opened determines how it is treated during input and output.

For historical reasons, it also is common on ASCII-based systems to think of text characters as being only those in the first half of the character set (that is, those with the high-order bit not set). However, 128 different characters have proved too few for modern applications, and many systems use almost all of the 256 characters for text. Consequently, the important matter is not the characters that a file contains, but whether or not it is viewed as consisting of lines. When a file is viewed as text, it is thought of as consisting of lines, while there is no such structure in binary files. Conceptually, a line is a sequence of characters followed by a line terminator. When a line is read, the sequence of characters up to the line terminator is returned and the line terminator is discarded. When the line is written, a line terminator is appended to become part of the file.

Unfortunately, not all computer systems use the same line terminator. On UNIX and the Amiga, lines are terminated by linefeed characters (hex 0A). On MS-DOS and the Atari ST, lines are terminated by two characters: return/linefeed pairs (hex 0D/hex 0A). On the Macintosh, lines are terminated by return characters (hex 0D). On some computer systems, the line terminator is not even composed of characters.

Notice that except for the characters actually in the file, the effect is the same when reading and writing lines, regardless of the nature of the line terminator: It is discarded on input and appended on output. As long as line-oriented input/output is done on text files, there is no need to worry about line terminators.

As mentioned previously, on UNIX systems line terminators are linefeed characters, which can be represented literally by "\n". For example,

write(line1, "\n", line2, "\n", line3)

writes three lines, since separating line terminators are provided. Suppose a pro-gram containing this expression is run on an MS-DOS system, where line termina-tors are pairs (represented literally as "\r\n"). It may be surprising to learn that a single "\n" works as a line terminator on MS-DOS also. This is because the input/output system that stands between Icon and the actual file translates line terminators automatically, converting (in MS-DOS) the linefeed to a return/line feed pair.

This translation is a property of the mode in which a file is opened. The translated mode is the default. This translation can be prevented by opening a file in the untranslated mode, using the "u" option, as in open("run.log", "uw"). The default translated mode can be given explicitly with the "t" option, and the same situation applies to opening a file for reading. Note that "u" and "t" options are irrelevant on systems for which the line terminator is the linefeed character. Standard input, standard output, and standard error output are translated.

Normally a text file is not opened in untranslated mode. However, in order to read or write a binary file on a system for which the line terminator is not the linefeed character, the file must be opened in untranslated mode. Otherwise, the data will be corrupted by translation. It is worth noting that some input/output systems treat characters other than line terminators in special ways. This is another reason for being careful to use the untranslated mode for binary data.

Binary input and output usually are done using reads() and writes(). Using reads() prevents line terminators, which may occur in binary data, from being discarded. In addition, reads() permits reading a binary file in fixed-sized pieces. And, of course, writes() prevents unwanted insertion of line terminators in binary data.

Using read() and write() with files opened in the translated mode, and using reads() and writes() with files opened in the untranslated mode, follows from the usual properties of files. It is not a physical or logical necessity. However, adhering to these conventions produces the correct results and avoids problems in most cases.

PIPES

Some operating systems (notably UNIX) support *pipes*, which allow the output of one process to be the input of another process ("piped into it"). In UNIX commands, pipes are indicated by the character | between processes. For example,

    ls | grep dat

is a command that pipes the output of ls into grep. The program ls writes the names of the files in the current directory, and grep writes only the ones containing the string in its argument (dat in this example).

On systems that support pipes, a command string can be opened as a pipe by using the open option "p". For example,

    iconfiles := open("ls *.icn", "p")

assigns a pipe to iconfiles corresponding to the command line above. Consequently,

    while write(read(iconfiles))

writes out the names of all files that end in .icn.

A pipe can be opened for reading ("pr") or writing ("pw"), but not both. Opening for reading is the default, and the "r" can be omitted.

An example of writing to a pipe is

    listprocs := open("grep procedure", "pw")

so that

    while write(listprocs, read())

pipes the lines from standard input into the command grep procedure, which writes only those containing the substring "procedure".

On systems that support pipes, opening command strings as pipes provides a very powerful technique for using other programs during the execution of an Icon program. The use of pipes in Icon programs, however, requires not only an understanding of the programs that are used, but also the system's command-line interpreter ("shell"), how programs work when connected by pipes, and how Icon's input and output work with pipes.

KEYBOARD FUNCTIONS

On systems that support console input and output, there are three keyboard functions.

The function getch() waits until a character is entered from the keyboard and then produces the corresponding one-character string. The character is not dis-played. The function getche() is the same as getch() except that the character is displayed.

The function kbhit() succeeds if a character is available for getch() or getche() but fails otherwise.

RANDOM-ACCESS INPUT AND OUTPUT

There are two functions related to random-access input and output. These functions allow data in files to be accessed non-sequentially.

The function seek(f, i) seeks to character i in file f. As with other positions in Icon, a nonpositive value of i can be used to reference a position relative to the end of f. i defaults to 1. The Icon form of position identification is used; the position of the first character of a file is 1, not 0 as it is in some other random-access facilities. seek(f, i) fails if an error occurs. The function where(f) produces the current character position in the file f.

Random-access input and output may produce peculiar results in the trans-lated mode on systems that have multi-character line terminators. Seeking only the positions previously produced by where(f) minimizes this risk.

OPERATIONS ON FILES

Files can be removed or renamed during program execution. The function remove(s) removes (deletes) the file named s. Subsequent attempts to open the file fail, unless it is created anew. If the file is open, the behavior of remove(s) is system dependent. remove(s) fails if it is unsuccessful.

The function rename(s1, s2) causes the file named s1 to be known subse-quently by the name s2. The file named s1 is effectively removed. If a file named s2 exists prior to the renaming, the behavior is system-dependent. rename(s1, s2) fails if unsuccessful, in which case if the file existed previously it is still known by its original name. Among possible causes of failure are a file currently open or a necessity to copy the file's contents to rename it.

NOTES

Library Resources

The Icon program library module io provides several procedures that may be helpful for matters related to files and reading and writing data.

12

An Overview of Graphics

Icon provides extensive facilities for creating and manipulating windows, drawing various geometric shapes, displaying text in a variety of type faces and sizes, accepting input from a mouse, and so on.

These facilities are too extensive to describe in detail here and are the subject of another book (Griswold, Jeffery, and Townsend, forthcoming). This chapter provides an overview to show the nature of the facilities and indicate what can be done with them.

WINDOW OPERATIONS AND ATTRIBUTES

A window is a rectangular area of the screen on which a program can draw, write text, and receive input. A window usually has a frame provided by the graphics system:

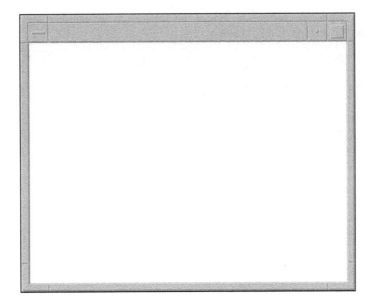

Locations in a window are measured in pixels ("picture elements"), which are small dots that can be illuminated and colored. The window shown above is 400 pixels wide and 300 pixels high.

In the window coordinate system, the upper-left pixel has x-y coordinates (0,0) and locations increase to the right (x-direction) and down (y-direction):

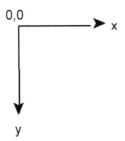

Consequently, the lower-right pixel in the window shown previously is numbered (399,299).

Windows can be opened and closed much in the manner of files. The function call

WOpen("size=400,300")

opens a 400×300 window like the one shown above.

The argument "size=400,300" is an attribute of the window and describes its size. Windows have many other attributes.

Two important attributes are the foreground color, in which drawing and text are displayed, and the background color, which initially fills the window. The default foreground and background colors are black and white, respectively. Other colors can be specified by using the attributes fg and bg, as in

WOpen("size=500, 300", "fg=blue", "bg=light gray")

which produces the window

Any subsequent drawing is done in blue.

The attributes of a window can be changed after a window is opened by using the function WAttrib(). For example, the foreground color can be changed to black by

WAttrib("fg=black")

Subsequent drawing is done in black.

DRAWING

Several drawing functions are available. A line can be drawn between two points by

DrawLine(x1, y1, x2, y2)

where x1 and y1 give the coordinates of the first point and x2 and y2 give the coordinates of the second point.

For example,

```
$define GridWidth      20
$define GridHeight     10

every x := GridWidth to 499 by GridWidth do
    DrawLine(x, 0, x, 299)
every y := GridHeight to 299 by GridHeight do
    DrawLine(0, y, 499, y)
```

produces

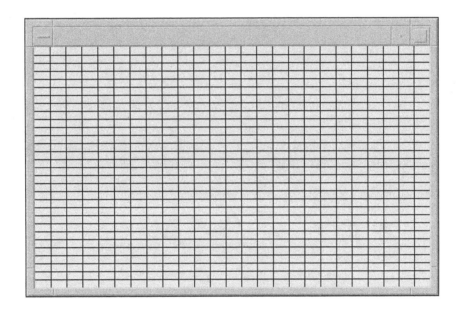

The function DrawRectangle(x, y, w, h) draws a rectangle whose upper-left corner is at x and y, whose width is w, and whose height is h. For example,

```
$define XIncr        35
$define YIncr        15
$define Width       200
$define Height      100
$define Iter          8

every i := 1 to Iter do
    DrawRectangle(i * XIncr, i * YIncr, Width, Height)
```

produces

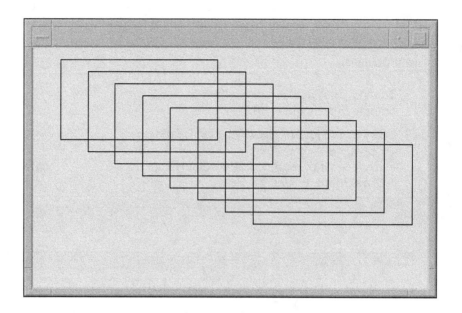

Circles are drawn by DrawCircle(x, y, r), where x and y specify the center of the circle and r its radius.

The following segment of code draws a sequence of circles with centers and radii chosen at random within a range:

```
$define Width        400
$define Height       400
$define Range        35
$define Min          5
$define Iter         50

WOpen("size=" || Width || "," || Height)

every 1 to Iter do
    DrawCircle(?Width, ?Height, ?Range + Min)
```

A typical result looks like this:

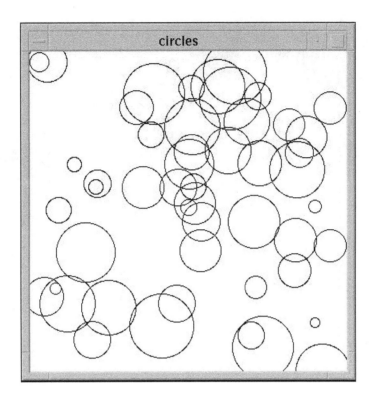

Note that the portions of circles that fall outside the window are not drawn. Drawing is confined to the window; anything that would be outside is "clipped" by the graphics system.

Closed figures can be filled with the background color as opposed to being drawn in outline as in the examples above. For example, FillCircle() draws a circle filled in the foreground color. A variation on the previous example is

```
$define Width        500
$define Height       300
$define Range         25
$define Min            9
$define Iter          25

WOpen("size=" || Width || "," || Height)

every 1 to Iter do
   DrawCircle(?Width, ?Height, ?Range + Min)

every 1 to Iter do
   FillCircle(?Width, ?Height, ?Range + Min)
```

which typically produces

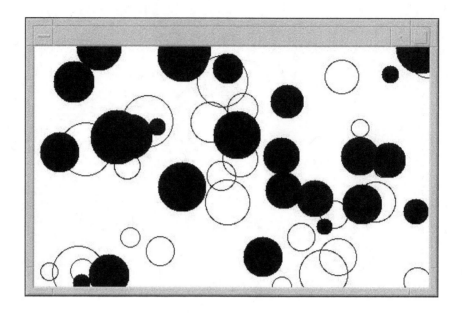

Other functions are provided for erasing portions of a window and drawing individual points, arcs, polygons, and smooth curves.

TEXT

Text is written to a window much in the manner it is written to a file. The position of text in a window is measured in rows and columns. The upper-left character is numbered (1,1).

The function WWrite(s) writes to the window. For example,

    WWrite(" Hello world")

produces the following result:

The initial blank in the string written provides space so that the H does not touch the frame.

One of the advantages of using a window for text is that the size and characteristics of the text can be specified. The characteristics of text are determined by a font, which consists of a type face that specifies its general appearance, a size in pixels, and its style characteristics. The font used for the image above is from a typeface called Times in a size of 12. The style is plain (known as "roman"). Other styles are bold, italic, bold italic, and so forth.

The font is specified by the font attribute, as in

    WAttrib("font=Helvetica,12,bold")

Helvetica is a "sans-serif" font without ornamentation and is used in this book for program material. For the window above,

    WWrite(" The subject of fonts is complex")

produces

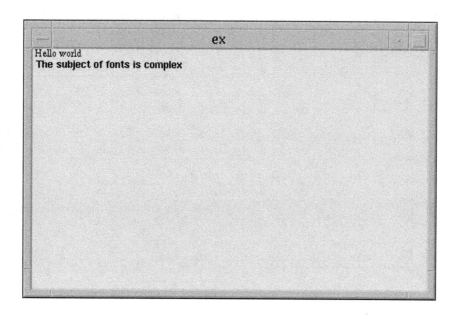

Notice that this line is written below the last line and starts at the left edge of the window. WWrite() produces an "end-of-line" in a manner similar to write() and advances the text position to the next line.

COLOR

Colors are named by English phrases using a system loosely based on Berk (1982). Examples are "brown", "yellowish green", and "moderate purple–gray". The syntax of a color name is

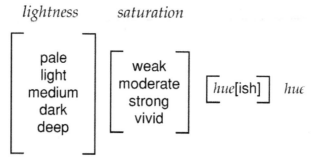

where choices enclosed in brackets are optional and *hue* can be one of black, gray, white, pink, violet, brown, red, orange, yellow, green, cyan, blue, purple, or magenta. A single hyphen or space separates each word from its neighbor.

Color names that are not recognized by Icon are passed to the graphics system for interpretation, allowing the use of system-dependent names.

Here is another variation on drawing circles, this time with colors, which are shown in gray here:

```
$define Width        500
$define Height       300
$define Range         25
$define Min            9
$define Iter          25

colors := ["dark gray", "light red", "light greenish blue", "vivid blue",
    "pale purple", "light brown", "medium brown", "orange", "black"]

WOpen("size=" || Width || "," || Height)

every 1 to Iter do {
  WAttrib("fg=" || ?colors)
  DrawCircle(?Width, ?Height, ?Range + Min)
   }

every 1 to Iter do {
  WAttrib("fg=" || ?colors)
  FillCircle(?Width, ?Height, ?Range + Min)
   }
```

A typical result is

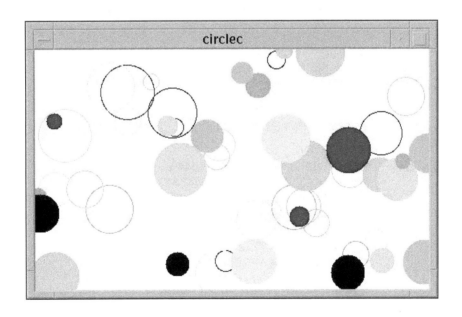

IMAGES

Icon provides facilities to draw arbitrarily complex images and to read and write image files.

Drawing Images

DrawImage(x, y, spec) draws an arbitrarily complex figure in a rectangular area by giving a value to each pixel in the area. x and y specify the upper left corner of the area. spec is a string of the form "*width,palette,data*" where *width* gives the width of the area to be drawn, *palette* chooses the set of colors to be used, and *data* specifies the pixel values.

Each character of *data* corresponds to one pixel in the output image. Pixels are written a row at a time, left to right, top to bottom. The amount of data determines the height of the area drawn. The area is always rectangular; the length of the data must be an integral multiple of the width.

The data characters are interpreted in paint-by-number fashion according to the selected palette. Spaces and commas can be used as punctuation to aid readabil-ity. The characters ~ and \377 specify transparent pixels that do not overwrite the pixels on the canvas when the image is drawn.

The following example uses DrawImage() to draw spheres randomly. The palette g16 contains 16 equally spaced shades of "gray" from black to white, labeled 0-9 and A-F. Transparent pixels are used for better appearance where the spheres overlap.

```
$define Width      400
$define Height     300
$define Iter       100
$define Margin      20

WOpen("size=" || Width || "," || Height)

sphere := "16,g16,_
  ~~~~B98788AE~~~~ ~~D865554446A~~~_
  ~D856886544339~~ E8579BA9643323A~_
  A569DECA7433215E 7569CDB86433211A_
  5579AA9643222108 4456776533221007_
  4444443332210007 4333333222100008_
  533322221100000A 822222111000003D_
  D41111100000019~ ~A200000000018E~_
  ~~A4000000028E~~ ~~~D9532248B~~~~"

every 1 to Iter do
  DrawImage(?(Width – Margin), ?(Height – Margin), sphere)
```

The result is shown below. The inset shows a magnified version of a single sphere.

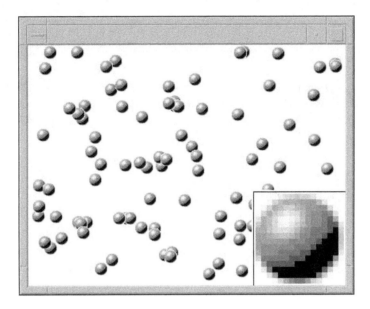

Image Files

Any rectangular portion of a window can be saved in an image file. Con-versely, image files can be read into a window. Icon supports GIF, the CompuServe Graphics Interchange Format (Murray and vanRyper, 1994). Additional image file formats are supported on some platforms.

An image can be loaded into a window when it is opened by using the image attribute with a file name as value, as in

    WOpen("image=kano.gif")

which opens a window using the image file kano.gif. The size of the window is set automatically to the size of the image. The result is:

EVENTS

A user of a program displaying a window can provide input to the program in a variety of ways. Typing a character or clicking a mouse button with the mouse cursor in the window produces an *event*. A program can detect the event, determine where in the window it occurred, and take different actions depending on the nature of the event.

The function Event() produces the next event. For example,

```
repeat {
  case Event() of {
    "c" : random_circle()
    "r" : random_rect()
    "q" : stop()
    "b" : break
    }
  }
```

is an event loop that performs different operations depending on the characters a user types: a "c" produces a random circle, an "r" a random rectangle, a "b" breaks out of the loop, and a "q" terminates program execution. All other events are ignored.

A mouse also can be used to produce events. A three-button mouse is standard, with left, middle, and right buttons that can be pressed and released, each of which produces an event. If the mouse is moved while a button is depressed, a third kind of event, "drag" is produced. Consequently there are nine possible mouse events in all. These events are represented by keywords:

&lpress	left mouse press
&ldrag	left mouse drag
&lrelease	left mouse release
&mpress	middle mouse press
&mdrag	middle mouse drag
&mrelease	middle mouse release
&rpress	right mouse press
&rdrag	right mouse drag
&rrelease	right mouse release

When an event is processed, the position in the window where the event occurred is automatically assigned to the keywords &x and &y.

Here is a simple event loop that draws a rectangle whose upper-left corner is the location where a mouse button is pressed and whose lower-right corner is the location where it is released:

```
repeat {
  case Event() of {
    &lpress | &mpress | &rpress: {
      x0 := &x                        # initial coordinates
      y0 := &y
      }
    &lrelease | &mrelease | &rrelease: {
      DrawRectangle(x0, y0, &x − x0, &y − y0)
      break
      }
    }
  }
```

DIALOGS

Dialogs are temporary windows that provide information to the user of a program and in which the user can enter information that the program needs. The simplest dialog is the notice dialog, which alerts the user to a situation such as an error and requires the user to acknowledge the notice. The function **Notice(s)** produces a dialog with the message **s**. For example,

$$\text{Notice("Unable to find specified resource.")}$$

produces the dialog

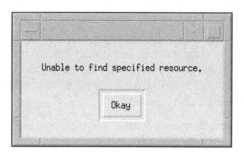

The dialog remains and the program waits until the user dismisses it by clicking on the **Okay** button. Other functions are provided for common situations, such as requesting the user to provide the name of a file to open. For example,

$$\text{OpenDialog("Open:", "points.drw")}$$

produces the dialog

The suggested name is highlighted. The user can edit the name if desired. Clicking on **Okay** dismisses the dialog and informs the program of the name of the file to open. Clicking on **Cancel** tells the program to cancel the request to open a file.

Other forms of dialogs allow the user to enter text in several fields, select one of several choices, turn switches on or off, and select colors interactively.

VISUAL INTERFACES

Interaction between a program and a user can be accomplished by mouse and keyboard events and by using dialogs as described in previous sections. A visual interface that organizes interaction using interface tools such as menus, buttons, and sliders makes an application easier to use and more attractive.

Interface Tools

Icon provides several kinds of interface tools:

- buttons with several kinds of functionality and in a variety of styles.
- menus in which the user can select an item from among several choices.
- text-entry fields in which the user can enter information.
- sliders and scroll bars that allow a user to specify a numerical value by moving a "thumb".

The dialogs in the last section showed examples of buttons and text-entry fields. Other interface tools are illustrated in the next section.

Building an Interface

A visual interface consists of a window containing various interface tools, identifying information, and areas in which the program can display text or images.

Icon provides a program, VIB (Townsend and Cameron, 1996), for building interfaces interactively: creating, positioning, and configuring individual interface tools; providing labels; and adding "decoration" such as lines to delineate areas. This painting program provides an example of a visual interface:

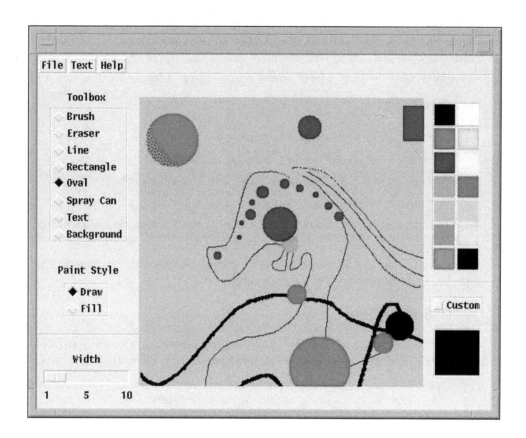

OTHER FEATURES

Icon provides many other graphics features, including:

- multiple windows
- automatic redrawing of windows when hidden parts are exposed
- hidden windows that do not appear on-screen until needed
- textures for filling figures
- "mutable" colors that allow all pixels of a given color to be changed to another color instantaneously
- graphic contexts that can be shared between windows

NOTES

Library Resources

The Icon program library contains many procedures related to graphics. The module graphics contains links to all the procedures necessary for running pro-grams that use graphics.

There also are several programs, ranging from useful applications to visual amusements. Examples are:

binpack	bin packing
colorbook	examining the colors for color names
kaleido	kaleidoscopic designs
travels	traveling-salesman problem
vib	visual interface builder
vqueens	n-queens problem (see Appendix I)

The program gxplor allows graphics facilities to be tested interactively.

13

Other Features

Like any programming language with an extensive computational repertoire, Icon has several features that do not fit neatly into any category. These features are described in this chapter. Some additional features for debugging are described in Chapter 16, and some features related to specific platforms are described in Appendix H.

SORTING STRUCTURES

The values in a record, list, set, or table can be sorted to produce a list with the values in order.

Sorting Records, Lists, and Sets

If X is a record, list, or set, the function sort(X) produces a list with the values in sorted order. If the list or set contains various types of values, the values are first sorted by type. The order of types in sorting is:

> the null value
> integers
> real numbers
> strings
> csets
> windows
> files

co-expressions
procedures, functions, and record constructors lists

sets
tables
record types

For example,

sort([[ ], &letters, 1, 2.0])

produces a new list with the values in the following order:

[1, 2.0, &letters, [ ]]

Integers and real numbers are sorted in nondecreasing numerical order, while strings and csets are sorted in nondecreasing lexical order. For example,

sort(["bcd", 3, 2, 'abc', "abc", 'bcd'])

produces

[2, 3, "abc", "bcd", 'abc', 'bcd']

Procedures, functions, and record constructors sort together by name. Within values of one structure type, values are sorted by time of creation, with the oldest first.

Sorting Tables

The function sort(T, i) produces a sorted list from the table T. The form of the result produced and the sorting order depends on the value of i.

If i is 1 or 2, the size of the sorted list is the same as the size of the table. Each value in the list is itself a list of two values: a key and its corresponding value. If i is 1, these lists are in the sorted order of the keys. If i is 2, the lists are in the sorted order of the corresponding values. If i is omitted, 1 is assumed.

If i is 3 or 4, the size of the sorted list is twice the size of the table and the values in the list are alternating keys and corresponding values for the elements in the table. If i is 3, the values are in the sorted order of the keys. If i is 4, the values are in the sorted order of the corresponding values. For example, the following program prints a count of word occurrences in the input file, using the procedure countwords() given previously:

```
procedure main()
    wlist := sort(countwords(), 3)
    while write(left(get(wlist), 12), right(get(wlist), 4))
end
```

Note that get() obtains a key first and then its corresponding value. The list is consumed in the process, but it is not needed for anything else.

Sorting by Field

The function sortf(X, i) is like sort() except that it applies only to records, lists, and sets. List and record values in X are ordered by comparing the values of their ith fields. For example, suppose personnel records are given by

```
record employee(name, job, salary)

office := employee("Joan", "supervisor", 56000)
cubicle1 := employee("Bert", "coder", 23000)
cubicle2 := employee("Melissa", "programmer",
35000) cubicle3 := employee("John", "writer", 25000)
nook := [cubicle1, cubicle2, cubicle3, office]
```

Then

```
sortf(nook, 3)
```

produces a list of the records in nook sorted by salary.

STRING NAMES

As described in Chapter 8, functions and procedures have string names. Operators also have string names that resemble their syntactic appearance. For example, "**" is the string name of the intersection operator. Operators, like functions and procedures, are values. Operator values are not, however, available as the values of global identifiers.

Function, procedure, and operator values can be obtained from their string names using the function proc(s, i), which produces the function, procedure, or operator named s but fails if s is not the name of one. The value of i is used to specify the number of arguments for operators. The default for i is 1. This second argument is not used for the names of procedures. For example, proc("repl") produces the function repl and proc("main") produces the main procedure. Similarly, proc("*", 1) produces the unary size operation, while proc("*", 2) produces the binary multipli-cation operation.

Since the value of an operator can be obtained in this way, it can be assigned to a variable, and the operator can be called like a function or procedure. For example, in

```
mult := proc("*",
2) write(mult(i, j))
```

writes the product of i and j.

The string names of prefix operators and infix operators consist of the operator symbols as indicated previously. Some operators have special forms. These opera-tors and their string names are:

operator	*string name*
s[i]	"[]"
s[i:j]	"[:]"
i to j by k	"..."

The value of i in proc(s, i) must be correct for the name of an operator. For example, proc("...", 3) produces the operator for to-by, but proc("...") fails, since the default value of the second argument is 1.

Although some control structures, such as alternation, are represented by an infix syntax in the same fashion as operators, they are not values and do not have string names. Field references and conjunction also are not values and do not have string names.

The function args(p) produces the number of arguments expected by the procedure p. args() produces –1 for a function, like write(), that accepts a variable number of arguments. For a declared procedure with a variable number of argu-ments, args() produces the negative of the number of formal parameters.

STRING INVOCATION

Functions, procedures, and operators can be invoked directly by using their string names.

Functions and Operators

A string name of a function can be used in place of the function itself. For example,

```
"write"(s)
```

has the same effect as

```
write(s)
```

Similarly, operators can be invoked like procedures by using their string names. For example,

"−"(i1, i2)

produces the difference of i1 and i2.

In string invocation, unary operators (which have operator symbols in prefix position) are distinguished from binary operators (which have operator symbols in infix position) by the number of arguments given. Thus,

"−"(i)

computes the negative of i.

Procedures

Procedures can be invoked by their string names in the same way as functions. However, the Icon compiler removes declarations in a program that are not explicitly referenced. For example, if the declaration

```
procedure alert(s)
  write("*** ", s, " ***")
  return
end
```

appears in a program, but there is no other appearance of the variable alert in the program, its declaration is deleted. If an attempt is made to call alert() by its string name, as in

```
messages := ["write", "alert", "stop"]
            ...
messages [2] ("no basis established")
```

a run-time error results because the procedure declaration for alert() has been deleted. (The string literal "alert" is not an explicit reference to the procedure alert() and hence does not prevent the removal of the procedure declaration.)

This problem can be avoided by using the invocable declaration, as in

```
invocable "alert"
```

which tells Icon that alert() may be called using string invocation.

If several procedures may be called by string invocation, their names can be given in a comma-separated list, as in

invocable "alert", "warning", "shutdown"

All procedures can be declared to be invocable by

invocable all

The invocable declaration is needed only for procedures, not for built-in functions and operators.

DYNAMIC LOADING

The function loadfunc(lib, func) loads the C function func from the library lib and returns a procedure. This procedure can be used to call the function in the usual manner.

For example, if the C function bitcount() counts the number of bits in the binary representation of an integer and is in /icon/lib/bits.so,

bitcount := loadfunc("/icon/lib/bits.so", "bitcount")

produces an Icon procedure bitcount(). For example,

bitcount(260)

produces 2.

Dynamic loading is not supported on all platforms, and the C functions must be specifically tailored for use with Icon. For more information about dynamic loading, see Griswold and Townsend (1995).

STORAGE MANAGEMENT

Storage is allocated automatically during program execution as strings and other objects are created. Garbage collection occurs automatically when more space is needed; it reclaims space used by objects that are no longer in use (Griswold and Griswold, 1986).

This automatic management of storage normally is transparent to persons writing and running Icon programs. However, Icon programs vary widely in their utilization of storage, and the amount of computer memory available to Icon programs varies from platform to platform. For these reasons, some understanding of how Icon manages storage may be useful.

Storage Regions

The storage that Icon allocates is divided into three parts:

1. static allocation for co-expressions and operating-system uses

2. strings

3. blocks for all other data objects (csets, lists, and so forth)

The default initial sizes of Icon's storage regions vary somewhat from implementation to implementation. For most implementations, the default sizes for the string and block regions are 500,000 bytes.

Appendix F describes how these default settings can be changed.

Four keywords can be used to measure the utilization of storage during program execution. The keyword &collections generates four values: the total number of garbage collections to date, followed by the number caused by allocations in the static, string, and block regions respectively. For example,

```
write(&collections)
```

writes the total number of garbage collections that have occurred.

Since &collections is a generator, using a list to collect its results may be helpful. For example, the following procedure writes all the values with identifying labels:

```
procedure notecol()
  local coll
  coll := [ ]
  every put(coll, &collections)
  write("static: ", coll[2])
  write("string: ", coll[3])
  write("block: ", coll[4])
  write("total: ", coll[1]) return

end
```

The keyword &regions generates the sizes of the static, string, and block regions. The value for the static region is not meaningful for most implementations of Icon.

The keyword &storage generates the amount of space currently occupied in the static, string, and block regions. The first value is not meaningful and is included only for consistency with &regions. The values produced by &storage give the space occupied; some of that space may be collectible.

The keyword &allocated generates the total amount of space allocated since the beginning of program execution. The first value is the total for all regions. The subsequent values are for the static, string, and block regions.

Forcing Garbage Collection

As mentioned earlier, garbage collection occurs automatically when there is not enough space available to satisfy an allocation request. When a garbage collection occurs, unused space is reclaimed in all regions.

Sometimes it is useful to force a garbage collection — for example, to find out how much space is available for future allocation. The function collect(i1, i2) causes a garbage collection, requesting i2 bytes of storage in region i1. The regions are identified by integers: 1 for the static region, 2 for the string region, and 3 for the block region. The function fails if i bytes are not available in the region after collection. If i1 is 0, a garbage collection is done, and contributes to the count of garbage collections, but no region is identified and i2 has no effect. Both i1 and i2 default to zero, so that collect() performs an "anonymous" collection and always succeeds.

Stacks

An Icon program uses two stacks: an evaluation stack and a system stack. The evaluation stack contains intermediate results of computations and procedure call information. The system stack contains calls of C functions (Icon is implemented in C). In addition, every co-expression has an evaluation stack and a system stack.

The evaluation stack grows as a result of procedure calls and suspended expressions. The system stack grows as a result of suspended expressions and during garbage collection.

The evaluation stack may overflow in programs with deeply nested (or runaway) procedure calls. The default size for the main evaluation stack usually is 10,000 words, which is ample for most programs. See Appendix F for information about changing the size of the evaluation stack.

The system stack may overflow if there are too many simultaneously sus-pended expressions. This may happen, for example, if there are many expressions in conjunction in string scanning. The system stack also may overflow if long chains of pointers are encountered during garbage collection.

The size of the system stack depends on the implementation. On a computer with a large amount of memory, the system stack usually is very large and overflow is unlikely. On personal computers with a limited amount of memory, the system stack may be small and overflow may be a problem.

Unfortunately, system stack overflow may not be detected. If this happens, adjacent memory may be overwritten, resulting in program or system malfunction.

The problem with stack overflow often is more severe in co-expressions. The default size for created co-expressions usually is 2,000 words, with the space divided evenly between an evaluation stack and a system stack. Thus, both are much smaller than for the program itself. Furthermore, overflow detection is less effective in co-expressions.

MISCELLANEOUS FACILITIES

Executing Commands

In command-line environments, the function **system(s)** executes the com-mand given by the string **s** as if it were entered on the command line. This facility allows an Icon program to execute other programs and in particular to perform platform-dependent operations that are not part of Icon itself. The value returned by **system(s)** is the exit status returned by the command-line interpreter. For example, with UNIX

> system("ls –l *.icn")

lists, in long form, the files whose names end in .icn. Exit codes vary considerably, depending on the platform and the specific program. The function **system()** is not available on all platforms.

Changing Directories

The function chdir(s) changes the current directory to **s** but fails if there is no such directory or the change cannot be made. For example, in UNIX

> chdir("..")

changes the directory to the one above the current one.

Environment Variables

Environment variables communicate information about the environment in which an Icon program executes. The function **getenv(s)** produces the value of the environment variable **s**, but fails if the environment variable **s** is not set. For example,

> write(getenv("TRACE"))

prints the value of the environment variable TRACE, provided it is set.

On platforms that do not support environment variables, **getenv()** always fails.

Date and Time

The value of &date is the current date in the form *yyyy/mm/dd*. For example, the value of &date for October 12, 1996 is "1996/10/12".

The value of &dateline is the date and time of day in a format that is easy to read. An example is

        Saturday, October 12, 1996 7:21 am

The value of **&clock** is the current time in the form *hh:mm:ss*. For example, the value of **&clock** for 7:21 p.m. is **19:21:00**.

The value of **&time** is the elapsed CPU time in milliseconds, measured from the beginning of program execution.

The function **delay**(i) delays program execution for i milliseconds.

Icon Identification

The value of **&host** identifies the computer on which Icon is running. The format of the information varies from implementation to implementation. An example is

        jupiter.cs.arizona.edu

The value of **&version** is the version number and creation date of the Icon implementation. An example is

        Icon Version 9.3. October 15, 1996

Program Termination

The execution of an Icon program may be terminated for several reasons: completion, programmer-specified termination, or error.

The normal way to terminate program execution is by return from the main procedure. This produces a normal exit code for the process whether the main procedure returns or fails.

Execution of the function **exit**(i) causes an Icon program to terminate with exit code of i. If i is omitted, the normal exit code is produced. This function is useful for terminating program execution in situations where it is not convenient to return to the main procedure.

The function **stop**(x1, x2, …, xn) writes output in the manner of **write**() and then terminates program execution with an error exit code. Output is written to standard error output unless another file is specified.

NOTES

Library Resources

The Icon program library contains several modules related to features de-scribed in this chapter. The most commonly needed ones are:

datetime	procedures related to date and time
sort	enhanced sorting

14

Running an Icon Program

The implementation of Icon is based on the concept of a virtual machine — an imaginary computer that executes instructions for Icon programs. The Icon com-piler translates Icon programs into assembly language for the virtual machine and then converts the assembly language into virtual machine code. This virtual ma-chine code is then "executed" on a real computer by an interpreter. This implemen-tation method allows Icon to run on many different computer platforms.

Compiling and running Icon programs is easy and it is not necessary to understand Icon's virtual machine, but knowing the nature of the implementation may help answer questions about what is going on in some situations. This chapter describes the rudiments of running Icon programs. More information is found in subsequent chapters and the appendices.

How Icon programs are run necessarily varies from platform to platform. On some platforms, Icon is run from the command line. On others, it is run interactively through a visual interface. This chapter describes how Icon is run in a command-line environment. Even for this environment, details depend on the platform. In any event, the user manual for a specific platform is the best guide to running Icon.

BASICS

The name of a file that contains an Icon source program must end with the suffix .icn, as in hello.icn. The .icn suffix is used by the Icon compiler to distinguish Icon source programs from other kinds of files.

The Icon compiler usually is named icont. To compile hello.icn, all that is needed is

    icont hello.icn

The suffix .icn is assumed if none is given, so that this can be written more simply as

    icont hello

The result is an executable *icode* file. The name of the icode file depends on the platform on which Icon is run. On some platforms, notably UNIX, the name is the same as the name of the source file, but without the suffix. On these platforms, the compilation of hello.icn produces an icode file named hello. On other platforms, such as MS-DOS, the icode file has the suffix .icn replaced by .exe, as in hello.exe. For MicroSoft Windows, the suffix is .cmd and so on.

After compilation, entering

    hello

runs the program.

An Icon program can be compiled and run in a single step using the −x option *following* the program name. For example,

    icont hello −x

compiles and executes hello.icn. An icode file also is created, and it can be executed subsequently without recompiling the source program.

There are command-line options for icont. Options must appear before file names on the icont command line. For example,

    icont −s hello

suppresses informative messages that icont ordinarily produces. Other command-line options are described in Chapter 15 and Appendix E.

INPUT AND OUTPUT REDIRECTION

In a command-line environment, most input and output is done using standard input, standard output, and standard error output. Standard input typically is read from the keyboard, while standard output and standard error output are written to the console.

Standard input and standard output can be redirected so that files can be used in place of the keyboard. For example,

```
hello < hello.dat > hello.out
```

executes hello with hello.dat as standard input and hello.out as standard output. (The directions that the angular brackets point relative to the program name are suggestive of the direction of data flow.)

COMMAND-LINE ARGUMENTS

Arguments on the command line following an icode file name are available to the executing Icon program in the form of a list of strings. This list is the argument to the main procedure. For example, suppose args.icn consists of

```
procedure main(arguments)

    every write(!arguments)

end
```

This program simply prints the arguments on the command line with which it executed. Thus,

```
icont args
args Hello world
```

writes

```
Hello
world
```

When —x is used, the arguments follow it, as in

```
icont args –x Hello world
```

Arguments are separated by blanks. The treatment of special characters, methods of embedding blanks in arguments, and so forth, varies from platform to platform.

ENVIRONMENT VARIABLES

Environment variables can be used to configure Icon and specify the location of files. For example, the environment variable IPATH can be used to specify the location of library modules. If graphics is in

/usr/icon/ipl/gprogs

and IPATH has that value, then

link graphics

will find it.

See Appendix F for a listing of the environment variables Icon uses.

NOTES

The Icon Optimizing Compiler

The compiler for the Icon virtual machine is fast, getting programs into execution quickly. Programs compiled for Icon's virtual machine run fast enough for most purposes.

There also is an optimizing compiler for Icon, Walker (1991) and Griswold (1996), that produces native code for platforms on which it runs. Programs compiled by the optimizing compiler take much longer to get into execution but run faster than those compiled for Icon's virtual machine; a factor of 2 or 3 is typical.

In addition to longer compilation time than the compiler for Icon's virtual machine, the optimizing compiler requires a large amount of memory and a C compiler for the platform on which it is run. For these reasons, the optimizing compiler is recommended only for short programs where execution speed is the paramount concern.

User Manuals

The best source of information for running Icon on a particular platform is the user manual for Icon for that platform. User manuals are included with distributions of Icon. They also are available on-line. See Appendix J.

15

Libraries

Procedures provide the primary method of extending Icon's built-in computational repertoire. Many procedures, of course, are specific to a particular program. Other procedures can be used in many programs.

This chapter describes procedure libraries: how to use them, the contents of some existing libraries, and how to create your own.

USING PROCEDURE LIBRARIES

Procedure libraries are files that are prepared for linking with programs. A library module is added to a program by a link declaration such as

    link graphics

as shown in the chapter on Icon's graphics facilities.

A module may contain one procedure or many. In order to link the procedures needed, it is necessary to know which ones are contained in a module or, conversely, what module contains the procedures required. In the case of graphics, it is enough to know that the module contains all the procedures needed to extend the built-in graphics repertoire. If the location of a library module is known, its complete path can be specified, as in

    link "/usr/icon/ipl/gprocs/graphics"

Note that quotation marks must enclose specifications that do not have the syntax of identifiers.

The path to use for linking also can be specified by the environment variable IPATH as described in the last chapter. The use of IPATH is preferred for program portability

THE ICON PROGRAM LIBRARY

The Icon program library is a large collection of programs, procedures, documenta-tion, data, and support tools that is available to all Icon programmers. The library is constantly changing. New material is added frequently and existing material is improved. What is described here is a snapshot as of the time this book was written. See Appendix J for instructions about obtaining the library.

Organization of the Icon Program Library

The main directories in the Icon program library hierarchy are:

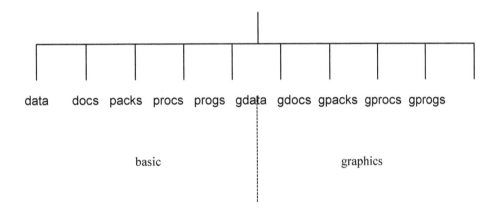

As indicated, the hierarchy has two main parts: basic material and graphics material. The initial character g indicates graphics material.

The source code for procedure modules is in the directories procs and gprocs. As one might expect, the source code for graphics is in gprocs. The directories progs and gprogs contain complete programs. The directories packs and gpacks contain large packages. For example, the visual interface builder, VIB, is in a subdirectory of gpacks.

Core Modules

The directories procs and gprocs contain hundreds of files, and in these there are thousands of procedures. Some procedures are useful only for specialized applications. Others provide commonly used facilities and are designated as "core" procedures. The core modules for the basic part of the library are:

convert	type conversion and formatting procedures
datetime	date and time procedures
factors	procedures related to factoring and prime numbers
io	procedures related to input and output
lists	list manipulation procedures
math	procedures for mathematical computation
numbers	procedures for numerical computation and formatting
random	procedures related to random numbers
records	procedures to manipulate records
scan	scanning procedures
sets	set manipulation procedures
sort	sorting procedures
strings	string manipulation procedures
tables	table manipulation procedures

Other Useful Procedures

Among all the procedures in the Icon program library, there are a few that are particularly useful. The following two procedures illustrate how library procedures can make programming easier. The code for these procedures is given in Appendix I.

Command-Line Options

As described in Chapter 14, when Icon is run from the command line, arguments are passed to the main procedure in the form of a list of strings, one string for each argument. This is the main way in which information is passed to a program that is run from the command line. For example, if a program named plot begins with

```
procedure main(args)

   shape := args[1]
   bound := args[2]
   points := args[3]

      ...
```

and plot is called as

```
plot lemniscate 10.0 1000
```

shape is set to "lemniscate" , bound is set to "10.0", and points is set to "1000". A more sophisticated program might issue an error message for an inappropriate value, convert the second and third arguments to real and integer, respectively, and provide defaults for omitted arguments.

Of course, command-line arguments can be used in any way one likes. The use above has the disadvantages that the arguments must be in a fixed order and there is only a hint in a call of what they mean.

The standard format that is used by the Icon program library identifies options by name, with a prefix − and follows the name by a value, if any. The program plot then might be called as

```
plot −s lemniscate −b 10.0 −p 1000
```

In this form, the options can carry identification and be given in any order.

It is not difficult to write a preamble to a program to handle named options. That is not necessary, however — the procedure options() in the Icon program library takes care of almost everything.

options(args, opts) processes command-line options in the list args according to the specifications given in the string opts. It returns a table with the option names as keys and with corresponding values from the command line. The options and values are deleted from args, leaving any remaining positional arguments for the program to process.

Using options(), the program plot might start as follows:

```
link options

procedure main(args)

    opt_tbl := options(args, "s:b.p+")
    shape := opt_tbl["s"]
    bound := opt_tbl["b"]
    points := opt_tbl["p"]

        ...
```

The option string consists of letters for the option names followed by a type flag. The flag ":" indicates the option value must be a string, "." indicates a real number, and "+" indicates an integer.

If an option appears on the command line, its value in the table is the result of converting to the specified type. Otherwise, it is the null value.

An option that does not take a value also can be specified. In this case, no type flag is specified. If such an option is given on the command line, its value in the table returned by options() is 1 (and hence nonnull); otherwise it is null. An example is

```
link options

procedure main(args)

    opt_tbl := options(args, "s:b.p+t")
    shape := opt_tbl["s"]
    bound := opt_tbl["b"]
    points := opt_tbl["p"]
    if \opt_tbl["t"] then &trace := −1

        ...
```

Here, the command-line option −t turns on tracing in plot.

A test for a table value being null can be used to set defaults, as in

```
link options

procedure main(args)

   opt_tbl := options(args, "s:b.p+t")
   shape := \opt_tbl["s"] | "circle"
   bound := \opt_tbl["b"] | 1.0 points
   := \opt_tbl["p"] | 100
   if \opt_tbl["t"] then &trace := −1
      ...
```

Multi-character option names are supported. They must be preceded in the option string by a − to distinguish them from single-character option names.

For the example above, this might take the form

```
link options

procedure main(args)

   opt_tbl := options(args, "−shape:−bound.−points+−trace")
   shape := opt_tbl["shape"] | "circle"
   bound := opt_tbl["bound"] | 1.0
   points := opt_tbl["points"] | 100
   if \opt_tbl["t"] then &trace := −1
      ...
```

where a command-line call might be

```
plot −shape lemniscate −bound 10.0 −points 1000
```

Many other features are supported by **options()**. The most important ones are:

- Options can appear in any order in the options string and on the command line.

- Blanks between single-character option names and the corresponding values are optional on the command line.

- If a command-line argument begins with an @, the subsequent string is taken to be the name of a file that contains options, one per line.

- **options()** removes option names and their values from the argument list, leaving anything else for subsequent processing by the program.

- The special argument − − terminates option processing, leaving the remaining values in the argument list.

- **options()** normally terminates with a run-time error if an option value cannot be converted to the specified type or if there is an unrecognized option on the command line.

- If a third procedure-valued argument is supplied in a call of options(), that procedure is called in case of an error instead of terminating execution

To include options() in a program,

```
link options
```

Structure Images

The procedure ximage(x) produces a string that describes x. If x is a structure, it shows the structure and its elements, and if an element is itself a structure, it shows that structure and so on. The result produced by ximage() resembles Icon code and hence is easy for Icon programmers to understand. Indentation and newlines are provided, so that if the result of ximage() is written, the output is nicely formatted.

It is easier to show what ximage() produces than it is to describe it. Suppose a program contains the following lines of code:

```
source := table()
basis := list(6, 0)
filter := list(10)
basis[1] := filter
basis[2] := basis
filter[3] := basis
source["basis"] := basis
source["filter"] := filter
```

For this, write(ximage(source)) produces:

```
T1 := table(&null)
  T1["basis"] := L1 := list(6,0)
    L1[1] := L2 := list(10,&null)
      L2[3] := L1
    L1[2] := L1
  T1["filter"] := L2
```

Several things about this output are worth noting. One is that each structure is given a name (tag). The first letter of the tag indicates its type, with the number following producing a unique identification. The value of each structure is shown in the style of assignment as a structure-creation function with its predominant element.

A table is shown with its default value. For example, most of the elements of basis (L1) are 0, while most of the elements of filter (L2) are null. Only the elements that are different from the predominant element are shown below the structure. The result is a compact but easily understood representation of structures.

Since every structure has a unique tag, pointer loops present no problem. For example,

```
node1 := []
node2 := []
put(node1, node2)
put(node2, node1)
put(node2, node2)

write(ximage(node1))
```

produces

```
L1 := list(1)
   L1[1] := L2 := list(2)
      L2[1] := L1
      L2[2] := L2
```

In addition to ximage(), there is a procedure xdump(x1, x2, ..., xn) that applies ximage() to x1, x2, ..., xn in succession and writes the results to standard error output. For example,

```
xdump("The basis:", basis)
```

writes

```
"The basis:"
L1 := list(6,0)
   L1[1] := L2 :=
      list(10,&null) L2[3] := L1
   L1[2] := L1
```

to standard error output.

To include ximage() and xdump() in a program,

```
link ximage
```

Finding Procedures

Various listings and cross-references exist to help locate procedures in the Icon program library. File listings provide brief summaries of each library file. A section of a listing for procs looks like this:

keyword	file	description
	...	
argument	apply	apply a list of functions to an argument
argument	pdae	programmer-defined argument evaluation
arguments	reduce	perform operation on list of arguments
arguments	sortff	sortf with multiple field arguments
arithmetic	complex	perform complex arithmetic

arithmetic	rational	arithmetic on rational numbers
arrange	colmize	arrange data into columns
array	progary	place program in a array
arrays	array	n-dimensional arrays
ascii	asciinam	ASCII name of unprintable character
ascii	ebcdic	convert between ASCII and EBCDIC
atomic	tclass	classify values as atomic or composite
backslash	slshupto	upto() with backslash escaping
backslashes	slashbal	balanced scanning with backslashes
balanced	slashbal	balanced scanning with backslashes
base	basename	produce base name of file
base	gettext	gettext (simple text-base routines)
based	ansi	ANSI-based terminal control
	…	

Procedure indexes provide information about specific procedures and the files in which they are located. A section of the index for procs looks like this:

keyword	*file:procedure*	*description*
	…	
character	strings:charcnt	character count
character	strings:comb	character combinations
character	strings:compress	character compression
characters	strings:csort	lexically ordered characters
characters	strings:deletec	delete characters
characters	strings:diffcnt	number of different characters
characters	strings:ochars	first appearance unique characters
characters	strings:replc	replicate characters
characters	strings:schars	lexical unique characters
characters	strings:selectp	select characters
characters	strings:transpose	transpose characters
chars	adjuncts:Strip	remove chars from string
closure	genrfncs:starseq	closure sequence
closure	graphpak:closure	transitive closure of graph
code	evtmap:evtmap	map event code name to event value
coefficient	math:binocoef	binomial coefficient
collation	strings:collate	string collation
combinations	lists:lcomb	list combinations
combinations	strings:comb	character combinations
	…	

Finally, each file itself contains detailed documentation about the procedures in it.

CREATING NEW LIBRARY MODULES

It is easy to create a new library module. To prepare a procedure or collection of procedures called, for example, mylibe, all that is needed is:

```
icont –c mylibe
```

where mylibe.icn contains the desired procedures. The –c option tells the Icon compiler to stop after translating the file instead of going on to link it to make an executable program. (Files for library modules normally do not contain a main procedure that is necessary to make an executable program.)

The result of using the –c option is to produce two "ucode" files with suffixes .u1 and .u2. In the example above, these would be mylibe.u1 and mylibe.u2. This pair of files is called a library module. (Since the names are paired, it is conventional to refer to them as if they were a single file.)

Once the ucode files are created, mylibe can be linked in a program using

```
link mylibe
```

NOTES

Library Path Searching

On most platforms the environment variable IPATH is a blank-separated list of paths, such as

```
/usr/icon/ipl/procs /usr/icon/ipl/gprocs
```

When Icon searches for the location of a library file specified in a link declaration, it always looks in the current directory first, regardless of the value of IPATH. If the library file is not found there, the paths in IPATH are searched from left to right.

More on Finding Things in the Library

Using World Wide Web is by far the easiest way to locate things in the Icon program library. A variety of indexes are available in addition to the ones described in this chapter. See Appendix J for information about Icon on the Web.

As an exercise in using the library, look in the progs directory for programs that can help: ibrow for browsing the library and ipldoc for printing summary informa-tion about the library.

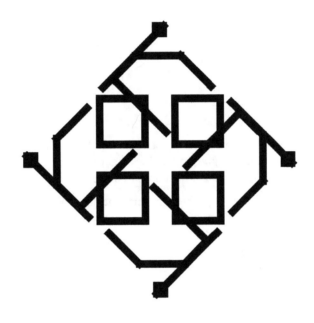

16

Errors and
Diagnostic Facilities

Errors are an inevitable by-product of programming. This chapter describes errors that are detected by Icon and the diagnostic facilities that can be used in detecting such errors, as well as program malfunctions that Icon doesn't detect.

Some of the features described in this chapter have applications other than debugging. They are included here because they usually are used for diagnostic purposes.

ERRORS

Errors may be detected during compilation, linking, or program execution. If an error is detected during compilation, linking is not performed. An error in compi-lation or linking prevents the production of an executable program. A program that compiles and links may, of course, encounter errors during execution.

Errors During Compilation

Syntactic errors in an Icon source program are detected during compilation. Each such error produces an explanatory message and the location at which the error was detected. Since some errors cannot be detected until after the point at which the actual error occurred, previous portions of the program should be examined if the problem at the specified location is not obvious.

Compilation continues following the detection of a syntax error, but ucode files are not produced. Since some kinds of errors cause a cascade of apparent errors in subsequent program text, it often is advisable to correct only the first error and attempt to compile the program again.

Errors During Linking

Inconsistent declarations may not be evident until ucode files from more than one source file are combined to form a single icode file. For example, there may be two declarations for a procedure or a procedure declaration and a record declaration with the same name. Such errors are detected by the linker and result in the error message

inconsistent redeclaration

This error prevents the production of an icode file.

Run-Time Errors

When a run-time error occurs, a diagnostic message is produced with an error number, a brief explanation, where in the program the error occurred, and, when possible, the offending value. Next, a traceback of procedure calls is given, followed by the offending expression.

For example, suppose the following program is contained in the file max.icn:

```
procedure main()

  i := max("a", 1)

end

procedure max(i, j)

  if i > j then i else j

end
```

The execution of this program produces the following output:

```
Run–time error 102
File max.icn; Line 9
numeric expected
offending value: "a"
Traceback:
  main()
  max("a",1) from line 3 in max.icn
  {"a" > 1} from line 9 in max.icn
```

ERROR CONVERSION

Most run-time errors can be converted to expression failure, rather than causing termination of program execution.

If the value of &error is zero (its initial value), errors cause program termination as shown above. If the value of &error is nonzero, errors are treated as failure of expression evaluation and &error is decremented. For example, if the value of &error had been nonzero when the expression i > j was executed in the previous example, the expression simply would have failed.

There are a few errors that cannot be converted to failure: arithmetic overflow and underflow, stack overflow, and errors during program initialization.

When an error is converted to failure, the value of &error is decremented and the values of three other keywords are set:

- &errornumber is the number of the error (for example, 101).
- &errortext is the error message (for example, "integer expected").
- &errorvalue is the offending value. References to &errorvalue fail if there is no offending value associated with the error.

A reference to any of these keywords fails if there has not been an error.

The function errorclear() removes the indication of the last error. Subsequent references to the keywords above fail until another error occurs.

Error conversion is illustrated by the following procedure, which could be used to process potential run-time errors:

```
procedure ErrorCheck()

   write("\nRun-time error ", &errornumber)
   write(&errortext)
   write("offending value: ", image(&errorvalue))
   writes("\nDo you want to continue? (n)")

   if map(read()) == ("y" | "yes") then return
   else exit(&errornumber)

end
```

For example,

```
&error := -1
   ...
write(s) | ErrorCheck()
```

could be used to check for an error during writing, while

```
(L := sort(T, 3)) | ErrorCheck()
```

could be used to detect failure to sort a table into a list (for lack of adequate storage).

A run-time error can be forced by the function runerr(i, x), which causes program execution to terminate with error number i as if a corresponding run-time error had occurred. If i is the number of a standard run-time error, the corresponding error text is printed; otherwise no error text is printed. The value of x is given as the offending value. If x is omitted, no offending value is printed.

This function makes it possible for library procedures to terminate in the same fashion as built-in operations. It is advisable to use error numbers for programmer-defined errors that are well outside the range of numbers used by Icon itself. Error number 500 has the predefined text "program malfunction" for use with runerr(). This number is not used by Icon itself.

A call of runerr() is subject to conversion to failure like any other run-time error.

STRING IMAGES

When debugging a program it often is useful to know what a value is. Its type can be determined by type(x), but this is not helpful if the actual value is of interest. Its value can be written, provided it is of a type that can be converted to a string, although there is no way to differentiate among types whose written values are the same, such as the integer 1 and the string "1". The function image(x) provides a string representation of x for all types.

If x is numeric, image(x) produces a string showing that numerical value. For example,

```
every write(image(30 | 10.7 | −150 | 2.37E20))
```

writes

```
30
10.7
−150
2.37e+20
```

Note that the image of real numbers may be in a different form from their literal representation in a program.

Integer values on the order of 10^{30} and larger are given in an approximate form as the nearest power of 10. For example, image(126 ^ 137) produces "~10^288".

If x is a string or cset, image(x) produces its string image with surrounding quotes and escape sequences, if necessary, as for string and cset literals. For example,

```
write(image("Hello world"))
```

writes "Hello world" (with the quotes). Similarly,

write(image('Hello world'))

writes ' Hdelorw'. Note that the characters in the image of a cset are in lexical order.

The data type, current size, and a serial number are given for structures. For example,

image([1, 4, 9, 16])

produces a result such as "list_10(4)". The number after the underscore is the serial number, which starts at 1 for the first list created during program execution and increases with each newly created list. Lists, sets, tables, and each record type have separate serial-number sequences.

The function serial(x) produces the serial number of x if x is a structure, co-expression, or window but fails otherwise.

Although functions and procedures have the same type ("procedure"), they are distinguished in string images. For example,

image(main)

produces "procedure main", while

image(trim)

produces "function trim".

In the case of a record declaration such as

record complex(rpart, ipart)

the record constructor is distinguished from functions, and

image(complex)

produces "record constructor complex". On the other hand, values of record types have the same kind of string images that other structures have:

image(complex(0.0, 0.0))

produces a result such as "record complex_5(2)".

Some built-in values have string images consisting of the keyword that produces the value. For example,

image()

produces "&null".

The image of a co-expression includes its serial number and the number of times it has been activated in parentheses. The serial number for &main is 1. For example,

image(&main)

produces "co-expression_1(1)", assuming &main has not been activated since its initial activation to start program execution.

PROGRAM INFORMATION

The values of the keywords &file and &line are, respectively, the name of the file and line number in that file for the currently executing expression.

For example,

write("File ", &file, "; Line ", &line)

writes out the current file name and the line number in it. Note that a program may consist of several parts that are compiled from different files.

The value of the keyword &progname is the name of the executing program.

TRACING

Tracing is the main debugging tool in Icon. Tracing is controlled by the value of the keyword &trace. See Appendices E and F for other ways of enabling tracing.

Tracing Procedures

If the value of &trace is nonzero, a diagnostic message is written to standard error output each time a procedure is called, returns, suspends, or is resumed. The value of &trace is decremented by 1 each time a message is written, so the value assigned to &trace can be used to limit the amount of trace output. On the other hand,

&trace := −1

allows tracing to continue indefinitely or until another value is assigned to &trace.

A diagnostic message produced by tracing shows the name of the file contain-ing the procedure, the line number in that file, the procedure called, the value returned, and so on. The vertical bars indicate, by way of indentation, the level of procedure call.

Suppose the following program is in the file fib.icn:

```
procedure main()

    &trace := -1

    write(fib(5))

end

procedure fib(i)

    if i = (1 | 2) then return 1
    else return fib(i - 1) + fib(i - 2)

end
```

The resulting trace output is:

```
fib.icn      :   5 |  fib(5)
fib.icn      :  12 | |  fib(4)
fib.icn      :  12 | | |  fib(3)
fib.icn      :  12 | | | |  fib(2)
fib.icn      :  11 | | | |  fib returned 1
fib.icn      :  12 | | | |  fib(1)
fib.icn      :  11 | | | |  fib returned 1
fib.icn      :  12 | | |  fib returned 2
fib.icn      :  12 | | |  fib(2)
fib.icn      :  11 | | |  fib returned 1
fib.icn      :  12 | |  fib returned 3
fib.icn      :  12 | |  fib(3)
fib.icn      :  12 | | |  fib(2)
fib.icn      :  11 | | |  fib returned 1
fib.icn      :  12 | | |  fib(1)
fib.icn      :  11 | | |  fib returned 1
fib.icn      :  12 | |  fib returned 2
fib.icn      :  12 |  fib returned 5
fib.icn      :   7  main failed
```

The keyword &level also gives the current level of procedure call. It starts at 1 for the initial call of the main procedure and increases and decreases as procedures are called and return.

Values in trace messages are shown in a manner similar to image(), but they show more detail. For example, the trace output resulting from

```
shape := ["cone", 0.0, 4.0, 1.2, 42.1, 11.3, &pi /
3] build(shape)
```

has the form

```
shape.icn : 123 | build(list_5 = ["cone",0.0,4.0,...,42.1,11.3,1.047197551])
```

Ellipses in trace messages indicate values omitted to prevent very long lines.

Tracing Co-Expressions

Co-expression activation and return also is traced if the value of **&trace** is non-zero. As for procedure calls and returns, the value of **&trace** is decremented for each trace message. The form of co-expression tracing is illustrated by the following program:

```
procedure main()
   local lower, upper

   &trace := −1

   lower := create !&lcase
   upper := create !&ucase

   while write(@lower, " ", @upper)

end
```

If this program is in the file trace.icn, the trace output is:

```
trace.icn   :   9 | main; co-expression_1 : &null @ co-expression_2
trace.icn   :   6 | main; co-expression_2 returned "a" to co-expression_1
trace.icn   :   9 | main; co-expression_1 : &null @ co-expression_3
trace.icn   :   7 | main; co-expression_3 returned "A" to co-expression_1
trace.icn   :   9 | main; co-expression_1 : &null @ co-expression_2
trace.icn   :   6 | main; co-expression_2 returned "b" to co-expression_1
trace.icn   :   9 | main; co-expression_1 : &null @ co-expression_3
trace.icn   :   7 | main; co-expression_3 returned "B" to co-expression_1
trace.icn   :   9 | main; co-expression_1 : &null @ co-expression_2
trace.icn   :   6 | main; co-expression_2 returned "c" to co-expression_1
trace.icn   :   9 | main; co-expression_1 : &null @ co-expression_3
trace.icn   :   7 | main; co-expression_3 returned "C" to co-expression_1

                      ...

trace.icn   :   9 | main; co-expression_1 : &null @ co-expression_2
trace.icn   :   6 | main; co-expression_2 returned "x" to co-expression_1
trace.icn   :   9 | main; co-expression_1 : &null @ co-expression_3
trace.icn   :   7 | main; co-expression_3 returned "X" to co-expression_1
trace.icn   :   9 | main; co-expression_1 : &null @ co-expression_2
```

```
trace.icn   :  6 | main; co-expression_2 returned "y" to co-expression_1
trace.icn   :  9 | main; co-expression_1 : &null @ co-expression_3
trace.icn   :  7 | main; co-expression_3 returned "Y" to co-expression_1
trace.icn   :  9 | main; co-expression_1 : &null @ co-expression_2
trace.icn   :  6 | main; co-expression_2 returned "z" to co-expression_1
trace.icn   :  9 | main; co-expression_1 : &null @ co-expression_3
trace.icn   :  7 | main; co-expression_3 returned "Z" to co-expression_1
trace.icn   :  9 | main; co-expression_1 : &null @ co-expression_2
trace.icn   :  6 | main; co-expression_2 failed to co-expression_1
trace.icn   : 11 main failed
```

THE VALUES OF VARIABLES

Displaying Variable Values

The function display(i, f) writes the image of the current co-expression, followed by a list of local identifiers and their values in i levels of procedure calls, starting at the current level, followed by the program's global identifiers and their values. The output is written to the file f. An omitted value of i defaults to &level, whose value is the current level of procedure. An omitted value of f defaults to &errout. The function call display(1) includes only local identifiers in the currently active procedure. The function call display(&level) includes local identifiers for all procedure calls leading to the current procedure call, while display(0) includes only global identifiers.

An example of the output of display() is given by the following program:

```
procedure main()
  local intext

  intext := open("build.dat") | stop("cannot open input file")

  write(linecount(intext))
end
procedure linecount(file)
  local count, line

  count := 0

  while line := read(file)
    do line ? {
      if ="stop" then break
      else count +:= 1
      }

  display()
```

```
        return count

    end
```

which produces the display output

```
    co–expression_1(1)

    linecount local identifiers:
      count = 39
      file = file(build.dat)
      line = "stop"
    main local identifiers:
      intext = file(build.dat)
    global identifiers:
      display = function display
      linecount = procedure linecount
      main = procedure main
      open = function open
      read = function read
      stop = function stop
      write = function write
```

Post-Mortem Dumps

If the keyword **&dump** has a nonzero value when program execution termi-nates, whether by normal termination or a run-time error, a listing of the values of variables in the style of display(1) is produced.

An example is

```
    procedure main()

      words := set()

      &dump := 1

      while line := read() do
        every word := genword(line)
          do put(words, word)

      every write(!sort(words))

    end

    procedure genword(s)

      s ? {
        while  tab(upto(&letters))  do  {
          word  :=  tab(many(&letters))
          suspend word
          }
```

```
        }
   end
```

Typical output on termination is:

```
   Run–time error 108
   File dump.icn; Line
   9 list expected
   offending value:
   set_1(0) Traceback:
     main()
     put(set_1(0),"Icon") from line 9 in dump.icn
```

```
   Termination dump:
```

```
   co-expression #1 (1)
   main local identifiers:
     line = "Icon Programming..."
     word = "Icon"
     words = set_1(0)
```

```
   global identifiers:
     genword = procedure genword
     main = procedure main
     many = function many
     put = function put read
     = function read set =
     function set
     sort = function sort
     tab = function tab
     upto = function upto
     write = function write
```

VARIABLES AND NAMES

Since references to variables usually are explicit in a program, they are obvious when reading a program. Sometimes, however, especially when debugging a program, it is useful to know the name of a variable. This is provided by name(v), which produces a string name for the variable v.

The names of identifiers and keywords are obvious. For example, name(main) produces "main" and name(&subject) produces "&subject".

For subscripted lists and tables, an indication of the type and subscript is given.

For subscripted string-valued variables, the variable name is given, followed by the subscript range. For example, if the value of noun is "piano", name(noun[2]) produces "noun[2:3]".

The record type, field name, and serial number are used in the name of a field reference. For example, in

```
record complex(r, i)
        ...
z := complex(2.0, 3.5)
```

name(z.r) produces a result such as "complex_4.r".

For identifiers and keywords that are variables, it is possible to get a variable from its name. The function variable(s) produces the variable whose name is s, provided s is an identifier or a keyword that is a variable. It fails otherwise. For example, if summary is a global identifier, then

```
variable("summary") := 1
```

assigns 1 to the global identifier summary.

Scope rules apply to variable(s). If s is the name of a local variable in the current procedure, the result is that local variable even if there is a global variable by the same name.

NOTES

Images of Integers

As noted earlier in this chapter, for very large integers the function image() produces a string showing the approximate value of the integer. This is done because of the amount of time needed to produce a string for the exact value for a very large integer, as mentioned in the **Notes** section of Chapter 10.

A consequence of using an approximation for very large integers is that

```
integer(image(i))
```

may fail, contrary to what might be expected.

Runaway Recursion

If a procedure calls itself endlessly, either directly or through a chain of calls to other procedures, Icon's evaluation stack eventually overflows.

When this happens, program execution terminates with a run-time error and a traceback is produced. Since Icon's evaluation stack is large, the traceback may be hundreds of lines long and very voluminous if the calls have many complicated arguments. On occasion, it may appear that the traceback is in a loop.

In the case of an extensive traceback, it may be useful to suspect runaway recursion first and start by examining the end of the traceback.

Using name() and variable()

The use of name() and variable() are illustrated by writing out the names and values of local identifiers. Consider the following procedure declaration:

```
procedure encapsulate(term, value)
   local i, j
      ...
```

Diagnostic lines such as

```
write("The value of term is: ", term)
```

could be provided in this procedure for each local identifier of interest. An interac-tive interface, such as

```
while var := read() do
   write("The value of ", var, " is: ", image(variable(var)))
    | write(var, " is not a variable")
```

allows the user to find the values of variables of interest.

Some kinds of diagnostic output can be simplified by taking advantage of the fact that name() and variable() are inverses for identifiers. For example,

```
every x := name(x1 | x2 | x3 | x4 | x5)
   do write(x, ":", image(variable(x)))
```

writes the names and values of x1, x2, x3, x4, and x5. It also is easy to change the identifiers in such an expression.

17

Programming with Generators

Generators in combination with iteration and goal-directed evaluation allow com-plex computations to be expressed in a concise and natural manner. In many cases they internalize computations that otherwise would require complicated loops, auxiliary identifiers, and tedious comparisons.

Few programming languages have generators. Consequently, using the full capacity of generators requires new programming techniques and unconventional ways of approaching problems. This chapter describes ways to use generators and provides several idioms for computations that are natural in Icon.

NESTED ITERATION

Many problems that require the production of all possible solutions can be formu-lated using nested iteration. For example, many word puzzles depend on the intersection of two words in a common character. In constructing or solving such puzzles, all the places that two words intersect may be of interest.

Given two words word1 and word2,

    i := upto(word2, word1)

produces the position in word1 of one intersection. In this expression, the string value of word2 is automatically converted to a cset consisting of the possible characters at which an intersection in word1 can occur. While i gives the position of such an intersection in word1, the position in word2 is needed also. The pair of positions can be determined by

```
if i := upto(word2, word1) then
j := upto(word1[i], word2)
```

This computation can be cast in terms of a procedure that locates the positions and displays the intersection:

```
procedure cross(word1,
  word2) local i, j

  if i := upto(word2, word1) then
    { j := upto(word1[i], word2)
    every write(right(word2[1 to j – 1],
    i)) write(word1)
    every write(right(word2[j + 1 to *word2],
    i)) write()
    }

  return

end
```

For example, cross("lottery", "boat") produces

```
        b
l o t t e r y a

        t
```

This approach produces at most one intersection. All intersections can be produced by using nested iteration:

```
every i := upto(word2, word1) do every
  j := upto(word1[i], word2) do {
    every write(right(word2[1 to j – 1],
    i)) write(word1)
    every write(right(word2[j + 1 to *word2],
    i)) write()
    }
```

In this procedure, i iterates over the positions in word1 at which there is a character in word2, while j iterates over the positions in word2 at which this character occurs. The results written for cross("lottery", "boat") are:

```
    b
lotterya

t

    b
    o
    a
lottery

      b
      o
      a
lottery
```

This nested iteration can be reformulated using a single iteration and conjunction:

```
every (i := upto(word2, word1)) & (j := upto(word1[i], word2)) do {
  every write(right(word2[1 to j − 1], i))
  write(word1)
  every write(right(word2[j + 1 to *word2],
  i)) write()
  }
```

The effect is the same as for nested iteration because suspended generators are resumed in a last-in, first-out manner. This is the same in a single iteration with conjunction as it is in nested iterations.

GOAL-DIRECTED EVALUATION AND SEARCHING

Goal-directed evaluation is one of the more powerful programming techniques for solving problems that involve searching through many possible combinations of values. Goal-directed evaluation is commonly used in Icon for "small-scale" com-putation, such as finding common positions in two strings. The real power of goal-directed evaluation is evident in larger problems in which solutions are best formulated in terms of searches over "solution spaces".

The classical problem of this kind consists of placing eight queens on a chessboard so that no two queens are on the same column, row, or diagonal. The solution to this problem involves generation of possible solutions: Goal-directed evaluation to find mutually consistent solutions and data backtracking to reuse previous partial solutions. One solution to this problem is:

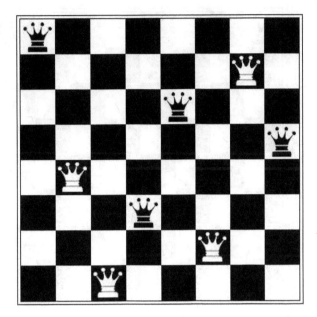

Since there can be only one queen in a column, a natural approach to solving this problem is to associate a queen with each column. The queens then can be placed consecutively, starting with the first queen in the first column.

The first queen can be placed in any row, since there are no other queens on the board yet. The natural place to put the first queen is in row one. The second queen cannot be placed in row one, since the first queen is in this row, nor in row two, since the first queen is on a diagonal through this position. Row three is an acceptable place for the second queen, however. Continuing this process, each successive queen is placed on the first free row. When an attempt is made to place the sixth queen, however, there are no free rows:

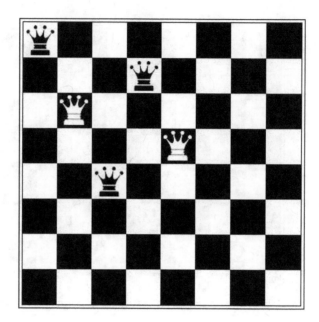

Some previously placed queen must be moved to another position. This is accom-plished by backtracking to the previously placed queen, which can be placed in row eight instead of row four:

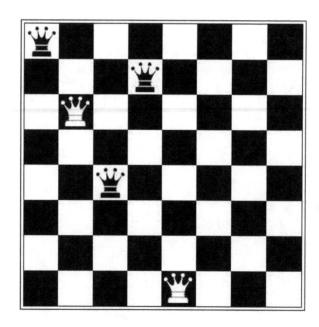

Another attempt is now made to place the sixth queen. No row is free, however, and backtracking takes place to the fifth queen again. There are no more free rows for the fifth queen, so backtracking takes place to the fourth queen, which is now placed in row seven:

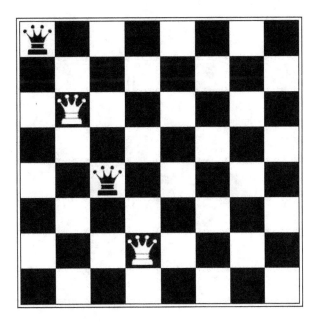

Now placement of the fifth queen is attempted again. Eventually, through backtracking, the positions are finally adjusted so that all eight queens are placed, as shown on the board at the beginning of this section. Notice that it is not necessary to try all queens in all positions; a queen is moved only when its position cannot lead to a final solution.

This informal description of the placement process corresponds to the way that arguments are evaluated in Icon: left-to-right evaluation with last-in, first-out resumption to obtain alternative results. The solution of the eight-queens problem therefore can be formulated in terms of procedures that place the queens according to the method described. A way of representing the chessboard and of determining free positions is needed, however.

The geometrical representation of the chessboard as an eight-by-eight array is not particularly useful. Instead, the important matter is the occupancy of columns, rows, and diagonals. The columns are taken care of by the assignment of one queen to each column. A list provides a natural way of representing the rows:

```
row := list(8, 0)
```

where row [i] is zero if there is no queen on it and nonzero otherwise.

The diagonals are slightly more difficult, since there are 30 of them in all. One approach is to divide the diagonals into two groups (see Dahl, Dijkstra, and Hoare, 1972). Fifteen of the diagonals are downward facing, with their left ends lower than their right ends:

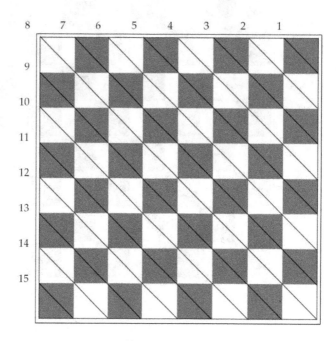

The other 15 diagonals are upward facing:

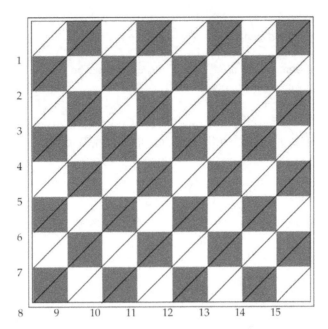

In each case, the diagonals can be represented by lists:

> down := list(15,
> 0) up := list(15, 0)

with zero or nonzero values assigned as they were for the rows.

In placing a queen c on row r, it is necessary to assure that row, down, and up for that position are zero. The expression

> $r + c - 1$

selects the correct downward facing diagonal, while

> $8 + r - c$

selects the correct upward facing diagonal. A queen c can be placed on row r if the following comparison succeeds:

> row[r] = down[r + c −1] = up[8 + r − c] = 0

To place a queen, a nonzero value is assigned to the corresponding positions in row, down, and up. The row number is a convenient value to use, since it records the row on which the queen is placed and can be used in displaying the resulting solution:

$$row[r] <- down[r + c - 1] <- up[8 + r - c] <- r$$

Reversible assignment is used so that the queen can be removed automatically during backtracking. The complete program is

```
procedure main()
  write(q(1), q(2), q(3), q(4), q(5), q(6), q(7), q(8))
end

procedure q(c)
  suspend place(1 to 8, c)   # look for a row
end

procedure place(r, c)
  static up, down, row
  initial {
    up := list(15, 0)
    down := list(15, 0)
    row := list(8, 0)

    }
  if row[r] = down[r + c -1] = up[8 + r - c] = 0     # place if free
  then suspend row[r] <- down[r + c - 1] <- up[8 + r - c] <-

r end
```

The procedure q(c) corresponds to the queen on column c. The procedure place(r, c) places queen c on row r if that position is free. If place(r, c) is successful, it suspends so that if it is resumed because the next queen cannot be placed, the queen is removed by reversing the assignment.

The expression

```
write(q(1), q(2), q(3), q(4), q(5), q(6), q(7), q(8))
```

serves to place the queens. When all the queens are successfully placed, the row positions are written:

```
15863724
```

All possible solutions can be obtained by iteration:

every write(q(1), q(2), q(3), q(4), q(5), q(6), q(7), q(8))

There are 92 solutions in all, although because of symmetries only 12 are unique.

See Appendix I for more general solutions to the *n*-queens problem.

RECURSIVE GENERATORS

Recursion is a powerful programming tool. While recursive procedure calls are widely used, the use of recursion in combination with generation is not as obvious.

Consider the problem of generating all the strings from a set of characters with the strings produced in the order of their length. For example, the results for "abc" would be "", "a", "b", "c", "aa", "ab", "ac", "ba", ... A procedure that produces these results is

```
procedure star(chars)
  suspend "" | (star(chars) || !chars)
end
```

In order to understand the sequence of results for this procedure, consider

```
star("abc")
```

The first result is the empty string, produced by suspending with "". The subsequent results consist of each result in the results for star("abc") followed by each character in "abc". Since !chars is repeatedly resumed for each value produced by star(chars), each character in chars is appended to the first value in the results for star(chars). Therefore, the results are "", "a", "b", "c", ... When star(chars) is resumed for its second result, it produces "a", onto which are appended in succession "a", "b", and "c", and so on.

Recursive generators also can be used to produce the sequences for many recursively defined functions. For example, the Fibonacci numbers are generated by fibseq(1, 1) using the following procedure:

```
procedure fibseq(i, j)
  suspend i | fibseq(j, i + j)
end
```

18

String Scanning and Pattern Matching

Although string scanning involves only a few functions and operations, its apparent simplicity is deceptive. Except for generators, string scanning adds more to the power of Icon and influences programming techniques more than any other feature of the language. Furthermore, some of the ways that string scanning can be used are not obvious. This chapter explores string scanning, concentrating on examples and techniques that exploit its potential and lead to good programming style.

ARITHMETIC EXPRESSIONS

Arithmetic expressions are usually written in infix form with operators between the arguments and with parentheses used for grouping. Rules of precedence and associativity for operators are used to avoid excessive numbers of parentheses. Icon's syntax itself is typical in this respect. Such a syntax is designed for human use. In computer processing, it is more convenient to dispense with precedence and associativity rules and to use parentheses to group all arguments with their operators or to use some other similar representation. Furthermore, it often is convenient to have operators appear before or after their arguments; that is, to have operations in prefix form or suffix form rather than the infix form that is easier for human beings to read. The conversion of strings from one form to another provides a good example of string scanning.

Some typical infix operators with their relative precedences and associativities are

operator	precedence	associativity
^	3	right to left
*	2	left to right
/	2	left to right
+	1	left to right
−	1	left to right

For example, the fully parenthesized form of

"x−y−z*delta"

is

"((x−y)−(z*delta))"

and

"u+v/n^e^2"

is equivalent to

"(u+(v/(n^(e^2))))"

The prefix forms of these two expressions are:

"−(−(x, y),*(z,delta))"
"+(u /(v,^(n,^(e,2))))"

Note that the variables and constants have the same form in both infix and prefix notation.

A typical problem is to convert infix expressions with the preceding operators into prefix form. There may be superfluous parentheses, but the infix expressions otherwise are assumed to be well formed (that is, syntactically correct). The general approach to the problem is recursive, with a procedure fix(exp) that converts an infix expression exp into prefix form. Therefore, the transformation has the form

expr1 operator expr2 → *operator* (fix(*expr1*), fix(*expr2*))

The first problem is to remove any outer parentheses that may occur around the argument of fix(). Since there may be superfluous parentheses, this process must be repeated. One approach is:

```
while exp ?:= {
   2(="(", tab(bal(')')), pos(−1))
   }
```

As long as exp begins with a left parenthesis, the balanced string up to a right parenthesis is matched, and pos(−1) checks that this parenthesis is the last character of the string being scanned. If the right parenthesis is the last character of the string being scanned, the scanning expression succeeds. The value produced by tab(bal(')')) is assigned to exp, and the while loop continues with exp being scanned again.

The next step is to analyze exp to get the proper operator for the pattern

expr1 operator expr2

This pattern may occur in an infix expression in many ways. For example, in

```
"x−y*2"
 − −
```

the pattern occurs in two ways, as indicated by the arrows beneath the operators. Precedence is used to select the correct operator. The first occurrence of the pattern is the correct one in this example, since multiplication has higher precedence than subtraction, and hence y is an argument of the multiplication, not the subtraction. The correct pattern therefore is obtained by looking for the operators of lowest precedence first.

A similar problem occurs in selecting among several operators of equal precedence. Therefore, in "x−y−z" there are two ways the pattern could be applied. Since subtraction is left-associative, this expression is equivalent to "(x−y)−z" and the rightmost left-associative operator is the correct one. On the other hand, the opposite is true of right-associative operators. For example, "x^e^2" is equivalent to "x^(e^2)".

In summary, there are two rules:

1. Look for the operator of lowest precedence first and then for operators with increasingly higher precedence.

2. Locate the rightmost left-associative operator but the leftmost right-asso-ciative operator.

Since string scanning operates from left to right, it is easiest to handle right-associative operators. A procedure is:

```
procedure rassoc(exp, op)

   return exp ? {
     form(tab(bal(op)), move(1), tab(0))
     }

end
```

where form(arg1, op, arg2) constructs the desired prefix expression:

```
procedure form(arg1, op, arg2)
   return op || "(" || fix(arg1) || "," || fix(arg2) ||
")" end
```

Note that form(arg1, op, arg2) performs the necessary rearrangement of the strings produced by scanning.

The rightmost left-associative operator can be located by iterating over the result sequence for the positions of all such operators to find the last one:

```
procedure lassoc(exp, op)
   local j

   return exp ? {
      every j := bal(op)
      form(tab(\j), move(1), tab(0))
      }
   end
```

The expression \j determines whether any value was assigned to j in the every loop. If bal(op) does not produce any result, the initial null value of j is not changed, tab(\j) fails, and lassoc() fails, indicating that op does not occur in exp.

The procedures rassoc() and lassoc() must be applied in the correct order. The obvious approach is:

```
if exp := lassoc(exp, '+ −') then return exp
else if exp := lassoc(exp, '*/') then return exp
else if exp := rassoc(exp, '^') then return exp
else return exp
```

Note that the second arguments of lassoc() and rassoc() are character sets, allowing all operators in a class to be processed at the same time. The final component of this expression returns exp unchanged if it contains no operators, that is, if it is an identifier or a constant. This presumes, of course, that exp is well formed.

The preceding program segment can be made considerably more concise by using goal-directed evaluation in the return expression:

```
return lassoc(exp,'+ −' | '*/') | rassoc(exp, '^') | exp
```

The argument of the return expression consists of the possible alternatives, which are evaluated from left to right. Notice that the argument of lassoc() also contains two alternatives, an application of the fact that p(*expr1*) | p(*expr2*)

and

p(*expr1* | *expr2*)

are equivalent.

The procedure to convert infix expressions into prefix form first removes outer parentheses and then applies lassoc() and rassoc(), as shown previously:

```
procedure fix(exp)
   while exp ?:= {
      2(="(", tab(bal(')'))), pos(-1))
      }
   return lassoc(exp, '+ -' | '*/') | rassoc(exp, '^') | exp
end
```

The rest of the program for infix-to-prefix conversion is:

```
procedure main()
   while write(fix(read()))
end

procedure lassoc(exp, op)
   local j

   return exp ? {
      every j := bal(op)
      form(tab(\j), move(1), tab(0))
      }
end

procedure rassoc(exp, op)
   return exp ? {
      form(tab(bal(op)), move(1), tab(0))
      }
end

procedure form(arg1, op, arg2)
   return op || "(" || fix(arg1) || "," || fix(arg2) || ")"
end
```

Note that the prefix form is determined in form(); suffix or fully parenthesized infix forms can be produced by rearranging the concatenation.

PATTERN MATCHING

The operations for transforming infix to prefix forms in the preceding sections use patterns such as

expr1 operator expr2

to describe the structure of the string and to identify its components.

A pattern is a powerful conceptual tool for describing the structure of strings. This section develops a methodology for describing and implementing patterns using string scanning.

Matching Expressions

The functions tab(i) and move(i) are called matching functions because they change the position in the subject and produce the substring of the subject between the old and new positions. While the value of i in tab(i) can be computed in many ways using string analysis functions, actual matching is done only by tab(i) and move(i).

Matching expressions that extend the repertoire of matching functions provide a way of expressing more complicated matching operations. Matching expressions must obey a protocol that allows them to be used like matching functions. The protocol for a matching expression *expr* is as follows:

1. Evaluation of *expr* does not change the subject.

2. If *expr* succeeds, it produces the substring of the subject between the positions before and after its evaluation.

3. If *expr* does not produce a result, it leaves the position where it was prior to the time *expr* was evaluated.

The first rule assumes that matching expressions all apply to the same subject. The second rule is concerned with the values produced by matching expressions, while the third rule assures that alternative matches start at the same place in the subject. The third rule includes the possibility that a matching expression may change the position but later restore it if a subsequent match is unsuccessful. The three rules are largely independent.

For example,

tab(upto(',')) || move(1)

is a matching expression, but

> tab(upto(',')) || move(−1)

is not, since the value it produces is not the substring between the old and new positions. Similarly,

> tab(upto(',')) & move(1)

is not a matching expression, since it does not produce the substring of the subject between the positions before tab(upto(',')) is evaluated and after move(1) is evalu-ated. The expression

> &subject[.&pos:&pos := upto(',')]

is not a matching expression either, since, if it is resumed, it does not restore the previous position. On the other hand,

> &subject[.&pos:&pos <− upto(',')]

is a matching expression, since, if it is resumed, the reversible assignment operation restores the previous position. Note that in both cases the first occurrence of &pos in the range specification must be dereferenced before a new value is assigned to &pos.

In general, bounded expressions prevent restoration of the position, so that

> {s := move(1); s || tab(0)}

is not a matching expression even though it produces the matched substring.

When using string scanning to do pattern matching, it is generally good practice to use matching expressions. Most pattern matching is done from left to right. In such cases,

> *expr1* || *expr2*

should be used instead of

> *expr1* & *expr2*

since the former expression produces the matched substring, while the latter does not. Both operations perform data backtracking, however. If production of matched substrings is not important, conjunction may be used in place of concatenation.

Matching Procedures

A *matching procedure* is a procedure that is a matching expression. As an example, consider a procedure that does what the function tab(i) does.

```
procedure tab(i)

    suspend .&subject[.&pos:&pos <- i]

end
```

Such a procedure is merely an encapsulation of a matching expression and satisfies all the rules of protocol for matching expressions. The value returned is dereferenced; otherwise the result would be a variable to which a value could be assigned to change the subject. The matching function move(i) can be written as a procedure in an analogous manner.

Using this technique, a variety of matching procedures can be written. For example,

```
procedure arb()

    suspend .&subject[.&pos:&pos <- &pos to *&subject + 1]

end
```

matches any string from the current position through the end of the subject. Note that arb() may generate more than one value. Therefore,

```
arb() || ="load" || arb() || ="r6"
```

matches any string that contains the substring "load" followed by the substring "r6"; "load" need not appear at the beginning of the subject, and "load" and "r6" need not be consecutive substrings.

A similar procedure that matches the longest possible string first is

```
procedure rarb()

    suspend .&subject[.&pos: &pos <- ((*&subject + 1) to &pos by -1)]

end
```

For example,

```
rarb() || ="."
```

matches the string up to and including the last period in the subject.

Another example is a matching procedure that matches any one of several strings in a list:

```
procedure lmatch(slist)
  suspend =!slist
end
```

For example,

```
lmatch(["black", "white", "gray"])
```

matches "black", "white", or "gray".

One advantage of using a matching procedure for high-level string processing is that a procedure is a value. As such, it can be used as an argument to other matching procedures. An example of such a use is given by:

```
procedure arbno(p)
  suspend "" | (p() || arbno(p))
end
```

The procedure arbno(p) matches zero or more instances of whatever p() matches. The first alternative, the empty string, corresponds to zero matches of p(). The second alternative matches whatever p() matches, concatenated with whatever arbno(p) matches: zero or more instances of whatever p() matches. For example, given

```
procedure shades()
  suspend arb() || lmatch(["black", "white",
  "gray"]) end
```

then arbno(shades) matches strings that contain zero or more occurrences of "black", "white", or "gray".

The argument of arbno() must be a matching procedure. It cannot be an arbitrary matching expression, since the argument is called in the body of the procedure for arbno(). For example, in

```
arbno(lmatch(["black", "white", "gray"]))
```

the call of lmatch() is evaluated before arbno() is called. Not only is this order of evaluation incorrect, but also the value assigned to the parameter p is a string, not a procedure.

Note that arbno() is a recursive generator. Compare it to star() given in Chapter 17.

GRAMMARS AND LANGUAGES

A pattern characterizes a set of strings — the strings that it matches. A set of strings is called a language. The strings in a language (its "sentences") are derived or described according to grammatical rules.

Natural languages, such as English, are very complex. The grammatical rules of such languages (their syntax) describe these languages only superficially. In fact, there are many aspects of natural languages that defy precise description. There are, however, many interesting languages, including programming languages, in which the structure can be defined by precise and comparatively simple grammatical rules.

Patterns and the grammars for languages have a close relationship. For some kinds of grammars, there is a direct mapping from the rules of the grammar to patterns that match strings in the corresponding language.

A language for a simple class of arithmetic expressions can be described informally in terms of mutually recursive definitions:

1. An *expression* is a *term* or a *term* followed by a + followed by an *expression*.

2. A *term* is an *element* or an *element* followed by a * followed by a *term*.

3. An *element* is one of the characters x, y, z or an *expression* enclosed in parentheses.

Words in italics, like *element*, describe sets of strings and are called nonterminal symbols. Specific strings, like x, are called terminal symbols.

These definitions can be expressed more formally in terms of a grammar as follows. Let X, T, and E stand for *expression*, *term*, and *element*, respectively. Then a grammar corresponding to the preceding definitions is:

```
X ::= T | T+X
T ::= E | E*T
E ::= x | y | z | (X)
```

Uppercase letters are used here to denote nonterminal symbols, while other charac-ters, including parentheses, stand for themselves. The symbol ::= stands for "is defined to be". The concatenation of symbols replaces "followed by" in the informal definition, and the vertical bar replaces "or". Note the similarity of this use of the vertical bar to the alternation control structure in Icon. In a grammar, the vertical bar has lower precedence than concatenation.

Each nonterminal symbol defines its own language: a language for expres-sions defined by X, a language for terms defined by T, and a language for elements defined by E. One nonterminal symbol is designated as a "goal" for the language of interest. X is the goal in the examples that follow.

In deriving the strings for the language defined by a nonterminal symbol, the symbol ::= in the grammar means that an instance of the nonterminal symbol on its left can be replaced by any one of the alternatives on the right. For example, T can be replaced by either E or E∗T. Starting with the goal symbol X, a possible derivation of a sentence is:

X	goal
T+X	second alternative for X
T+T	first alternative for X
E+T	first alternative for first instance of T
x+T	first alternative for E
x+E	first alternative for T
x+(X)	fourth alternative for E
x+(T)	first alternative for X
x+(E∗T)	second alternative for T
x+(y∗T)	second alternative for E
x+(y∗E)	first alternative for T
x+(y∗z)	third alternative for E

Since there are no more nonterminal symbols in this string, x+(y∗z) is a sentence in the language defined by X.

The alternatives in the preceding derivation were chosen at random. Applica-tion of all the rules in all possible ways produces all strings in the language. As in most interesting languages, the language for X contains an infinite number of strings.

Recognizers

Recognition is the process of determining whether or not a string belongs to a language and is the converse of derivation. In the present context, this amounts to matching the strings that are in a language and only those strings.

In the case of grammars like the preceding one, there is a straightforward and mechanical way of producing patterns that match the strings in the language:

1. Terminal symbols are matched by corresponding matching expressions for the specific strings. For example, x is matched by ="x".

2. Nonterminal symbols are matched by matching procedures. For example, X is matched by X(). The form of such matching procedures is given later.

3. A concatenation of symbols is matched by the concatenation of the match-ing expressions for the individual symbols. For example, T+X is matched by

$$T() \parallel =\text{"+"} \parallel X()$$

4. Alternatives are matched by the alternation of matching expressions. For example,

$$E|E*T$$

is matched by

$$E() \mid (E() \parallel =\text{"*"} \parallel T())$$

5. A matching procedure encapsulates the matching expression for the corresponding nonterminal symbol. For example, the matching procedure for

$$X ::= T|T+X$$

is:

```
procedure X()
  suspend T() | (T() || ="+" || X())
end
```

These rules can be used to convert any context-free grammar of the kind given previously directly into matching procedures.

The procedure for the nonterminal goal symbol is called within a scanning expression. Since recognition requires that the entire string be matched, not just an initial substring of it, the scanning operation has the form

```
line ? {
   X() & pos(0)
   }
```

A program to recognize strings in the language defined by X is:

```
procedure main()
   while writes(line := read())
     do if line ? {
        X() & pos(0)
        }
     then write(" accepted") else write(" rejected")
end
```

The kind of recognizer given here is called a top-down, recursive-descent recognizer with backtracking. Recognizers of this kind have two problems: they are inefficient, and they cannot handle left recursion in the grammar. Left recursion occurs when the definition of a nonterminal symbol has an alternative that begins with a nonterminal symbol leading back to itself. For example, in a rule such as

$$X ::= X+T \mid T$$

the matching procedure

```
procedure X()
    suspend (X() || ="+" || T()) | T()
end
```

calls itself indefinitely, which causes internal stack overflow and program termina-tion with an error message.

Despite these problems, this approach to recognizing strings is sometimes useful. It also provides insights into the relationship between grammars and pattern matching.

There are other possibilities. The previous matching procedures have no arguments. By adding arguments, recognizers can be constructed for classes of languages that are more general than context-free ones. Consider, for example, the program

```
procedure main()
    while writes(line := read())
        do if line ? {
            ABC("") & pos(0)
            }
        then write(" accepted") else write(" rejected")
end

procedure ABC(s)
    suspend =s | (="a" || ABC("b" || s) || ="c")
end
```

This program matches sentences in the language $a^n b^n c^n$ for $n = 0, 1, \ldots$: the empty string, abc, aabbcc, aaabbbccc, ... This is a well-known context-sensitive lan-guage, which cannot be derived from any context-free grammar. While there are more obvious ways of recognizing such strings than the procedure given above, it is representative of a general class of recognizers for context-sensitive languages.

Tracing provides insight into the matching process. For the input line aaabbbccc, the trace output for the procedure ABC() is:

```
abc.icn:    5  | ABC("")
abc.icn:   13  | ABC suspended ""
abc.icn:    5  | ABC resumed
abc.icn:   13  || ABC("b")
abc.icn:   13  || | ABC("bb")
abc.icn:   13  || | | ABC("bbb")
abc.icn:   13  || | | ABC suspended "bbb"
abc.icn:   13  || | | ABC suspended "abbbc"
abc.icn:   13  || ABC suspended "aabbbcc"
abc.icn: 13s   | ABC suspended "aaabbbccc"
```

Parsers

The process of recognizing strings in a language has limited usefulness. Recognition produces only a "yes" or a "no", but no information is produced about how the string is matched or how its structure is related to the grammar.

It is relatively easy to convert matching procedures like those given previously into parsing procedures that produce a "parse tree" that retains the structure of the match. The technique produces lists of matched strings rather than concatenations of matched strings. A matching procedure such as

```
procedure X()

   suspend T() | (T() || ="+" || X())

end
```

can be rewritten as a parsing procedure:

```
procedure X()

   suspend [ T()] | [ T(), ="+", X()]

end
```

Since parsing procedures produce lists, the result is a list of lists, or a tree, that shows the details of the parse. For example, the value produced for the string "x+(y*z)" is

[[["x"]], "+", [[["(", [[["y"], "*", [["z"]]]], ")"]]]]

Such a list is more easily understood if it is drawn as a tree:

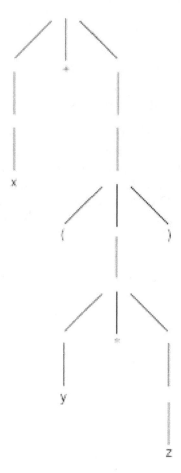

It may be useful to provide a tag as the first value in each list in order to identify the nonterminal symbol. With this addition, the parsing procedures for the gram-mar in the preceding section are:

```
procedure T()
    suspend ["T", E()] | ["T", E(), ="*",
T()] end

procedure E()
    suspend ["E", =!"xyz"] | ["E", ="(", X(), =")"]
end

procedure X()
    suspend ["X", T()] | ["X", T(), ="+", X()]
end
```

Note that the more compact formulation

=!"xyz"

is used in place of the direct translation

="x" | ="y" | ="z"

The tree produced for the preceding example is:

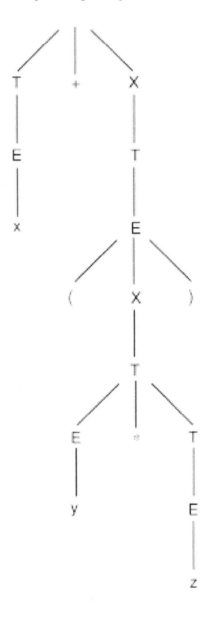

19

Using Structures

Icon provides the facilities that are needed for processing structures, such as the parse trees that were developed in Chapter 18. This chapter describes how records, lists, sets, and tables can be used for representing and manipulating trees, graphs, and other structures.

TREES

A tree is a collection of nodes connected by directed arcs. At most one arc can be directed into any node, although there may be many arcs directed out of a node. One node, the *root*, has no arcs directed into it. Nodes that have no arcs directed out of them are *leaves*. A value usually is associated with each node.

A common way to represent trees with strings corresponds to the way that arithmetic expressions are given in prefix form (see Chapter 18). For example, the arithmetic expression

   "(a/b)+(c–d)"

has the prefix form

   "+(/(a,b),–(c,d))"

and corresponds to the tree

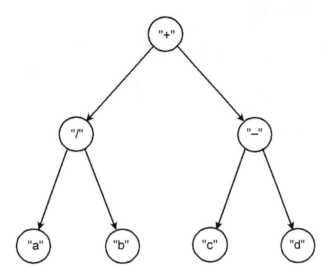

As shown here, trees usually are drawn with the root at the top. This is a binary tree. That is, there are two arcs out of all nodes except the leaves.

When a tree is represented by a string, the parentheses and commas indicate the structural relationships. The string representation of a tree is compact, but it is awkward to process for many purposes. There are several ways that a tree can be represented with structures. A natural method uses lists, as in

["+", ["/", ["a"], ["b"]], ["−", ["c"], ["d"]]]

In this representation each node of the tree is represented by a list. The first value in each list is the value that is associated with the node, and subsequent values in a list correspond to arcs to other nodes. Note that this representation is somewhat different from the one used for parse trees in Chapter 18. In that representation, leaves are represented by strings, not lists. The representation here is more general.

A more structured way of representing a binary tree is to use records for the nodes:

record node(value, lptr, rptr)

where the lptr and rptr fields contain pointers to the left and right subtrees, respectively.

Using this representation, the tree shown above can be constructed as follows:

```
leaf1 := node("a")
leaf2 := node("b")
leaf3 := node("c")
```

```
leaf4 := node("d")
inode1 := node("/",  leaf1,  leaf2)
inode2 := node("–",  leaf3,  leaf4)
root := node("+", inode1, inode2)
```

Of course, this tree could be constructed in a single large expression.

While such a representation of a tree is useful for processing data within a program, information read into a program and written out of a program consists of strings. Consequently, procedures are needed to convert between the string and record representations of trees. A procedure to do this is naturally recursive, since the structure of a tree is recursive.

A procedure to convert the string representation of a tree to its corresponding record representation is:

```
procedure rtree(stree)
  local R

  stree ? {
    if R := node(tab(upto('('))) then {        # new node
      move(1)                                  # skip paren
      R.lptr := rtree(tab(bal(',')))           # left subtree
      move(1)                                  # skip comma
      R.rptr := rtree(tab(bal(')')))           # right subtree
      }
    else R := node(tab(0))                     # leaf
    }

  return R

end
```

This formulation assumes that the string representation of the tree is well-formed. The two branches of the selection expression differentiate between interior and leaf nodes. For interior nodes, rtree() is called recursively to construct the subtrees. Note that the fields lptr and rptr have null values for leaf nodes.

Conversion from the record representation of a tree to the corresponding string representation is similar in structure, with concatenation replacing assign-ments to fields:

```
procedure stree(rtree)

  if /rtree.lptr then return rtree.value       # leaf
  else return rtree.value || "(" || stree(rtree.lptr) || "," || stree(rtree.rptr) ||

")" end
```

This formulation assumes that if one pointer from a node is null the other one is also.

For some purposes it is useful to be able to visit all the nodes (subtrees) of a tree. This can be done easily with a recursive generator:

```
procedure visit(rtree)

  suspend rtree
  suspend visit(\(rtree.lptr | rtree.rptr)) # not leaf, continue

end
```

Note that this procedure reflects the recursive definition of a tree. The root node itself is produced first, followed by the nodes for its subtrees. Here it is more convenient to check that each pointer is non-null.

The procedure visit(rtree) can be used in a variety of ways. For example,

```
every write(stree(visit(rtree)))
```

writes all the subtrees in rtree, while

```
every write(visit(rtree).value)
```

writes the values of all nodes in the tree. Similarly,

```
every R := visit(rtree) do
  if /R.lptr then write(R.value)
```

writes the values of all leaves in rtree.

Sometimes it is necessary to know whether or not two trees have the same structure and the same node values, that is, if they are equivalent. The operation

```
R1 === R2
```

does not determine whether or not two trees are equivalent, but only if they are identical; that is, if R1 and R2 are the same record (see Chapter 10). A procedure to compare two trees for equivalence is

```
procedure rtreeq(R1,R2)

  if R1 === R2 then return R2              # identical subtrees
  else if /(R1 | R2) then fail            # only one is null
  else if {
    R1.value === R2.value &               # check values and subtrees
    rtreeq(R1.lptr, R2.lptr) &
    rtreeq(R1.rtpr, R2.rptr)
    }
  then return R2
```

              else fail

       . end

The first test checks whether R1 and R2 are identical. If they are, it is not necessary to check anything else. If this fails, the values and subtrees are checked for equivalence, calling rtreeq() recursively. The recursion terminates for equivalent trees when null-valued pointers (for leaf nodes) are compared. If all subtrees are the same, R2 is returned, conforming to the convention for built-in comparison opera-tions.

DAGS

A directed acyclic graph, or *dag*, is a graph in which there are no loops leading from a node back to itself. A *rooted* dag is like a tree except that there may be several arcs directed into any node other than the root. Rooted dags occur, for example, as the result of common subexpression elimination, where a subtree that is the same as another is eliminated and the two arcs are directed to one of the subtrees. For example, the infix expression

      (a/b)+((a/b)−b)

has the tree

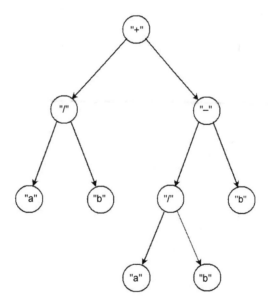

Duplicate subtrees can be eliminated by converting this tree to a dag:

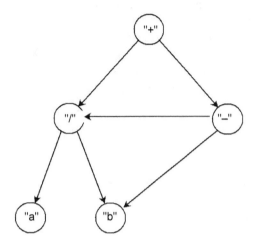

Instead of converting a tree to a dag, it is easier to construct the dag in the first place. The technique used here is to tabulate the parts of the structure that have been built already and to direct arcs to them rather than constructing equivalent parts:

```
procedure rdag(stree,done)
  local R

  /done := table()                          # new table

  if R := \done[stree] then return R        # return part already done

  stree ? {
    if R := node(tab(upto('('))) then {      # new node
      move(1)                               # skip paren
      R.lptr := rdag(tab(bal(',')), done)   # left subdag
      move(1)                               # skip comma
      R.rptr := rdag(tab(bal(')')), done)   # right subdag
      }
    else R := node(tab(0))                   # leaf
    }

  return done[stree] := R

end
```

The table **done** keeps track of portions of the dag that already have been constructed. Its keys are strings and its values point to the corresponding nodes. When rdag() is called to construct a dag for **stree**, the second argument is omitted, since no parts of the dag have been constructed yet. Thus, the table is created on the initial call of rdag(). The recursive call of rdag() includes the table **done** as its second argument, passing the table of the parts that have been constructed. Finally, the newly constructed dag is added as the value corresponding to the key stree.

The method of handling the table of constructed parts deserves note. Since the table done is created at the "top-level" call of rdag() and subsequently passed as an argument to recursive calls of rdag(), done is local to the processing of a particular tree. If it were global instead, independent uses of rdag() might interfere with each other. The table cannot be constructed in an initial clause for the same reason.

Note that the tree-processing functions in the preceding section all work properly on rooted dags. The procedure stree() processes dags as well as trees, effectively "unfolding" them. Similarly, rtreeq() works properly on dags. The procedure visit() works on dags, although nodes with more than one arc into them are visited once for each arc. This causes a dag to appear to be a tree.

GRAPHS

In general, directed graphs have cycles and unconnected subgraphs, as in:

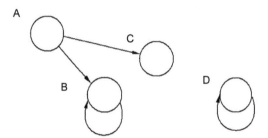

One way to build the corresponding structure is to represent each node in the graph by a set. Then the values in the set are pointers — arcs to the nodes to which the node points. For example, the program structures for the graph shown above are:

```
A := set() B
:= set() C :=
set() D :=
set()
insert(A, B)
insert(A, C)
insert(B, B)
insert(D, D)
```

The important conceptual point is that a set is a collection of pointers to other sets. A slightly different visualization of the structures in the programming domain illustrates this:

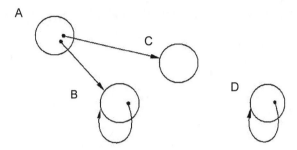

Thus, an arc is represented by (a pointer to) a set and a node is represented by the values in the set.

The ease of manipulating this representation of graphs is illustrated by a procedure to compute the transitive closure of a node (the node and all nodes reachable from it by a succession of arcs):

```
procedure closure(n,
  S) local n1

  /S := set()

  insert(S, n)

  every n1 := !n do
      member(S, n1) | closure(n1, S)

  return S

end
```

Note that a set also is used to keep track of nodes as they accumulate.

Several problems arise in computations on graphs that may require a some-what more sophisticated representation of structures. For example, values may be associated with arcs:

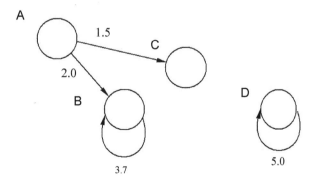

In this case, the set-of-sets approach is inadequate. However, a record type can be used for arcs, as in

record arc(value, node)

where the value field contains the value associated with the arc and the node field contains the set to which the arc points. Then the graph can be represented in a program as follows:

```
insert(A,  arc(2.0,  B))
insert(A,  arc(1.5,  C))
insert(B,  arc(3.7,  B))
insert(D, arc(5.0, D))
```

TWO-WAY TABLES

Programs that manipulate graphs generally need to be able to read a representation of a graph in string form and write the results in string form. For example, the (unweighted) form of the graph in the preceding section might be represented by strings such as:

```
"A–>B"
"A–>C"
"B–>B"
"D–>D"
```

One problem is associating labels for the nodes with corresponding program structures. The natural solution in Icon is to use a table in which the keys are the labels and the corresponding values are the corresponding sets. Written out expli-citly for the graph above, this might be:

```
Node := table()
Node["A"] := A
Node["B"] := B
Node["C"] := C
Node["D"] := D
```

Consequently, Node["A"] produces the node (set) labeled A. Such a table might be used, for example, in constructing a graph from its string representation.

On the other hand, the converse association may be needed. For example, in writing out the results of a computation on a graph (such as the transitive closure of a node), the labels associated with nodes may be needed.

Since any kind of value can be used as a key, a table with the keys and corresponding values reversed can be used:

```
Label := table()
Label[A] := "A"
Label[B] := "B"
Label[C] := "C"
Label[D] := "D"
```

It is not necessary to have two tables, however. Since the keys in a table need not all be of the same type, the same table can be keyed with both the labels and the nodes (sets):

```
Graph := table()
Graph["A"] := A
Graph["B"] := B
Graph["C"] := C
Graph["D"] := D
Graph[A] := "A"
Graph[B] := "B"
Graph[C] := "C"
Graph[D] := "D"
```

Such a "two-way" table keeps all the information needed to associate labels with nodes and vice versa in one structure. Subscripting it with a label produces the corresponding node, and subscripting it with a node produces the corresponding label.

20

Mappings and Labelings

MAPPING TECHNIQUES

The function map(s1, s2, s3) normally is used to perform a character substitution on s1 by replacing characters in s1 that occur in s2 by the characters of s3 that are in corresponding positions to those in s2. In this kind of use, s2 and s3 are parameters that characterize the substitution, and s1 varies, as in

> map(line, "aeiou", "*****")

which replaces all lowercase vowels in line by asterisks.

If s1 and s2 are considered to be parameters and s3 is allowed to vary, some surprising results are possible.

Transpositions

If the value of labels is a string of distinct characters (that is, containing no duplicates), and the value of trans is a rearrangement, or *transposition*, of the value of labels, then

> map(trans, labels, s3)

produces the corresponding transposition of s3. For example, map("654321", "123456", s3)

produces the reversal of the value of s3. Suppose the value of s3 is "quotas" as in

map("654321", "123456", "quotas")

Then the "6" in the first argument is replaced by the character corresponding to the "6" in the second argument, that is, "s". Similarly, the character "5" in the first argument is replaced by the character corresponding to the "5" in the second argument, that is, "a", and so on:

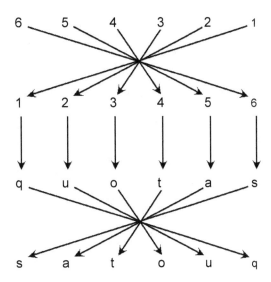

The value produced is "satouq", the reversal of "quotas", since the specified transposition, "654321", is the reversal of the labeling string, "123456". If the transposition is different, as in

map("561234", "123456", s3)

the result produced is correspondingly different. In this case it is the rotation of s3 two characters to the right (or four to the left).

Any characters can be used for the labeling as long as there are no duplicates. The maximum size of a transposition is limited to 256. The more important restriction is that the sizes of the second and third arguments must be the same. Therefore,

map("654321", "123456", s3)

only can be used to reverse six-character strings. In many cases, however, the transposition of longer strings can be performed piece by piece. That is,

reverse(s1 || s2) == (reverse(s2) || reverse(s1))

Although there is a built-in function reverse(s), a corresponding procedure using mapping techniques provides a model for a variety of transpositions. A procedure is:

```
procedure reverse(s)
  static labels, trans, max

  initial {
    labels  :=  "abcdefghijklmnopqrstuvwxyz"
    trans   :=  "zyxwvutsrqponmlkjihgfedcba"
    max := *labels
    }

  if *s <= max then return map(right(trans, *s), left(labels, *s), s)
  else return reverse(right(s, *s − max)) || map(trans, labels, left(s, max))

end
```

The values chosen for labels and trans are two strings of reasonable size that are easy to write. If s is not too long, it can be reversed by one application of map(). The expression

left(labels, *s)

truncates s at the right and produces a labeling of the correct length. The expression

right(trans, *s)

produces the corresponding transposition from the other end of trans. Subscripting expressions also could also be used for these purposes.

If s is too long to be reversed by one application of map(), recursion is used. Piece-by-piece reversals of long strings can be done iteratively, of course; recursion simply provides a more compact solution for the purposes of illustration.

The reversal process is more efficient for longer values of labels and trans. The longest possible labeling is 256, as mentioned earlier. Strings of all 256 characters are impractical to write out literally, but they can be computed by

```
labels := string(&cset)
trans := ""
every trans := !labels || trans
```

A more sophisticated approach is to obtain the longest labeling and transpo-sition strings by bootstrapping, starting with short labeling and transposition strings. For example,

```
labels := "12"
trans := "21"
```

characterizes reversal. The procedure reverse() can be modified to perform the bootstrapping in its initial clause:

```
procedure reverse(s)
  static labels, trans, max

  initial {
    labels := "12"                           # short label
    trans := "21"                            # short transposition
    max := *labels
    trans := reverse(string(&cset))          # long transposition
    labels := string(&cset)                  # long label
    max := *labels                           # new length
    }
        ...
```

When reverse() is called the first time, it calls itself to change short values of labels and trans to the longest possible values. Note that labels, trans, and max must be defined consistently when reverse() calls itself in its initial clause.

The two strings

```
labels := "12"
trans := "21"
```

characterize the reversal of two-character strings. The extension of this transposition to the reversal of strings of arbitrary length depends on the way substrings of labels and trans are selected and on the handling of the case in which s is too long to be transposed by a single call of map(). Consider a transposition in which every odd-numbered character is swapped with its even-numbered neighbor. For six-character strings, this has the form

```
map("214365", "123456", s3)
```

This transposition also can be characterized by

```
labels := "12"
trans := "21"
```

which is the same labeling as used for reversal. The procedure to swap characters is very similar to reverse(). The two procedures differ in the way that substrings of labels and trans are selected and in the handling of strings that are too long to be transposed by a single call of map(), which is based on

$$\text{swap(s1 || s2) == (swap(s1) || swap(s2))}$$

The complete procedure for swapping adjacent characters is:

```
procedure swap(s)

   static labels, trans, max
   initial {
      labels := "12"
      trans := "21"
      max := *labels
      trans := swap(string(&cset))
      labels := string(&cset)
      max := *labels
      }

   if *s <= max then return map(left(trans, *s), left(labels, *s), s)
   else return swap(left(s, *s – max)) || map(trans, labels, right(s, max))

end
```

This procedure only works properly if the size of s is even.

It is reasonable to question the use of mapping techniques for transpositions of this kind, since the procedures are relatively complicated and many transposi-tions can be written concisely using more conventional techniques. Mapping techniques have two advantages. First, they are fast, especially when the same transposition is performed many times, overcoming the initialization overhead for procedures. Second, mapping techniques also provide a clear characterization of the transposition process.

Positional Transformations

For transpositions like

map(trans, labels, s3)

labels cannot contain duplicate characters and trans must be a transposition of labels. If these two constraints are relaxed, other kinds of *positional transformations* are possible (see Gimpel, 1976).

The strings trans and labels do not have to be the same size. If some characters in labels are omitted from trans, the corresponding characters in s3 are omitted from the result. For example, map("124578", "12345678", s3)

deletes the third and sixth characters of an eight-character string, s3. Therefore,

    map("124578", "12345678", "03:56:42")

produces "035642". In cases like this, labels that are more mnemonic make the intent clearer. Furthermore, the labels that correspond to deleted characters can be anything; they need not be distinct. An equivalent positional transformation is:

    map("HhMmSs", "Hh:Mm:Ss", s3)

If there are characters in trans that do not occur in labels, these characters are added to the result. Consequently,

    map("Hh:Mm:Ss", "HhMmSs", "035642")

produces "03:56:42".

If labels contains duplicate characters, the rightmost correspondences with characters in s3 apply. For example,

    map("be", "beeeeee", s3)

produces the first and last characters of strings s3 of length seven.

Characters in labels also can be duplicated in trans. For instance,

    map("123321", "123", s3)

produces the three-character string s3 followed by its reversal. An example is:

    map("123321", "123", "–*|")

which produces " – *||* –" .

LABELINGS

In the preceding sections, characters are used as labels to identify positions of characters in strings. Characters can also be used to stand for objects. Since there are only 256 different characters, their use for labeling objects is limited, but when they can be used they often allow a compact representation and efficient manipulation. Two examples follow.

Manipulating Decks of Cards

Since a standard deck of playing cards consists of 52 different cards, it is a natural candidate for representation by characters, such as

```
deck := string(&letters)
```

In this string, the correspondence between characters and individual playing cards is arbitrary. For example, "a" might correspond to the ace of clubs, "b" to the two of clubs, "n" to the ace of diamonds, and so on.

To illustrate the ease of performing computations on such a representation, consider shuffling a deck of cards. One approach is:

```
procedure shuffle(deck)
  local i

  every i := *deck to 2 by −1
    do deck[?i] :=: deck[i]

  return deck

end
```

In order to display a shuffled deck or any hand of cards, the implied correspondence between characters and cards must be converted to a readable format. Suppose that in a "fresh" deck the first 13 characters are clubs, the second 13 are diamonds, and so on. Then if

```
fresh := string(&letters)
```

and

```
suits := repl("C", 13) || repl("D", 13) || repl("H", 13) || repl("S", 13)
```

the mapping

```
map(deck, fresh, suits)
```

produces a string showing the suit of each card in deck. Similarly, if the denomina-tions in each suit of a fresh deck are arranged with the ace first, followed by the two, and so on through the jack, queen, and king, then

```
denoms := repl("A23456789TJQK", 4)
```

used in the mapping

```
map(deck, fresh, denoms)
```

produces a string showing the denomination of each card in deck. A complete procedure for displaying the cards with suits on one line and denominations below is:

```
procedure disp(deck)
  static fresh, suits, denoms

  initial {
    fresh := string(&letters)
    suits := repl("C", 13) || repl("D", 13) || repl("H", 13) || repl("S",
    13) denoms := repl("A23456789TJQK", 4)
    }
  write(map(deck, fresh, suits))          # suits
  write(map(deck, fresh, denoms))         #denominations

end
```

A typical display might be:

```
C D C H S S ...
5 3 K T Q 8 ...
```

While such a display is understandable, it is not attractive. Consider the problem of displaying a bridge hand in the conventional way, with each suit given separately. One way to extract all the cards of a given suit from a hand is to map all characters that are not in that suit into a single character. A blank provides a convenient representation for all cards in the suits that are not of interest. If the first 13 cards in a fresh deck are clubs, then in ASCII

```
clubs := "ABCDEFGHIJKLM" || repl(" ", 39)
```

characterizes the clubs. If hand contains characters from fresh, then

```
map(hand, fresh, clubs)
```

maps all clubs in hand into distinct characters and all other characters in hand into spaces. Characters that do not correspond to clubs are "filtered out". Diamonds can be obtained by using

```
diamonds := repl(" ", 13) || "ABCDEFGHIJKLM" || repl(" ", 26)
```

in a similar manner. Since the same string is used to label the characters in both suits, corresponding clubs and diamonds are mapped into the same characters. These characters correspond to the ranks of the card in the suit: Cards of the same rank in different suits are mapped into the same character. Furthermore

```
string(cset(map(hand, fresh, clubs)))
```

places the clubs in order. Any blanks are condensed into a single blank which, because of the order of the ASCII characters, is at the beginning of the resulting string. This blank is essentially "invisible".

Manipulating Graphs

Chapter 19 presented a general way of representing directed graphs. In many cases, a considerably more concise representation is possible. If the number of nodes in a graph is small and only the structural properties of graphs are of interest, a graph can be represented by labeling each node with a different character. An arc from one node to another can be represented by the two characters for the nodes, in order according to the direction of the arc. For example, the graph

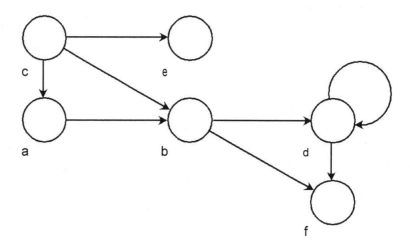

can be represented by the string

g := "abbdbfcacbcedddf"

where "ab" represents the arc from a to b, "bd" represents the arc from b to d, and so on.

Many computations are particularly simple if such a representation is used. For example, the number of arcs in a graph g is given by

*g / 2

and the number of nodes is given by

*cset(g)

This representation assumes there is no isolated node that has no arc into it or out of it. If such a node exists, a separate list of nodes is necessary.

Computing transitive closure illustrates the methods of manipulating this representation of directed graphs. The first step in determining transitive closure is to obtain the immediate successors of a set of nodes (those to which there is an arc from any of the nodes in the set):

```
procedure successors(graph, nodes)
   local snodes

   snodes := ''                    # start with none

   graph ? repeat {
     if tab(any(nodes)) then snodes ++:= move(1)
     else move(2) | break # exit at end of string
     }

   return snodes

end
```

The successor of every odd-numbered character in graph that is contained in nodes is added to snodes by the augmented assignment operation.

Transitive closure starts with the single node of interest and successively expands the set of nodes that can be reached from it until no new nodes are added:

```
procedure closure(graph, nodes)
   local snodes

   snodes := nodes          # start with given nodes

   while snodes ~=== (nodes ++:= successors(graph, nodes)) do
      snodes := nodes           # update if changed

   return nodes

end
```

Note that at each step all the successors that can be reached from any node currently in the closure are added to the closure.

A

Syntax

The description of the syntax of Icon that follows uses an italic typeface to denote syntactic classes, such as *program*, and a sans serif typeface to denote literal program text, such as global. An optional symbol is denoted by the subscript *opt*, so that

$$(expression_{opt})$$

denotes an optional expression that is enclosed in parentheses.

Alternatives are denoted by vertical stacking. For example,

program:
    declaration
    declaration program

defines a *program* to be a *declaration* or a *declaration* followed by a *program*. In effect, a program is a sequence of one or more declarations.

PROGRAMS

declaration: global-
declaration invocable-
declaration link-
declaration
procedure-declaration
record-declaration

invocable-declaration:
invocable **all**
invocable proc-list

proc-list: string-
literal
string-literal , proc-list

global-declaration:
global *identifier-list*

identifier-list:
identifier
identifier , identifier-list

link-declaration:
link *link-list*

link-list: file-
name
file-name , link-list

file-name:
identifier
string-literal

procedure-declaration:
header locals$_{opt}$ initial-clause$_{opt}$ expression-sequence$_{opt}$ **end**

header:
procedure *identifier (parameter-list$_{opt}$)* ;

parameter-list:
identifier-list
identifier-list , identifier [ ]
identifier [ ]

locals:
>   *local-specification identifier-list* ; *local-specification identifier-list* ; *locals*

local-specification:
>   local
>   static

initial-clause:
>   initial *expression* ;

record-declaration:
>   record *identifier* (*field-list*$_{opt}$)

field-list: field-name
>   *field-name* , *field-list*

expression-sequence:

>   *expression*$_{opt}$
>   *expression*$_{opt}$; *expression-sequence*

expression: parenthesized-expression compound-expression list-expression field-reference-expression subscripting-expression invocation-expression mutual-evaluation-expression prefix-expression infix-expression to-by-expression create-expression return-expression break-expression next-expression case-expression if-then-else-expression loop-expression

>   *identifier*
>   *keyword*
>   *literal*

parenthesized-expression:

    ($expression_{opt}$)

compound-expression:
    { *expression-sequence* }

list-expression:
    [*expression-list*]

expression-list:

    $expression_{opt}$

    $expression_{opt}$, *expression-list*

field-reference-expression:
    expression . field-name

subscripting-expression:
    expression [*expression-list*]
    expression [*range-specification*]

range-specification:
    expression : *expression*
    expression +: *expression*
    expression −: *expression*

invocation-expression:

    $expression_{opt}$ (*expression-list*)

    $expression_{opt}$ { *expression-list* }

mutual-evaluation-expression:
    (*expression-list*)

prefix-expression prefix-
    operator expression

infix-expression
    expression infix-operator expression

to-by expression:

    expression to *expression* $by\text{-}clause_{opt}$

by-clause:
    by *expression*

create-expression:
> create *expression*

return-expression return

> *expression*$_{opt}$
> suspend *expression*$_{opt}$ *do-clause*$_{opt}$
> fail

do-clause:
> do *expression*

break-expression:

> break *expression*$_{opt}$

next-expression:
> next

case-expression:
> case *expression* of { *case-list* }

case-list: case-
> *clause*
> *case-clause* ; *case-list*

case-clause:
> *expression* : *expression*
> default : *expression*

if-then-else expression:

> if *expression* then *expression* *else-clause*$_{opt}$

else-clause:
> else *expression*

loop-expression:
> repeat *expression*
> while *expression* *do-clause*$_{opt}$
> until *expression* *do-clause*$_{opt}$
> every *expression* *do-clause*$_{opt}$

LANGUAGE ELEMENTS

The most elementary components of Icon expressions are identifiers, reserved words, keywords, and literals.

Identifiers

An identifier must begin with a letter or an underscore, which may be followed by any number of letters, underscores, and digits. Upper- and lowercase letters are distinct. The syntax for field names is the same as the syntax for identifiers.

Reserved Words

Reserved words may not be used as identifiers or field names. Reserved words are all lowercase. The reserved words are:

break	global	record
by	if	repeat
case	initial	return
create	invocable	static
default	link	suspend
do	local	then
else	next	to
end	not	until
every	of	while
fail	procedure	

Keywords

Keywords consist of an ampersand followed by one of a selected set of identifiers. Keyword meanings are summarized in Appendix D. The keywords, which are lowercase, are:

&allocated	&errorvalue	&phi
&ascii	&errout	&pi
&clock	&fail	&pos
&collections	&features	&progname
&cset	&file	&random
&current	&host	&regions
&date	&input	&source
&dateline	&lcase	&storage
&digits	&letters	&subject
&dump	&level	&time
&e	&line	&trace
&error	&main	&ucase
&errornumber	&null	&version
&errortext	&output	

Note: Keywords related to graphics are not included in the list above.

Literals

There are two categories of literals:

> *literal: numeric-*
>   *literal quoted-*
>   *literal*

Numeric literals, in turn, are divided into two categories:

> *numeric-literal:*
>   *integer-literal*
>   *real-literal*

Integer literals have two forms:

> *integer-literal:*
>   *digit-literal*
>   *radix-literal*

Digit literals consist of one or more digits. Radix literals allow the radix for digits to be specified:

> *radix-literal:*
>   *digit-literal radix-specification digit-specification*

> *radix-specification:*
>   r
>   R

The value of the digit literal specifies the radix and must be between 2 and 36, inclusive. The digit specification consists of a sequence of digits and letters, where a stands for 10, b stands for 11, and so forth through z. Upper- and lowercase letters in digit specifications are equivalent. The characters in digit specifications must stand for values that are less than the radix.

Real literals have two forms:

> *real-literal:*
>   *decimal-literal*
>   *exponent-literal*

> *decimal-literal:*
>   *digit-literal . digit-literal$_{opt}$*
>   *digit-literal$_{opt}$. digit-literal*

exponent-literal:

     digit-literal exponent-specification sign$_{opt}$ *digit-literal*

     decimal-literal exponent-specification sign$_{opt}$ *digit-literal*

exponent-specification:

          e

          E

sign:

          +

          −

Quoted literals are divided into two categories:

quoted-literal:
    cset-literal
    string-literal

A cset literal consists of a string of characters enclosed in single quotes. A single quote may not appear within the enclosing quotes unless it is escaped. Escape sequences are described below.

A string literal consists of a string of characters enclosed in double quotes. A double quote may not appear within the enclosing quotes unless it is escaped.

Escape sequences allow characters to be included in string literals that other-wise would be awkward or impossible to include. An escape sequence consists of a backslash followed by one or more characters that have special meanings. The escape sequences and the characters that they stand for are:

\b	backspace
\d	delete
\e	escape
\f	formfeed
\l	linefeed
\n	newline
\r	return
\t	horizontal tab
\v	vertical tab
\'	single quote
\"	double quote
\\	backslash
\ddd	*octal code*
\xdd	*hexadecimal code*
\^c	*control code*

The linefeed and newline characters are the same in ASCII; both are included to accommodate the terminologies of different computer systems.

The sequence \ddd stands for the character with octal code ddd, where d is an octal digit 0, 1, ..., 7. The sequence \xdd stands for the character with hexadecimal code dd, where d is a hexadecimal digit 0, 1, ..., a, ... f. Upper- and lowercase hexadecimal digits, such as a and A, are equivalent. Only enough digits need to be given to specify the desired octal or hexadecimal number, provided the characters that follow cannot be interpreted as part of the escape sequence. For example, \43 specifies the ASCII character #, and \xa is equivalent to \x0a.

The control code sequence \^c stands for the ASCII character control-c. For example, \^A stands for control-A. Specifically, \^c stands for the character corresponding to the five low-order bits of c.

If the character following a backslash is not one of those in the preceding list, the backslash is ignored. Therefore, \a stands for a.

PROGRAM LAYOUT

White Space

Program text that has no meaning in itself is collectively called "white space". Except in quoted literals, blanks and tabs serve as white space to separate tokens that otherwise could be construed as a single token. For example,

> ifnot expr1 then expr2

is syntactically erroneous, since ifnot is interpreted as an identifier rather than two reserved words.

Blanks and tabs otherwise have no significance. For example, blanks and tabs can appear between a prefix operator and its argument. Blanks and tabs can also be used as optional separators to improve the visual appearance of a program. Blanks or tabs are necessary to separate infix operators from prefix operators in situations that are ambiguous. For example,

> expr1||expr2

might be interpreted in two ways, as concatenation or as alternation followed by repeated alternation of the second expression. The Icon compiler resolves such potential ambiguities by taking the longest legal sequence of operator symbols to be a single token, so this example is interpreted as concatenation. A blank between the two bars would cause the expression to be interpreted as alternation followed by repeated alternation.

A #, except in a quoted literal, introduces a comment, which terminates at the end of the line. A comment is considered to be white space by the Icon compiler.

Semicolons and Line Breaks

The Icon compiler generally is indifferent to program layout, but it automati-cally inserts a semicolon at the end of a line if an expression ends on that line and the next line begins with another expression. Therefore,

```
x := 1
y := 2
z := 0
```

is equivalent to

```
x := 1; y := 2; z := 0
```

Because the compiler inserts semicolons at the ends of lines where possible, it usually is not necessary to use semicolons explicitly. However, care must be taken in splitting an expression between two lines. In the case of an infix operation, the operator should be placed at the end of the first line, not the beginning of the second. Therefore,

$$expr1 \parallel expr2$$

should be split as

$$expr1 \parallel$$
$$expr2$$

The compiler does not insert a semicolon at the end of the first line, since the expression at the end of that line is not complete. However, in

$$expr1$$
$$\parallel expr2$$

a semicolon is inserted at the end of the first line, since

$$expr1; \parallel expr2$$

is syntactically correct. Here $\parallel$ is two prefix repeated alternation operators.

Identifiers can be arbitrarily long, but they must be contained on one line. A quoted literal can be continued from one line to the next by placing an underscore after the last character of the literal on a line and omitting the closing quote. If a quoted literal is continued in this way, the underscore as well as any white space at the beginning of the next line are ignored. For example,

```
cons := "abcdfghjklmno_
    pqrstvwxyz"
```

is equivalent to

```
cons := "abcdfghjklmnopqrstvwxyz"
```

PRECEDENCE AND ASSOCIATIVITY

Icon has many operators. Precedence determines how different operators, in combination, group with their arguments. Associativity determines whether operations group to the left or to the right.

The list that follows gives operators by precedence from highest to lowest. Operators with the same precedence are grouped together; lines separate groups. Most infix operators are left-associative. Those that associate to the right are marked as such.

(expr)
{ expr1; expr2; ... }
[expr1, expr2, ...]
expr. f
expr1 [expr2, expr3, ...]
expr1 [expr2 : expr3]
expr1 [expr2 +: expr3]
expr1 [expr2 −: expr3]
expr (expr1, expr2, ...)
expr { expr1, expr2, ... }

---

not *expr*
| expr
! expr
∗ expr
+ expr
− expr
. expr /
*expr   *
expr   =
expr   ?
expr   ~
expr   @
expr   ^
expr

---

expr1 \ *expr2*
expr1 @ *expr2*
expr1 ! *expr2*

---

expr1 ∧ *expr2*   (right associative)

---

expr1 * *expr2*
expr1 / *expr2*
expr1 % *expr2*
expr1 ** *expr2*

---

expr1 + *expr2*
expr1 − *expr2*
expr1 ++ *expr2*
expr1 − − *expr2*

---

expr1 || *expr2*
expr1 ||| *expr2*

---

expr1 < *expr2*
expr1 <= *expr2*
expr1 = *expr2*
expr1 >= *expr2*
expr1 > *expr2*
expr1 ~= *expr2*
expr1 << *expr2*
expr1 <<= *expr2*
expr1 == *expr2*
expr1 >>= *expr2*
expr1 >> *expr2*
expr1 ~== *expr2*
expr1 === *expr2*
expr1 ~=== *expr2*

---

expr1 | *expr2*

---

expr1 to *expr2* by *expr3*

---

expr1 := *expr2*   (right associative)
expr1 <– *expr2*   (right associative)
expr1 :=: *expr2*   (right associative)
expr1 <–> *expr2*   (right associative)
expr1 *op*:= *expr2*   (right associative)

---

expr1 ? *expr2*

---

expr1 & *expr2*

---

break *expr*
case *expr* of { *expr1* : *expr2*; *expr3* : *expr4*; …
} create *expr*
every *expr1* do
expr2 fail
if *expr1* then *expr2* else
expr3 next
repeat *expr*
return *expr*
suspend *expr1* do *expr2*
until *expr1* do *expr2*
while *expr1* do *expr2*

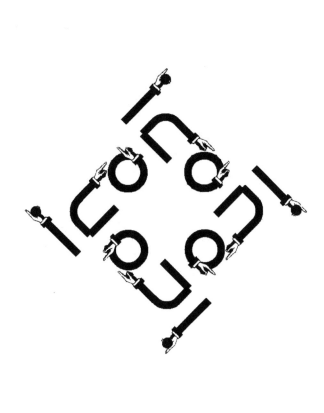

B

Characters

Characters serve two purposes: the representation of text using glyphs and control operations.

GLYPHS

The glyphs assigned to character codes associate meaning with the codes. Many sets of glyphs are used for purposes ranging from textual material to pictograms and printer's ornaments.

For textual material, on most computer platforms the underlying interpreta-tion for letters, digits, and common punctuation marks is based on the 7-bit ASCII character set (American National Standards Institute, 1986) that assigns glyphs and other interpretations to the first 128 characters.

Various computer platforms extend ASCII in different ways, using different glyphs or associating them with different character codes.

It is now common to assign glyphs to the 128 remaining characters. This allows the use of characters from various languages, as well as various symbols. A collection of glyphs is called a font. Thousands of different fonts are available for various computer platforms.

One standard set of glyphs, which includes ASCII as a subset, is defined by ISO8859-1 (ISO, 1987) and is called Latin-1. This set is used on most UNIX worksta-tions.

Another set of glyphs, called ECS ("extended character set") (Microsoft, 1991) is used by MS-DOS in the absence of other fonts.

Finally, there is the EBCDIC character set (Ralston and Reilly, 1993) used on IBM mainframes. It assigns glyphs for letters, digits, and common punctuation marks to different character codes than ASCII does. Several different versions of EBCDIC are in use. The most commonly used one is shown in the table in this appendix.

In the table that follows, columns one through three show the decimal, octal, and hexadecimal values for codes. The Latin-1 encoding is shown in column four. Columns five and six show typical text fonts for the Macintosh and Microsoft Windows. The seventh column shows ECS, and the eighth EBCDIC. Finally, the last two columns show the Macintosh versions of symbols and printer ornaments ("dingbats").

dec.	oct.	hex.	Latin-1	Macintosh	Windows	ECS	EBCDIC	symbols	dingbats
000	000	00							
001	001	01				b			
002	002	02				a			
003	003	03				c			
004	004	04				d			
005	005	05				e			
006	006	06				f			
007	007	07				g			
008	010	08				h			
009	011	09				i			
010	012	0a				j			
011	013	0b				k			
012	014	0c				l			
013	015	0d				m			
014	016	0e				n			
015	017	0f				o			
016	020	10				p			
017	021	11				q			
018	022	12				r			
019	023	13				s			
020	024	14				t			
021	025	15				u			
022	026	16				v			
023	027	17				w			
024	030	18				x			
025	031	19				y			
026	032	1a				z			
027	033	1b				{			
028	034	1c								
029	035	1d				}			
030	036	1e				~			
031	037	1f				0			

dec.	oct.	hex.	Latin-1	Macintosh	Windows	ECS	EBCDIC	symbols	dingbats
032	040	20	*blank*	*blank*	*blank*	*blank*		*blank*	*blank*
033	041	21	!	!	!	!		!	✂
034	042	22	"	"	"	"		∀	✄
035	043	23	#	#	#	#		#	✁
036	044	24	$	$	$	$		∃	✄
037	045	25	%	%	%	%		%	☎
038	046	26	&	&	&	&		&	✆
039	047	27	'	'	'	'		∋	✇
040	050	28	(	(	(	(		(	✈
041	051	29	)	)	)	)		)	✉
042	052	2a	*	*	*	*		*	☛
043	053	2b	+	+	+	+		+	☞
044	054	2c	,	,	,	,		,	✌
045	055	2d	--	-	-	-		--	✍
046	056	2e	.	.	.	.		.	✎
047	057	2f	/	/	/	/		/	✏
048	060	30	0	0	0	0		0	✐
049	061	31	1	1	1	1		1	✑
050	062	32	2	2	2	2		2	➔
051	063	33	3	3	3	3		3	✓
052	064	34	4	4	4	4		4	✔
053	065	35	5	5	5	5		5	✕
054	066	36	6	6	6	6		6	✖
055	067	37	7	7	7	7		7	✗
056	070	38	8	8	8	8		8	✘
057	071	39	9	9	9	9		9	✙
058	072	3a	:	:	:	:		:	✚
059	073	3b	;	;	;	;		;	✛
060	074	3c	<	<	<	<		<	✜
061	075	3d	=	=	=	=		=	✝
062	076	3e	>	>	>	>		>	✞
063	077	3f	?	?	?	?		?	✟
064	100	40	@	@	@	@	*blank*	≅	✠
065	101	41	A	A	A	A		A	✡
066	102	42	B	B	B	B		B	✢
067	103	43	C	C	C	C		X	✣
068	104	44	D	D	D	D		Δ	✤
069	105	45	E	E	E	E		E	✥
070	106	46	F	F	F	F		Φ	✦
071	107	47	G	G	G	G		Γ	✧
072	110	48	H	H	H	H		H	★
073	111	49	I	I	I	I		I	✩
074	112	4a	J	J	J	J	¢	ϑ	✪
075	113	4b	K	K	K	K	.	K	✫
076	114	4c	L	L	L	L	<	Λ	✬
077	115	4d	M	M	M	M	(	M	✭
078	116	4e	N	N	N	N	+	N	✮
079	117	4f	O	O	O	O	!	O	✯

dec.	oct.	hex.	Latin-1	Macintosh	Windows	ECS	EBCDIC	symbols	dingbats
080	120	50	P	P	P	P	&	Π	☆
081	121	51	Q	Q	Q	Q		Θ	✳
082	122	52	R	R	R	R		P	✲
083	123	53	S	S	S	S		Σ	✳
084	124	54	T	T	T	T		T	✳
085	125	55	U	U	U	U		Υ	✳
086	126	56	V	V	V	V		ς	✳
087	127	57	W	W	W	W		Ω	✳
088	130	58	X	X	X	X		Ξ	✳
089	131	59	Y	Y	Y	Y		Ψ	✳
090	132	5a	Z	Z	Z	Z	!	Z	✳
091	133	5b	[	[	[	[	$	[	✳
092	134	5c	\	\	\	\	*	∴	✳
093	135	5d	]	]	]	]	)	]	✳
094	136	5e	^	^	^	^	;	⊥	✿
095	137	5f	_	_	_	_	¬	_	✿
096	140	60	`	`	`	`	−		✿
097	141	61	a	a	a	a	/	α	✿
098	142	62	b	b	b	b		β	✳
099	143	63	c	c	c	c		χ	✳
100	144	64	d	d	d	d		δ	✳
101	145	65	e	e	e	e		ε	✳
102	146	66	f	f	f	f		φ	✳
103	147	67	g	g	g	g		γ	✳
104	150	68	h	h	h	h		η	✳
105	151	69	i	i	i	i		ι	✳
106	152	6a	j	j	j	j		φ	✳
107	153	6b	k	k	k	k	,	κ	✳
108	154	6c	l	l	l	l	%	λ	●
109	155	6d	m	m	m	m	_	μ	○
110	156	6e	n	n	n	n	>	ν	■
111	157	6f	o	o	o	o	?	ο	❑
112	160	70	p	p	p	p		π	❐
113	161	71	q	q	q	q		θ	❑
114	162	72	r	r	r	r		ρ	❐
115	163	73	s	s	s	s		σ	▲
116	164	74	t	t	t	t		τ	▼
117	165	75	u	u	u	u		υ	◆
118	166	76	v	v	v	v		ϖ	❖
119	167	77	w	w	w	w		ω	❘
120	170	78	x	x	x	x		ξ	❙
121	171	79	y	y	y	y		ψ	❙
122	172	7a	z	z	z	z	:	ζ	❚
123	173	7b	{	{	{	{	#	{	'
124	174	7c	|	|	|	|	@	|	'
125	175	7d	}	}	}	}	`	}	"
126	176	7e	~	~	~	~	=	~	"
127	177	7f					"		

dec.	oct.	hex.	Latin-1	Macintosh	Windows	ECS	EBCDIC	symbols	dingbats
128	200	80		Ä		Ç			❨
129	201	81		Å		ü	a		❩
130	202	82		Ç	‚	é	b		❪
131	203	83		É	ƒ	â	c		❫
132	204	84		Ñ	„	ä	d		❨
133	205	85		Ö	…	à	e		❩
134	206	86		Ü	†	å	f		❬
135	207	87		á	‡	ç	g		❭
136	210	88		à	^	ê	h		❲
137	211	89		â	‰	ë	i		❳
138	212	8a		ä	Š	è			❴
139	213	8b		ã	‹	ï			❵
140	214	8c		å	Œ	î			❴
141	215	8d		ç		ì			❵
142	216	8e		é		Ä			
143	217	8f		è		Å			
144	220	90		ê		É			
145	221	91		ë	'	æ	j		
146	222	92		í	'	Æ	k		
147	223	93		ì	"	ô	l		
148	224	94		î	"	ö	m		
149	225	95		ï	•	ò	n		
150	226	96		ñ	–	û	o		
151	227	97		ó	—	ù	p		
152	230	98		ò	˜	ÿ	q		
153	231	99		ô	™	Ö			
154	232	9a		ö	š	Ü			
155	233	9b		õ	›	¢			
156	234	9c		ú	œ	£			
157	235	9d		ù		¥			
158	236	9e		û		₧			
159	237	9f		ü	Ÿ	ƒ			
160	240	a0		†		á			¶
161	241	a1	¡	°	¡	í	~	Υ	❣
162	242	a2	¢	¢	¢	ó	s	′	❢
163	243	a3	£	£	£	ú	t	≤	❤
164	244	a4	¤	§	¤	ñ	u	/	❥
165	245	a5	¥	•	¥	Ñ	v	∞	❦
166	246	a6	¦	¶	¦	ª	w	ƒ	❧
167	247	a7	§	ß	§	º	x	♣	♣
168	250	a8	¨	®	¨	¿	y	♦	♣
169	251	a9	©	©	©	⌐	z	♥	♦
170	252	aa	ª	™	ª	¬		♠	♥
171	253	ab	«	´	«	½		↔	♠
172	254	ac	¬	¨	¬	¼		←	①
173	255	ad		≠		¡	[	↑	②
174	256	ae	®	Æ	®	«		→	③
175	257	af	¯	Ø	¯	»		↓	④

dec.	oct.	hex.	Latin-1	Macintosh	Windows	ECS	EBCDIC	symbols	dingbats
176	260	b0	º	∞	º	∞		º	⑤
177	261	b1	±	±	±	±		±	⑥
178	262	b2	²	≤	²	≤		″	⑦
179	263	b3	³	≥	³	≥		≥	⑧
180	264	b4	´	¥	´	⊣		×	⑨
181	265	b5	µ	µ	µ	µ		∝	⑩
182	266	b6	¶	∂	¶	∂		∂	❶
183	267	b7	·	Σ	·	Σ		•	❷
184	270	b8	¸	Π	¸	Π		÷	❸
185	271	b9	¹	π	¹	π		≠	❹
186	272	ba	º	∫	º	∫		≡	❺
187	273	bb	»	ª	»	]		≈	❻
188	274	bc	¼	º	¼			…	❼
189	275	bd	½	Ω	½	Ω	⌉	⏐	❽
190	276	be	¾	æ	¾	⌋		—	❾
191	277	bf	¿	ø	¿	⌊		⌟	❿
192	300	c0	À	¿	À	⌊	{	ℵ	①
193	301	c1	Á	¡	Á	⊥	A	ℑ	②
194	302	c2	Â	¬	Â	T√	B	ℜ	③
195	303	c3	Ã	√	Ã	⊤√	C	℘	②
196	304	c4	Ä	ƒ	Ä	—	D	⊗	⑤
197	305	c5	Å	≈	Å	≈	E	⊕	⑥
198	306	c6	Æ	Δ	Æ	Δ	F	∅	⑥
199	307	c7	Ç	«	Ç	⫿	G	∩	⑧
200	310	c8	È	»	È	⫿	H	∪	⑨
201	311	c9	É	…	É	⟦	I	⊃	⑩
202	312	ca	Ê		Ê	═		⊇	❶
203	313	cb	Ë	À	Ë	⫿		⊄	❷
204	314	cc	Ì	Ã	Ì	⊨		⊂	❸
205	315	cd	Í	Õ	Í	═		⊆	❹
206	316	ce	Î	Œ	Î	⫿		∈	❺
207	317	cf	Ï	œ	Ï	⊔		∉	❻
208	320	d0	Ð	–	Ð	⊔	{	∠	❼
209	321	d1	Ñ	—	Ñ	⊤	J	∇	❽
210	322	d2	Ò	"	Ò	⫿	K	®	❾
211	323	d3	Ó	"	Ó	⊩	L	©	❿
212	324	d4	Ô	'	Ô	⊢	M	™	→
213	325	d5	Õ	'	Õ	F	N	Π	⇢
214	326	d6	Ö	÷	Ö	÷	O	√	↔
215	327	d7	×	◊	×	◊	P	·	↕
216	330	d8	Ø	ÿ	Ø	‡	Q	¬	↘
217	331	d9	Ù	Ÿ	Ù	⊣	R	∧	→
218	332	da	Ú	⁄	Ú	⌈		∨	↗
219	333	db	Û	¤	Û	■		⇔	⇒
220	334	dc	Ü	‹	Ü	▪		⇐	➔
221	335	dd	Ý	›	Ý	⎜		⇑	→
222	336	de	Þ	fi	Þ	!		⇒	→
223	337	df	ß	fl	ß	■		⇓	→

dec.	oct.	hex.	Latin-1	Macintosh	Windows	ECS	EBCDIC	symbols	dingbats
224	340	e0	à	‡	à	α	\	◊	⇢
225	341	e1	á	·	á	β		⟨	➡
226	342	e2	â	‚	â	Γ	S	®	➢
227	343	e3	ã	„	ã	π	T	©	➣
228	344	e4	ä	‰	ä	Σ	U	™	➤
229	345	e5	å	Â	å	σ	V	Σ	➥
230	346	e6	æ	Ê	æ	μ	W	⎧	➦
231	347	e7	ç	Á	ç	T	X	⎨	◗
232	350	e8	è	Ë	è	Φ	Y	⎩	➨
233	351	e9	é	È	é	θ	Z	⎡	⇨
234	352	ea	ê	Í	ê	Ω			⇨
235	353	eb	ë	Î	ë	δ		⎣	⇦
236	354	ec	ì	Ï	ì	∞		⎧	⇐
237	355	ed	í	Ì	í	Ø			⇨
238	356	ee	î	Ó	î	∈		⎩	⇨
239	357	ef	ï	Ô	ï	∩			⇨
240	360	f0	ð		ð	≡	0		⇨
241	361	f1	ñ	Ò	ñ	±	1	⎫	⇨
242	362	f2	ò	Ú	ò	≥	2	⎬	⊃
243	363	f3	ó	Û	ó	≤	3	⎡	➺
244	364	f4	ô	Ù	ô	⌠	4		➴
245	365	f5	õ	ı	õ	⌡	5	⎦	➶
246	366	f6	ö	^	ö	÷	6	⎞	➷
247	367	f7	÷	~	÷	≈	7	⎟	➴
248	370	f8	ø	¯	ø	°	8	⎬	➵
249	371	f9	ù	˘	ù	•	9	⎫	➹
250	372	fa	ú	˙	ú	·			→
251	373	fb	û	˚	û	√		⎦	↔
252	374	fc	ü	¸	ü	^{n}		⎫	➻
253	375	fd	ý	˝	ý	^{2}		⎬	➼
254	376	fe	þ	˛	þ	■		⎭	⇒
255	377	ff	ÿ	ˇ	ÿ				

ASCII CONTROL CHARACTERS

The first 32 characters in ASCII are called control characters and are entered by depressing the control key while typing another character. These characters have associated names and functions, such as backspacing and tabbing. These are shown in the following table.

dec.	oct.	hex.	escape seq.	coding	function
000	000	00		control-@	null
001	001	01		control-a	
002	002	02		control-b	
003	003	03		control-c	
004	004	04		control-d	
005	005	05		control-e	
006	006	06		control-f	
007	007	07		control-g	bell
008	010	08	\b	control-h	backspace
009	011	09	\t	control-i	tab
010	012	0a	\n	control-j	linefeed
011	013	0b	\v	control-k	vertical tab
012	014	0c	\f	control-l	formfeed
013	015	0d	\r	control-m	return
014	016	0e		control-n	
015	017	0f		control-o	
016	020	10		control-p	
017	021	11		control-q	
018	022	12		control-r	
019	023	13		control-s	
020	024	14		control-t	
021	025	15		control-u	
022	026	16		control-v	
023	027	17		control-w	
024	030	18		control-x	
025	031	19		control-y	
026	032	1a		control-z	
027	033	1b	\e	control-[	escape
028	034	1c		control-\	
029	035	1d		control-]	
030	036	1e		control-^	
031	037	1f		control-_	

C

Preprocessing

All Icon source code passes through a preprocessor before compilation. Preproces-sor directives control the actions of the preprocessor and are not passed to the Icon compiler. If no preprocessor directives are present, the source code passes through the preprocessor unaltered.

A source line is a preprocessor directive if its first non-white-space character is a $ and if that $ is not followed by another punctuation character. The general form of a preprocessor directive is

$directive arguments   # comment

White space separates tokens when needed, and case is significant, as in Icon proper. The entire preprocessor directive must appear on a single line, which cannot be continued but can be arbitrarily long. The comment portion is optional. An invalid preprocessor directive produces an error except when skipped by condi-tional compilation.

Preprocessor directives can appear anywhere in an Icon source file without regard to procedure, declaration, or expression boundaries.

INCLUDE DIRECTIVES

An include directive has the form

$include *filename*

An include directive causes the contents of the specified file to be interpolated in the source file. The file name must be quoted if it is not in the form of an Icon identifier.

Included files may be nested to arbitrary depth, but a file may not include itself either directly or indirectly. File names are looked for first in the current directory and then in the directories listed in the environment variable LPATH. Relative paths are interpreted in the preprocessor's context and not in relation to the including file's location.

LINE DIRECTIVES

A line directive has the form

$$\text{\$line } n \text{ } filename_{opt}$$

The line containing the preprocessing directive is considered to be line n of the given file (or the current file, if unspecified) for diagnostic and other purposes. The line number is a simple unsigned integer. The file name must be quoted if it is not in the form of an Icon identifier.

DEFINE DIRECTIVES

A define directive has the form

$$\text{\$define } name \text{ } text$$

The define directive defines the text to be substituted for later occurrences of the identifier *name* in the source code. *text* is any sequence of characters except that any string or cset literals must be properly terminated within the definition. Leading and trailing white space are not part of the definition. The text can be empty.

Duplicate definition of a name is allowed if the new text is exactly the same as the old text. This prevents problems from arising if a file of definitions is included more than once. The text must match exactly: For example, 3.0 is not the same as 3.000.

Definitions remain in effect through the end of the current original source file, crossing include boundaries, but they do not persist from one source file to another.

If the text begins with a left parenthesis, it must be separated from the name by at least one space. Note that the Icon preprocessor does not provide parameterized definitions.

It is possible to define replacement text for Icon reserved words or keywords, but this generally is dangerous and ill-advised.

UNDEFINE DIRECTIVES

An undefine directive has the form

   $undef *name*

The current definition of *name* is removed, allowing its redefinition if desired. It is not an error to undefine a nonexistent name.

PREDEFINED SYMBOLS

At the start of each source file, several symbols are automatically defined to indicate the Icon system configuration. If a feature is present, the symbol is defined with a value of 1. If a feature is absent, the symbol is not defined. The most commonly used predefined symbols are listed below. See Griswold, Jeffery, and Townsend (1996) for a complete list.

predefined symbol	&features value
_MACINTOSH	Macintosh
_MSDOS	MS-DOS
_MSDOS_386	MS-DOS/386
_MS_WINDOWS_NT	MS Windows NT
_OS2	OS/2
_UNIX	UNIX
_VMS	VMS
_WINDOW_FUNCTIONS	window functions
_MS_WINDOWS	MS Windows
_PRESENTATION_MGR	Presentation Manager
_X_WINDOW_SYSTEM	X Windows
_PIPES	pipes
_SYSTEM_FUNCTION	system function

Predefined symbols have no special status. Like other symbols, they can be undefined and redefined.

SUBSTITUTION

As input is read, each identifier is checked to see if it matches a previously defined symbol. If it does, the value replaces the identifier in the input stream.

No white space is added or deleted when a definition is inserted. The replacement text is scanned for defined identifiers, possibly causing further substi-tution, but recognition of the original identifier name is disabled to prevent infinite recursion.

Occurrences of defined names within comments, literals, or preprocessor directives are not altered. The preprocessor is ignorant of multi-line string literals, however, and it potentially can be fooled by these.

Substitution cannot produce a preprocessor directive. By then it is too late.

CONDITIONAL COMPILATION

Conditional compilation directives have the form

> $ifdef *name*

and

> $ifndef *name*

$ifdef or $ifndef cause subsequent code to be accepted or skipped depending on whether *name* has been previously defined. $ifdef succeeds if a definition exists; $ifndef succeeds if a definition does not exist. The value of the definition does not matter.

A conditional block has this general form:

```
$ifdef name  or  $ifndef name
    ... code to use if test succeeds ...
$else
    ... code to use if test fails ...
$endif
```

The $else section is optional. Conditional blocks can be nested provided that all of the $if/$else/$endif directives for a particular block are in the same source file. This does not prevent the conditional inclusion of other files via $include as long as any included conditional blocks are similarly self-contained.

ERROR DIRECTIVES

An error directive has the form

> $error *text*

An $error directive forces a fatal compilation error displaying the given text. This is typically used with conditional compilation to indicate an improper set of defini-tions.

D

Language Reference Manual

This reference manual summarizes Icon's built-in repertoire. The descriptions are brief; they are intended for reference only. Operations related to graphics are not included.

The operations fall into four main categories: functions, operators, keywords, and control structures. Functions, operators, and keywords perform computations; control structures determine the order of expression evaluation. Function names provide a vocabulary with a common syntax in which computations are performed on argument lists. Different operators, on the other hand, have different syntactic forms. They are divided into prefix (unary) operators, infix (binary) operators, and operators with distinctive syntax. Keywords all have a common syntax.

Data types are important in Icon, especially the types of data a function or operator expects and the type it returns. Types are indicated by letters as follows:

c	cset	C	co-expression
f	file	L	list
i	integer	N	numeric (i or r)
n	null	R	record (any record type)
p	procedure	S	set
r	real	T	table
s	string	X	any structure type (R, L, S, or T)
x	any type		

In addition, the symbol v indicates a situation in which a variable is required or always produced.

Numeric suffixes are used to distinguish different arguments of the same type. For example,

center(s1, i, s2)

indicates that center() has three arguments. The first and third are strings; the second is an integer.

The type of the result produced by a function follows the function prototype, with a separating colon. For example,

center(s1, i, s2) : s3

indicates that center() produces a string. The format of entries for operators and keywords is similar.

The results for generators are indicated by a sequence, as in

!s : s1, s2, ..., sn

Icon performs type conversion automatically if an argument does not have the expected type, so the types of arguments may be different from the expected type and still be acceptable. For example, center(s1, 10, s2) and center(s1, "10", s2) produce the same result, since the string "10" is converted to the integer 10.

Default values are provided automatically in some cases when an argument is omitted (or has the null value). For example, the default for the second argument of center() is 1, while the third argument defaults to a single blank. Consequently, center(s1) is equivalent to center(s1, 1, " "). Refer to the entry for center() to see how this information is shown.

Errors may occur for a variety of reasons. The possible errors and their causes are listed for each function and operation. Again, see the entry for center() for examples. In particular, note that a phrase such as "s not string" means s is neither a string nor a type that can be converted to a string.

In addition to the errors listed in the entries that follow, an error also can occur if there is not enough memory to convert an argument to the expected type. For example, converting a very long string to an integer for use in a numerical compu-tation conceivably could run out of memory. Such errors are unlikely and are not listed.

Cross references among entries have two forms. Most cross references refer to functions and operators that perform related computations, such as center(), left(), and right(). There also are cross references among operators and control structures with similar syntax, such as *x and N1 * N2, even though the computations per-formed are not related.

A list of generators appears at the end of this appendix.

FUNCTIONS

The arguments of functions are evaluated from left to right. If the evaluation of an argument fails, the function is not called. Some functions may generate a sequence of results for a given set of arguments. If an argument generates more than one value, the function may be called repeatedly with different argument values.

---

abs(N1) : N2   compute absolute value

abs(N1) produces the absolute value of N1.

Error: 102   N1 not numeric

---

acos(r1) : r2   compute arc cosine

acos(r1) produces the arc cosine of r1 in the range of 0 to π for r1 in the range of -1 to 1.

Errors: 102   r1 not real
              205 |r1| greater than 1

See also: cos()

---

any(c, s, i1, i2) : i3   locate initial character

any(c, s, i1, i2) succeeds and produces the position of the first character in s[i1:i2] if that character is in c; otherwise it fails.

Defaults: s   &subject
              i1   &pos if s is defaulted, otherwise 1
              i2   0

Errors: 101   i1 or i2 not integer
              103   s not string
              104   c not cset

See also: many() and match()

---

args(p) : i   get number of procedure arguments

args(p) produces the number of arguments for procedure p. For procedures with a variable number of arguments, the value returned is the negative of the number of formal parameters.

Error: 106   p not procedure

See also: proc()

---

asin(r1) : r2   compute arc sine

asin(r1) produces the arc sine of r1 in the range of $-\pi/2$ to $\pi/2$ for r1 in the range -1 to 1.

Errors: 102   r1 not real
              205 |r1| greater than 1

See also: sin()

---

atan(r1, r2) : r3   compute arc tangent

atan(r1, r2) produces the arc tangent of r1 / r2 in the range of $-\pi$ to π with the sign of r1.

Default: r2   1.0

Error: 102   r1 or r2 not real

See also: tan()

---

bal(c1, c2, c3, s, i1, i2) : i3, i4, ..., in   locate balanced characters

bal(c1, c2, c3, s, i1, i2) generates the sequence of integer positions in s preceding a character of c1 in s[i1:i2] that is balanced with respect to characters in c2 and c3, but fails if there is no such position.

Defaults: c1   &cset
           c2   '('
           c3   ')'
           s   &subject
           i1   &pos if s is defaulted, otherwise 1
           i2   0

Errors: 101   i1 or i2 not integer
               103   s not string
               104   c1, c2, or c3 not cset

See also: find() and upto()

---

center(s1, i, s2) : s3   position string at center

center(s1, i, s2) produces a string of size i in which s1 is centered, with s2 used for padding at left and right as necessary.

Defaults: i   1
              s2   " " (blank)

Errors: 101   i not integer
              103   s1 or s2 not string
              205   i < 0

See also: left() and right()

---

char(i) : s   produce character

char(i) produces a one-character string whose internal representation is i.

Errors: 101   i not integer
              205   i not between 0 and 255, inclusive

See also: ord()

---

chdir(s) : n   change directory

chdir(s) changes the current directory to s but fails if there is no such directory or if the change cannot be made. Whether the change in directory persists after program termination depends on the operating system.

Error: 103   s not string

---

close(f) : x   close file

close(f) closes f. If f is an ordinary file, the value returned is f. If f is a pipe, the value returned is the exit code.

Error: 105   f not file

See also: flush() and open()

---

collect(i1, i2) : n   perform garbage collection

collect(i1, i2) causes a garbage collection in region i1, requesting i2 bytes of space in that region. It fails if the requested space is not available. The regions are identified as follows:

i1	*region*
1	static
2	string
3	block

If i1 is 0, a collection is done, but no region is identified and i2 has no effect. The value of i2 is ignored for the static region.

Defaults:	i1	0
	i2	0

Errors:	101	i1 or i2 not integer
	205	i1 not between 0 and 3 inclusive or i2 < 0.

---

copy(x1) : x2   copy value

copy(x1) produces a copy of x1 if x1 is a structure; otherwise it produces x1.

---

cos(r1) : r2   compute cosine

cos(r1) produces the cosine of r1 in radians.

Error: 102   r1 not real

See also: cos()

---

cset(x) : c   convert to cset

cset(x) produces a cset resulting from converting x, but fails if the conversion is not possible.

---

delay(i) : n   delay execution

delay() delays program execution i milliseconds.

Error: 101   i not integer

---

delete(X, x) : X   delete element

If X is a set, delete(X, x) deletes x from X. If X is a table, delete(X, x) deletes the element for key x from X. delete(X, x) produces X.

Error: 122   X not set or table.

See also: insert() and member()

---

detab(s1, i1, i2, ..., in) : s2   replace tabs by blanks

detab(s1, i1, i2, ..., in) produces a string based on s1 in which each tab character is replaced by one or more blanks. Tab stops are at i1, i2, ..., in, with additional stops obtained by repeating the last interval.

Default: i1   9

Errors: 101   i1, i2, ..., in not integer
              103   s1 not string
              210   i1, i2, ..., in not positive or in increasing sequence

See also: entab()

---

display(i, f) : n   display variables

display(i, f) writes the image of the current co-expression and the values of the local variables in the current procedure call. If i is greater than 0, the local variables in the i preceding procedure calls are displayed as well. After all local variables are displayed, the values of global variables are displayed. Output is written to f.

Defaults: i   &level
             f   &errout

Errors: 101   i not integer
              105   f not file
              205   i < 0
              213   f not open for writing

---

dtor(r1) : r2   convert degrees to radians

dtor(r1) produces the radian equivalent of r1 given in degrees.

Error: 102   r1 not real

See also: rtod()

---

entab(s1, i1, i2, ..., in) : s2   replace blanks by tabs

entab(s1, i1, i2, ..., in) produces a string based on s1 in which runs of blanks are replaced by tabs. Tab stops are at i1, i2, ..., in, with additional stops obtained by repeating the last interval.

Default: i1   9

Errors: 101   i1, i2, ..., in not integer
               103   s1 not string
               210   i1, i2, ..., in not positive or in increasing sequence

See also: detab()

---

errorclear() : n   clear error indication

errorclear() clears the indications of the last error.

See also: &error

---

exit(i)   exit program

exit(i) terminates program execution with exit status i.

Default: i   normal exit (machine dependent)

Error: 101   i not integer

See also: stop()

---

exp(r1) : r2   compute exponential

exp(r1) produces *e* raised to the power r1.

Errors: 102   r1 not real
               204   overflow

See also: log() and N1 ^ N2

---

find(s1, s2, i1, i2) : i3, i4, ..., in   find string

find(s1, s2, i1, i2) generates the sequence of integer positions in s2 at which s1 occurs as a substring in s2[i1:i2], but fails if there is no such position.

Defaults: s2   &subject
             i1   &pos if s2 is defaulted, otherwise 1
             i2   0

Errors: 101   i1 or i2 not integer
             103   s1 or s2 not string

See also: bal(), match(), and upto()

---

flush(f) : f   flush output

flush() flushes any accumulated output for file f.

See also: close()

---

function() : s1, s2, ..., sn   generate function names

function() generates the names of the Icon (built-in) functions.

---

get(L) : x   get value from list

get(L) produces the leftmost element of L and removes it from L, but fails if L is empty. get is a synonym for pop.

Error: 108   L not list

See also: pop(), pull(), push(), and put()

---

getch() : s   get character

getch() waits until a character has been entered from the keyboard and then produces the corresponding one-character string. The character is not displayed. The function fails on an end of file.

See also: getche() and kbhit()

---

getche() : s   get and echo character

getche() waits until a character has been entered from the keyboard and then produces the corresponding one-character string. The character is displayed. The function fails on an end of file.

See also: getch() and kbhit()

---

getenv(s1) : s2   get value of environment variable

getenv(s1) produces the value of the environment variable s1, but fails if s1 is not set.

Error: 103   s1 not string

---

iand(i1, i2) : i3   compute bitwise *and*

iand(i1, i2) produces an integer consisting of the bitwise *and* of i1 and i2.

Error: 101   i1 or i2 not integer

See also: icom(), ior(), ishift(), and ixor()

---

icom(i1) : i2   compute bitwise complement

icom(i1) produces the bitwise complement of i1.

Error: 101   i1 not integer

See also: iand(), ior(), ishift(), and ixor()

---

image(x) : s   produce string image

image(x) produces the string image for x.

---

insert(X, x1, x2) : X   insert element

If X is a   table, insert(X, x1, x2) inserts key x1 with value x2 into X. If X is a set, insert(X, x1) inserts x1 into X. insert(X, x1, x2) produces X.

Default: x2   &null

Errors: 122   X not set or table

See also: delete() and member()

---

integer(x) : i   convert to integer

integer(x) produces the integer resulting from converting x, but fails if the conver-sion is not possible.

See also: numeric() and real()

---

ior(i1, i2) : i3   compute bitwise inclusive *or*

ior(i1, i2) produces the bitwise inclusive *or* of i1 and i2.

Error: 101   i1 or i2 not integer

See also: iand(), icom(), ishift(), and ixor()

---

ishift(i1, i2) : i3   shift bits

ishift(i1, i2) produces the result of shifting the bits in i1 by i2 positions. Positive values of i2 shift to the left with zero fill; negative values shift to the right with sign extension. Vacated bit positions are zero-filled.

Error: 101   i1 or i2 not integer

See also: iand(), icom(), ior(), and ixor()

---

ixor(i1, i2) : i3   compute bitwise exclusive *or*

ixor(i1, i2) produces the bitwise exclusive *or* of i1 and i2.

Error: 101 i1 or i2 not integer

See also: iand(), icom(), ior(), and ishift()

---

kbhit() : n   check for keyboard character

kbhit() succeeds if a character is available for getch() or getche() but fails otherwise.

See also: getch() and getche()

---

key(T) : x1, x2, ..., xn   generate keys from table

key(T) generates the keys in table T.

Error: 124   T not table

---

left(s1, i, s2) : s3   position string at left

left(s1, i, s2) produces a string of size i in which s1 is positioned at the left, with s2 used for padding at the right as necessary.

Defaults: i   1
             s2   " " (blank)

Errors: 101   i not integer
               103   s1 or s2 not string
               205   i < 0

See also: center() and right()

---

list(i, x) : L   create list

list(i, x) produces a list of size i in which each value is x.

Defaults: i   0
               x   &null

Errors: 101   i not integer
               205   i < 0

---

loadfunc(s1, s2) : p   load external function

loadfunc(s1, s2) loads the function named s2 from the library file s1 and produces a procedure for it. s2 must be a C or compatible function that provides a particular interface expected by loadfunc().

Errors: 216   function not found
               103   s1 or s2 not string

---

log(r1, r2) : r3   compute logarithm

log(r1, r2) produces the logarithm of r1 to the base r2.

Default: r2 e

Errors: 102   r1 or r2 not real
               205   r1 <= 0 or r2 <= 1

See also: exp()

---

many(c, s, i1, i2) : i3   locate many characters

many(c, s, i1, i2) succeeds and produces the position in s after the longest initial sequence of characters in c within s[i1:i2]. It fails if s[i1] is not in c.

Defaults: s   &subject
          i1   &pos if s is defaulted, otherwise 1
          i2   0

Errors: 101 i1 or i2 not integer
     103 s not string
     104 c not cset

See also: any() and match()

---

map(s1, s2, s3) : s4   map characters

map(s1, s2, s3) produces a string of size *s1 obtained by mapping characters of s1 that occur in s2 into corresponding characters in s3.

Defaults: s2 string(&ucase)
      s3 string(&lcase)

Errors: 103 s1, s2, or s3 not string
      208 *s2 ~= *s3

---

match(s1, s2, i1, i2) : i3   match initial string

match(s1, s2, i1, i2) produces the position beyond the initial substring of s2[i1:i2], if any, that is equal to s1; otherwise it fails.

Defaults: s2 &subject
      i1 &pos if s2 is defaulted, otherwise 1
      i2 0

Errors: 101 i1 or i2 not integer
      103 s1 or s2 not string

See also: =s, any(), and many()

---

member(X, x) : x   test for membership

If X is a set, member(X, x) succeeds if x is a member of X but fails otherwise. If X is a table, member(X, x) succeeds if x is a key of an element in X but fails otherwise. member(X, x) produces x if it succeeds.

Error: 122 X not set or table

See also: delete() and insert()

---

move(i) : s   move scanning position

move(i) produces &subject[&pos:&pos + i] and assigns &pos + i to &pos, but fails if i is out of range. move(i) reverses the assignment to &pos if it is resumed.

Error: 101   i not integer

See also: tab()

---

name(v) : s   produce name

name(v) produces the name of the variable v. If v is an identifier or a keyword that is a variable, the name of the identifier or keyword is produced. If v is a record field reference, the record type and field name are produced with a separating period. If v is a string, the name of the string and the subscript range are shown. If v is a subscripted list or table, the type name followed by the subscripting expression is produced.

Error: 111   v not a variable

See also: variable()

---

numeric(x) : N   convert to numeric

numeric(x) produces an integer or real number resulting from converting x, but fails if the conversion is not possible.

See also: integer() and real()

---

open(s1, s2) : f   open file

open(s1, s2) produces a file resulting from opening s1 according to options given in s2, but fails if the file cannot be opened. The options are:

character	effect
"r"	open for reading
"w"	open for writing
"a"	open for writing in append mode
"b"	open for reading and writing
"p"	open a pipe
"c"	create
"t"	translate line termination sequences to linefeeds
"u"	do not translate line termination sequences to linefeeds

The default mode is to translate line termination sequences to linefeeds on input and conversely on output. The untranslated mode should be used when reading and writing binary files.

Default: s2   "rt"

Errors: 103   s1 or s2 not string
               209   invalid option

See also: close()

---

ord(s) : i   produce ordinal

ord(s) produces an integer (ordinal) between 0 and 255 that is the character code for the one-character string s.

Errors: 103   s not string
               205   *s not 1

See also: char()

---

pop(L) : x   pop from list

pop(L) produces the leftmost element of L and removes it from L, but fails if L is empty. pop is a synonym for get.

Error: 108   L not list

See also: get(), pull(), push(), and put()

---

pos(i1) : i2   test scanning position

pos(i1) produces &pos if i1 or its positive equivalent is equal to &pos, but fails otherwise.

Error: 101   i1 not integer

See also: &pos and &subject

---

proc(s, i) : p   convert to procedure

proc(s, i) produces the procedure, function, or operator corresponding to s, but fails if s is not the name of one. If s is the string name of an operator, i specifies the number of arguments: 1 for unary (prefix), 2 for binary (infix), and 3 for ternary. proc(s, 0) produces the built-in function named s even if the global identifier having that name has been assigned another value. proc(s, 0) fails if s is not the name of a function.

The first argument of proc() may be a procedure, function, or operator, in which case proc() simply returns the first argument.

Default: i   1

Errors: 101   i not integer
               205   i not 0, 1, 2, or 3

See also: args()

---

pull(L) : x   pull from list

pull(L) produces the rightmost element of L and removes it from L, but fails if L is empty.

Error: 108   L not list

See also: get(), pop(), push(), and put()

---

push(L, x1, x2, ..., xn) : L   push onto list

push(L, x1, x2, ..., xn) pushes x1, x2, ..., onto the left end of L. Values are pushed in order from left to right, so xn becomes the first (leftmost) value of L. push(L) with no second argument pushes a null value onto L.

Errors: 108   L not list

See also: get(), pop(), pull(), and put()

---

put(L, x1, x2, ..., xn) : L   put onto list

put(L, x1, x2, ..., xn) puts x1, x2, ..., xn onto the right end of L. Values are added in order from left to right, so xn becomes the last (rightmost) value of L. put(L) with no second argument puts a null value onto L.

Errors: 108   L not list

See also: get(), pop(), pull(), and push()

---

read(f) : s   read line

read(f) produces the next line from f but fails on an end of file.

Default: f   &input

Errors: 105   f not file
               212   f not open for reading

See also: reads()

---

reads(f, i) : s   read string

reads(f, i) produces a string consisting of the next i characters from f, or the remaining characters of f if fewer remain, but fails on an end of file. In reads(), unlike read(), line termination sequences have no special significance. reads() should be used for reading binary data.

Defaults: f   &input
             i   1

Errors: 101   i not integer
             105   f not file
             205   i <= 0
             212   f not open for reading

See also: read()

---

real(x) : r   convert to real

real(x) produces a real number resulting from converting x, but fails if the conver-sion is not possible.

See also: integer() and numeric()

---

remove(s) : n   remove file

remove(s) removes (deletes) the file named s, but fails if s cannot be removed.

Error: 103   s not string

See also: rename()

---

rename(s1, s2) : n   rename file

rename(s1, s2) renames the file named s1 to be s2, but fails if the renaming cannot be done.

Error: 103   s1 or s2 not string

See also: remove()

---

repl(s1, i) : s2   replicate string

repl(s1, i) produces a string consisting of i concatenations of s1.

Errors: 101   i not integer
               103   s1 not string
               205   i < 0

---

reverse(s1) : s2   reverse string

reverse(s1) produces a string consisting of the reversal of s1.

Errors: 103   s1 not string

---

right(s1, i, s2) : s3   position string at right

right(s1, i, s2) produces a string of size i in which s1 is positioned at the right, with s2 used for padding at the left as necessary.

Defaults: i   1
               s2   " " (blank)

Errors: 101   i not integer
               103   s1 or s2 not string
               205   i < 0

See also: center() and left()

---

rtod(r1) : r2   convert radians to degrees

rtod(r1) produces the degree equivalent of r1 given in radians.

Error: 102   r1 not real

See also: dtor()

---

runerr(i, x)   terminate with run-time error

runerr(i, x) terminates program execution with error i and offending value x.

Default: x   no offending value

---

seek(f, i) : f   seek to position in file

seek(f, i) seeks to position i in f but fails if the seek cannot be performed. The first byte in the file is at position 1. seek(f, 0) seeks to the end of file f.

Errors: 101   i not integer
               105   f not file

See also: where()

---

seq(i1, i2) : i3, i4, ...   generate sequence of integers

seq(i1, i2) generates an endless sequence of integers starting at i1 with increments of i2.

Defaults: i1   1
               i2   1

Errors: 101   i1 or i2 not integer
               211   i2 = 0

See also: i1 to i2 by i3

---

serial(x) : i   produce serial number

serial(x) produces the serial number of x if it is a type that has one but fails otherwise.

---

set(L) : S   create set

set(L) produces a set whose members are the distinct values in the list L.

Default: L   [ ]

Errors: 108   L not list

---

sin(r1) : r2   compute sine

sin(r1) produces the sine of r1 given in radians.

Error: 102   r1 not real

See also: asin()

---

sort(X, i) : L   sort structure

sort(X, i) produces a list containing values from x. If X is a record, list, or set, sort(X, i) produces the values of X in sorted order. If X is a table, sort(X, i) produces a list obtained by sorting the elements of X, depending on the value of i. For i = 1 or 2, the list elements are two-element lists of key/value pairs. For i = 3 or 4, the list elements are alternative keys and values. Sorting is by keys for i odd, by values for i even.

Default:	i	1

Errors:	101	i not integer
	115	X not list, set, table, or a record
	205	i not 1, 2, 3, or 4

See also: sortf()

---

sortf(X, i) : L   sort structure by field

sortf(X, i) produces a sorted list of the values from the record, list, or set X. List and record values in X are ordered by comparing the values of their ith fields. The value of i can be negative but not zero. Two structure values in X having equal ith fields are ordered as they would be in regular sorting, but structures lacking an ith field appear before structures having them.

Default:	i	1

Errors:	101	i not integer
	125	X not list, set, or a record
	205	i = 0

See also: sort()

---

sqrt(r1) : r2   compute square root

sqrt(r1) produces the square root of r1.

Errors:	102	r1 not real
	205	r1 < 0

See also: N1 ^ N2

---

stop(x1, x2, ..., xn)   stop execution

stop(x1, x2, ..., xn) terminates program execution with an error exit status after writing strings x1, x2, ..., xn. If xi is a file, subsequent output is to xi. Initial output is to standard error output.

Default:	xi	"" (empty string)

Errors:	109	xi not string or file
	213	xi file not open for writing

See also: exit() and write()

---

string(x) : s   convert to string

string(x) produces a string resulting from converting x, but fails if the conversion is not possible.

---

system(s) : i   call system function

system(s) calls the C library function *system* to execute s and produces the resulting integer exit status.

Error: 103   s not string

---

tab(i) : s   set scanning position

tab(i) produces &subject[&pos:i] and assigns i to &pos, but fails if i is out of range. It reverses the assignment to &pos if it is resumed.

Error: 101   i not integer

See also: move()

---

table(x) : T   create table

table(x) produces a table with a default value x.

Default: x   &null

---

tan(r1) : r2   compute tangent

tan(r1) produces the tangent of r1 given in radians.

Errors: 102   r1 not real
               204   r1 a singular point of tangent

See also: atan()

---

trim(s1, c) : s2   trim string

trim(s1, c) produces a string consisting of the characters of s1 up to the trailing characters contained in c.

Default: c   ' ' (blank)

Errors: 103   s1 not string
                 104   c not cset

---

type(x) : s   produce type name

type(x) produces a string corresponding to the type of x.

---

upto(c, s, i1, i2) : i3, i4, ... in   locate characters

upto(c, s, i1, i2) generates the sequence of integer positions in s preceding a character of c in s[i1:i2]. It fails if there is no such position.

Defaults: s   &subject
              i1   &pos if s is defaulted, otherwise 1
              i2   0

Errors: 101   i1 or i2 not integer
              103   s not string
              104   c not cset

See also: bal() and find()

---

variable(s) : v   produce variable

Produces the variable for the identifier or keyword named s, but it fails if there is no such variable. Local identifiers override global identifiers.

Error: 103   s not string

See also: name()

---

where(f) : i   produce position in file

where(f) produces the current byte position in f. The first byte in the file is at position 1.

Error: 105   f not file

See also: seek()

---

write(x1, x2, ..., xn) : xn   write line

write(x1, x2, ..., xn) writes strings x1, x2, ..., xn with a line termination sequence added at the end or when switching files. If xi is a file, subsequent output is to xi. Initial output is to standard output.

Default: xi   "" (empty string)

Errors: 109   xi not string or file
              213   xi file not open for writing

See also: writes()

---

writes(x1, x2, ..., xn) : xn   write string

writes(x1, x2, ..., xn) writes strings x1, x2, ..., xn without a line termination sequence added at the end. If xi is a file, subsequent output is to xi. Initial output is to standard output.

Default: xi   "" (empty string)

Errors: 109   xi not string or file
              213   xi file not open for writing

See also: write()

PREFIX OPERATIONS

In a prefix operation, the operator symbol appears before the argument on which it operates. If evaluation of the argument fails, the operation is not performed. If the argument generates a sequence of results, the operation may be performed several times.

There are comparatively few prefix operations. They are listed in the order of the types of arguments: numeric, cset, string, co-expression, and then those that apply to arguments of several different types.

+N : N   compute positive

+N produces the numeric value of N.

Error: 102   N not integer or real

See also: N1 + N2

–N : N   compute negative

–N produces the negative of N.

Errors: 102   N not integer or real
               203   integer overflow

See also: N1 – N2

~c1 : c2   compute cset complement

~c1 produces the cset complement of c1 with respect to &cset.

Errors: 104   c1 not cset

=s : s   match string in scanning

=s is equivalent to tab(match(s)).

Error: 103   s1 not string

See also: match(), tab(), and N1 = N2

@C : x   activate co-expression

@C produces the outcome of activating C.

Error: 118   C not co–expression

See also: x @ C

---

^C1 : C2   create refreshed co-expression

^C1 produces a refreshed copy of C1.

Errors: 118   C1 not co–expression

See also: N1 ^ N2

∗x : i   compute size

∗x produces the size of x.

Error: 112   x not cset, string, co–expression, or a structure

See also: N1 ∗ N2

?x1 : x2   generate random value

If x1 is an integer, ?x1 produces a number from a pseudorandom sequence. If x1 > 0, it produces an integer in range 1 to x1, inclusive. If x1 = 0, it produces a real number in range 0.0 to 1.0.

If x1 is a string, ?x1 produces a randomly selected one-character substring of x1 that is a variable if x1 is a variable.

If x1 is a list or record, ?x1 produces a randomly selected element, which is a variable, from x1.

If x1 is a set, ?x1 produces a randomly selected member of x1.

If x1 is a table, ?x1 produces the value of a randomly selected element of x1 as a variable.

Errors: 113   x1 not **integer**, **string**, or a structure
               205   x1 < 0

See also: **s** ? *expr*

!x1 : x2, x3, ..., xn   generate values

If x1 is a file, !x1 generates the remaining lines of x1.

If x1 is a string, !x1 generates the one-character substrings of x1, and produces variables if x1 is a variable.

If x1 is a list or record, !x1 generates the elements of x1, which are variables. The order of generation is from the beginning to the end.

If x1 is a set, !x1 generates the members of x1 in no predictable order.

If x1 is a table, !x1 generates the elements of x1 as variables in no predictable order.

Errors: 103   x1 originally **string**, but type changed between resumptions
               116   x1 not **string**, **file**, or a structure
               212   x1 is **file** but not open for reading

/x : x   check for null value

/x produces x if the value of x is the null value, but fails otherwise. It produces a variable if x is a variable.

See also: **N1 / N2**

\x : x   check for non-null value

\x produces x if the value of x is not the null value, but fails otherwise. It produces a variable if x is a variable.

See also: *expr* \ i

.x : x   dereference variable

.x produces the value of x.

See also: R. *f*

INFIX OPERATIONS

In an infix operation, an operator symbol stands between the two arguments on which it operates. If evaluation of an argument fails, the operation is not performed. If an argument generates a sequence of results, the operation may be performed several times.

There are many infix operations. They are listed first by those that perform computations (such as N1 + N2) and then by those that perform comparisons (such as N1 < N2). Assignment operations are listed last. See the index, if necessary.

N1 + N2 : N3   compute sum

N1 + N2 produces the sum of N1 and N2.

Errors: 102   N1 or N2 not integer or real
             203   integer overflow
             204   real overflow or underflow

See also: +N

N1 − N2 : N3   compute difference

N1 − N2 produces the difference of N1 and N2.

Errors: 102   N1 or N2 not integer or real
             203   integer overflow
             204   real overflow or underflow

See also: −N

N1 * N2 : N3

compute product

N1 * N2 produces the product of N1 and N2.

Errors: 102   N1 or N2 not integer or real
             203   integer overflow
             204   real overflow or underflow

See also: *x

N1 / N2 : N3

compute quotient

N1 / N2 produces the quotient of N1 and N2.

Errors: 102   N1 or N2 not integer or real
             201   N2 = 0
             204   real overflow or underflow

See also: /x

N1 % N2 : N3

compute remainder

N1 % N2 produces the remainder of N1 divided by N2. The sign of the result is the sign of N1.

Errors: 102   N1 or N2 not integer or real
             202   N2 = 0
             204   real overflow or underflow

N1 ^ N2 : N3

compute exponential

N1 ^ N2 produces N1 raised to the power N2.

Errors: 102   N1 or N2 not integer or real
             204   real overflow, underflow, or N1 = 0 and N2 <= 0
             206   N1 < 0 and N2 real

See also: ^C, exp(), and sqrt()

---

x1 ++ x2 : x3

compute cset or set union

x1 ++ x2 produces the cset or set union of x1 and x2.

Errors: 120   x1 and x2 not both cset or both set

---

x1 − − x2 : x3   compute cset or set difference

x1 − − x2 produces the cset or set difference of x1 and x2.

Errors: 120   x1 and x2 not both **cset** or both **set**

---

x1 ** x2 : x3   cset or set intersection

x1 ** x2 produces the cset or set intersection of x1 and x2.

Error: 120   x1 and x2 not both **cset** or both **set**

---

s1 || s2 : s3   concatenate strings

s1 || s2 produces a string consisting of s1 followed by s2.

Errors: 103   s1 or s2 not **string**

See also: L1 ||| L2

L1 ||| L2 : L3   concatenate lists

L1 ||| L2 produces a list consisting of the values in L1 followed by the values in L2.

Errors: 108   L1 or L2 not **list**

See also: s1 || s2

R.f : x   get field of record

R.f produces a variable for the f field of record R.

Errors: 107   R not a record type
                 207   R does not have field f

See also: .x

---

x1 @ C : x2   transmit value to co-expression

x1 @ C activates C, transmitting the value of x1 to it; it produces the outcome of activating C.

Error: 118   C not co-expression

See also: @C

---

x1 & x2 : x2   evaluate in conjunction

x1 & x2 produces x2. It produces a variable if x2 is a variable.

N1 > N2 : N2   numerically greater than
N1 >= N2 : N2   numerically greater than or equal
N1 = N2 : N2   numerically equal
N1 <= N2 : N2   numerically less than or equal
N1 < N2 : N2   numerically less than
N1 ~= N2 : N2   numerically not equal

The numerical comparison operators produce N2 if the condition is satisfied, but fail otherwise.

Error: 102   N1 or N2 not integer or real

---

s1 >> s2 : s2   lexically greater than
s1 >>= s2 : s2   lexically greater than or equal
s1== s2 : s2   lexically equal
s1 <<= s2 : s2   lexically less than or equal
s1 << s2 : s2   lexically less than
s1 ~== s2 : s2   lexically not equal

The lexical comparison operators produce s2 if the condition is satisfied, but fail otherwise.

Error: 103   s1 or s2 not string

---

x1 === x2 : x2   value equal
x1 ~=== x2 : x2   value not equal

The value comparison operators produce x2 if the condition is satisfied, but fail otherwise.

---

v := x : v   assign value

v := x assigns the value of x to v and produces the variable v.

Errors:	101	v requires integer, but x not integer
	103	v requires string, but x not string
	111	v not a variable

See also: v *op*:= x, v1 :=: v2, v <− x2, and v1 <−> v2

---

v *op*:= x : v   augmented assignment

v *op*:= x performs the operation v *op* x and assigns the result to v; it produces the variable v. For example, i1 +:= i2 produces the same result as i1 := i1 + i2. There are augmented assignment operators for all infix operations except assignment opera-tions. The error conditions for augmented assignment operations are the same as for the basic operations.

Error:	101	v requires integer, but x not integer
	103	v requires string, but x not string
	111	v not variable

See also: v := x

---

v1 :=: v2 : v1   exchange values

v1 :=: v2 exchanges the values of v1 and v2 and produces the variable v1.

Errors:	101	v1 or v2 requires integer, but other argument not integer
	103	v1 or v2 requires string, but other argument not string
	111	v1 or v2 not a variable

See also: v := x and v1 <−> v2

---

v <− x : v   assign value reversibly

v <− x assigns the value of x to v and produces the variable v. It reverses the assignment if it is resumed.

Errors:	101	v requires integer, but x not integer
	103	v requires string, but x not string
	111	v not a variable

See also: v := x and v1 <−> v2

---

v1 <–> v2 : v1   exchange values reversibly

v1 <–> v2 exchanges the values v1 and v2 and produces the variable v1. It reverses the exchange if it is resumed.

Errors: 101   v1 or v2 requires integer, but other argument not integer
                103   v1 or v2 requires string, but other argument not string
                111   v1 or v2 not a variable

See also: v <– x and v1 :=: v2

OTHER OPERATIONS

The operations on the following pages have varying types of syntax. Some have more than two arguments. If evaluation of an argument fails, the operation is not performed. If an argument generates a sequence of results, the operation may be performed several times.

---

i1 to i2 by i3 : i1, ..., in   generate integers in sequence

i1 to i2 by i3 generates the sequence of integers from i1 to i2 in increments of i3.

Default: i3   1 if by clause is omitted

Errors: 101   i1, i2, or i3 not integer
                211   i3 = 0

See also: seq()

[x1, x2, ..., xn] : L   create list

[x1, x2, ..., xn] produces a list containing the values x1, x2, ..., xn. [ ] produces an empty list.

See also: list()

---

x1[x2] : x3   subscript

If x1 is a string, x1[x2] produces a one-character string consisting of character x2 of x1. x1[x2] produces a variable if x1 is a variable.

If x1 is a list or record, x1[x2] produces element x2 of x1.

If x1 is a table, x1[x2] produces the element corresponding to key x2 of x1.

In all cases, x2 may be nonpositive.

In all cases, the subscripting operation fails if the subscript is out of range.

Errors: 101   x1 is string, list, or a record, but x2 not integer
               114   x1 not string, list, table, or record

See also: x[x1, x2, ..., xn], x[i1:i2], x[i1+i2], and x[i1−:i2]

---

x[x1, x2, ..., xn] : Xn   multiple subscript

x[x1, x2, ..., xn] is equivalent to x[x1, x2, ..., xn].

See also: x[x1]

---

x1[i1:i2] : x2   produce substring or list section

If x1 is a string, x1[i1:i2] produces the substring of x1 between i1 and i2. x1[i1:i2] produces a variable if x1 is a variable.

If x1 is a list, x1[i1:i2] produces a list consisting of the values of x1 in the given range.

In either case, i1 and i2 may be nonpositive.

In either case, the subscripting operation fails if a subscript is out of range.

Errors: 101   i1 or i2 not integer
               114   x1 not string or list

See also: x1[x2], x[i1+:i2], and x[i1−:i2]

---

x1[i1+:i2] : x2   produce substring or list section

If x1 is a string, x1[i1+:i2] produces the substring of x1 between i1 and i1 + i2. x1[i1+:i2] produces a variable if x1 is a variable.

If x1 is a list, x1[i1+:i2] produces a list consisting of the values of x1 in the given range.

In either case, i1 and i2 may be nonpositive.

In either case, the subscripting operation fails if a subscript is out of range.

Errors: 101   i1 or i2 not integer
               114   x1 not string or list

See also: x1[x2], x[i1:i2], and x[i1−:i2]

---

x1[i1–:i2] : x2   produce substring or list section

If x1 is a string, x1[i1–:i2] produces the substring of x1 between i1 and i1 − i2. x1[i1–:i2] produces a variable if x1 is a variable.

If x1 is a list, x1[i1–:i2] produces a list consisting of the values of x1 in the given range.

In either case, i1 and i2 may be nonpositive.

In either case, the subscripting operation fails if a subscript is out of range.

Errors: 101   i1 or i2 not integer
            114   x1 not string or list

See also: x1[x2], x[i1:i2], and x[i1+:i2]

---

x(x1, x2, ..., xn) : xm   process argument list

If x is a function or procedure, x(x1, x2, ..., xn) produces the outcome of calling x with arguments x1, x2, ..., xn.

If x is an integer, x(x1, x2, ..., xn) produces the outcome of xi, but fails if i is out of the range 1, ..., n. In this case, it produces a variable if xi is a variable; i may be nonpositive.

Default: x   −1

Errors: 106   x not procedure or integer
            117   x is main, but there is no main procedure (during startup)

See also: x ! X, x{...}

---

x1 ! X : x2   process argument list

If x1 is a function or procedure, x1 ! X produces the outcome of calling x1 with the arguments in the list or record X. If x1 is an integer, x1 ! X produces X[x1] but fails if x1 is out of range of X.

Errors: 106   x not procedure or integer
            108   X not list or record

See also: x(...)

---

x{x1, x2, ..., xn} : xm   process argument list as co-expressions

x{x1, x2, ..., xn} is equivalent to x([create x1, create x2, ..., create xn]).

Error: 106   x not procedure or integer

See also: x(...)

KEYWORDS

Keywords are listed in alphabetical order.

Some keywords are variables; values may be assigned to these. However, the allowable type depends on the keyword. See the assignment operations for error conditions.

&allocated : i1, i2, i3, i4   cumulative allocation

&allocated generates the total amount of space, in bytes, allocated since the begin-ning of program execution. The first value is the total for all regions, followed by the totals for the static, string, and block regions, respectively. The space allocated in the static region is always given as zero. Note: &allocated gives the cumulative alloca-tion; &storage gives the current allocation; that is, the amount that has not been freed by garbage collection.

&ascii : c   ASCII characters

The value of &ascii is a cset consisting of the 128 ASCII characters.

&clock : s   time of day

The value of &clock is a string consisting of the current time of day, as in "19:21:00".

&collections : i1, i2, i3, i4   garbage collections

&collections generates the total number of garbage collections followed by the numbers caused by allocation in the static, string, and block regions, respectively.

&cset : c   all characters

The value of &cset is a cset consisting of all 256 characters.

&current : C   current co-expression

The value of &current is the currently active co-expression.

&date : s   date

The value of &date is the current date, as in "1996/10/15".

&dateline : s   date and time of day

The value of &dateline is the current date and time of day, as in "Tuesday, October 15, 1996 7:21 p.m.".

&digits : c   digits

The value of &digits is a cset containing the ten digits.

&dump : i   termination dump

If the value of &dump is nonzero when program execution terminates, a dump in the style of display() is provided.

&e : r   base of natural logarithms

The value of &e is the base of the natural logarithms, 2.71828... .

&error : i   control error conversion

If the value of &error is nonzero, a run-time error is converted to expression failure and &error is decremented. &error is zero initially. &error is a variable.

&errornumber : i   number of last error

The value of &errornumber is the number of the last error converted to failure. &errornumber fails if no error has occurred.

&errortext : s   description of last error

The value of &errortext is the error message corresponding to the last error converted to failure. &errortext fails if no error has occurred.

&errorvalue : x   value causing last error

The value of &errorvalue is the value that caused the last error converted to failure. &errorvalue fails if no error has occurred or no specific value caused the error.

&errout : f   standard error output

The value of &errout is the standard error output file.

&fail   failure

&fail produces no result.

&features : s1, s2, ..., sn   implementation features

The value of &features generates strings identifying the features of the executing version of Icon.

&file : s   source file

The value of &file is the name of the file from which the current program line was compiled.

&host : s   host system

The value of &host is a string that identifies the host system on which Icon is running.

&input : f   standard input

The value of &input is the standard input file.

&lcase : c   lowercase letters

The value of &lcase is a cset consisting of the 26 lowercase letters.

&letters : c   letters

The value of &letters is a cset consisting of the 52 upper- and lowercase letters.

&level : i   procedure level

The value of &level is the level of the current procedure call.

&line : i   source line number

The value of &line is the number of the source-program line in which it appears.

&main : C   main co-expression

The value of &main is the co-expression for the main procedure.

&null : n   null value

The value of &null is the null value.

&output : f   standard output

The value of &output is the standard output file.

&phi : r   golden ratio

The value of &phi is the golden ratio, 1.61803... .

&pi : r   ratio of circumference to diameter of a circle

The value of &pi is the ratio of the circumference of a circle to its diameter, 3.14159... .

&pos : i   scanning position

The value of **&pos** is the position of scanning in **&subject**. The scanning position may be changed by assignment to **&pos**. Such an assignment fails if it would be out of range of **&subject**. **&pos** is a variable.

&progname : s   program name

The value of **&progname** is the file name of the executing program. A string value can be assigned to **&progname** to replace its initial value.

&random : i   random seed

The value of **&random** is the seed for the pseudorandom sequence. The seed may be changed by assignment to **&random**. **&random** is zero initially. **&random** is a variable.

&regions : i1, i2, i3   storage regions

&region generates the current sizes of the static, string, and block regions, respec-tively. The size of the static region may not be meaningful.

&source : C   source co-expression

The value of **&source** is the co-expression for the activator of the current co-expression.

&storage : i1, i2, i3   storage utilization

&storage generates the current amount of space used in the static, string, and block regions, respectively. The space used in the static region may not be meaningful.

&subject : s   subject of scanning

The value of **&subject** is the string being scanned. The subject of scanning may be changed by assignment to **&subject**. **&subject** is a variable.

&time : i   elapsed time

The value of &time is the number of milliseconds of CPU time since the beginning of program execution.

&trace : i   procedure tracing

If the value of &trace is nonzero, a trace message is produced when a co-expression is activated or a procedure is called, returns, suspends, or is resumed. &trace is decremented for each message produced. &trace is zero initially. &trace is a variable.

&ucase : c   uppercase letters

The value of &ucase is a cset consisting of the 26 uppercase letters.

&version : s   Icon version

The value of &version is a string identifying the version of Icon.

CONTROL STRUCTURES

The way that arguments of a control structure are evaluated depends on the control structure; in fact, that is what distinguishes a control structure from a function or operation.

Most control structures are identified by reserved words. They are arranged alphabetically on the following pages, with the few control structures that use operator symbols appearing at the end.

---

break *expr* **: x**   break out of loop

break *expr* exits from the enclosing loop and produces the outcome of *expr*.

Default: *expr*   &null

See also: next

---

case *expr* **of { ... } : x**   select according to value

case *expr* of { ... } produces the outcome of the case clause that is selected by the value of *expr*.

create *expr* : **C**   create co-expression

create *expr* produces a co-expression for *expr*.

See also: ^C

---

every *expr1* **do** *expr2*   generate every result

every *expr1* **do** *expr2* evaluates *expr2* for each result generated by *expr1*; it fails when *expr1* does not produce a result. The **do** clause is optional.

---

fail   fail from procedure

fail returns from the current procedure, causing the call to fail.

See also: **return** and **suspend**

---

if *expr1* **then** *expr2* **else** *expr3* : **x**   select according to outcome

if *expr1* **then** *expr2* **else** *expr3* produces the outcome of *expr2* if *expr1* succeeds, otherwise the outcome of *expr3*. The **else** clause is optional.

---

next   go to beginning of loop

next transfers control to the beginning of the enclosing loop.

See also: **break**

---

not *expr* : **n**   invert failure

not *expr* produces the null value if *expr* fails, but fails if *expr* succeeds.

---

repeat *expr*   evaluate repeatedly

repeat *expr* evaluates *expr* repeatedly.

---

return *expr*   return from procedure

return *expr* returns from the current procedure, producing the outcome of *expr*.

Default: *expr*   &null

See also: fail and suspend

---

suspend *expr1* **do** *expr2*   suspend from procedure

suspend *expr1* do *expr2* suspends from the current procedure, producing each result generated by *expr1*. If suspend is resumed, *expr2* is evaluated before resuming *expr1*. The do clause is optional.

Default: *expr1*   &null (only if the do clause is omitted)

See also: fail and return

---

until *expr1* **do** *expr2*   loop until result

until *expr1* do *expr2* evaluates *expr2* each time *expr1* fails; it fails when *expr1* succeeds. The do clause is optional.

See also: while *expr1* do *expr2*

---

while *expr1* **do** *expr2*   loop while result

while *expr1* do *expr2* evaluates *expr2* each time *expr1* succeeds; it fails when *expr1* fails. The do clause is optional.

See also: until *expr1* do *expr2*

---

expr1 | *expr2* : **x1, x2, ...**   evaluate alternatives

expr1 | *expr2* generates the results for *expr1* followed by the results for *expr2*.

See also: |*expr*

|*expr* : **x1, x2, ...**   evaluate repeatedly

|*expr* generates the results for *expr* repeatedly, terminating if *expr* fails.

See also: *expr1* | *expr2*

---

expr \ i : **x1, x2, ..., xi**   limit generator

expr \ i generates at most i results from the outcome for *expr*.

Errors: 101   i not integer
              205   i < 0

See also: \x

---

s ? *expr* : **x**   scan string

s ? *expr* saves the current subject and position and then sets them to the values of **s** and 1, respectively. It then evaluates *expr*. The outcome is the outcome of *expr*. The saved values of the subject and position are restored on exit from *expr*.

Error: 103   **s** not string

See also: ?x

GENERATORS

The following expressions may produce more than one result if the context in which they are evaluated requires it.

bal(c1, c2, c3, s, i1, i2)	&allocated
find(s1, s2, i1, i2)	&collections
function()	&features
key(T)	&regions
seq(i1, i 2)	&storage
upto(c, s, i1, i2)	|*expr*
!x	*expr1* | *expr2*
i1 to i2 by i3	

E

Command-Line Options

The following command-line options are recognized by the Icon compiler, icont:

−c		Stop after producing ucode files and do not delete them.
−e *file*		Redirect standard error output to *file*.
−f s		Enable full string invocation.
−o *name*		Name the output file *name*.
−s		Suppress informative messages. Normally, both informative messages and error messages are sent to standard error output.
−t		Set **&trace** to an initial value of −1.
−u		Issue warning messages for undeclared identifiers.
−v *i*		Set verbosity level of informative messages to *i*.
−E		Direct the results of preprocessing to standard output and inhibit further processing.

See user manuals for information about platform-specific command-line options.

F

Environment Variables

Most operating systems support environment variables. (There are different names for environment variables on different systems, but the facilities generally are the same.)

Since environment variables are used by Icon primarily to set run-time parameters such as storage region sizes, the absence of environment variables usually does not, in itself, directly affect Icon programs. Systems that do not support environment variables usually provide another way of setting run-time parameters.

When an Icon program is executed, several environment variables are exam-ined to determine certain execution parameters. Values in parentheses are the defaults; other values can be set.

BLKSIZE (500000)	The initial size of the allocated block region, in bytes.
COEXPSIZE (2000)	The size, in words, of each co-expression.
IPATH (*undefined*)	The location of ucode files specified in link declarations for the Icon compiler. IPATH is a blank–separated list of directories. The current directory is always searched first, regardless of the value of IPATH.

LPATH (*undefined*)   The location of source files specified in prepro-
                             cessor $include directives. LPATH is otherwise
                             similar to IPATH.

MSTKSIZE (10000)   The size, in words, of the main interpreter
                             stack.

NOERRBUF (*undefined*)   By default, &errout is buffered. If this variable
                             is set, &errout is not buffered.

STRSIZE (500000)   The initial size of the allocated string region, in
                             bytes.

TRACE (*undefined*)   The initial value of &trace. If this variable has
                             a value, it overrides the −t option to icont.

See user manuals for information about platform-specific environment vari-ables.

G

Error Messages

Chapter 16 describes the various kinds of errors that may occur when compiling, linking, and running Icon programs. The corresponding error messages are de-signed to be self-explanatory. They are listed here for reference.

PREPROCESSOR ERRORS

The messages for preprecessor errors are:

$define: "(" after name requires preceding space
$define: missing name
$define: unterminated literal
$ifdef/$ifndef: missing name
$ifdef/$ifndef: too many arguments
$include: invalid file name
$include: too many arguments
$line: invalid file name
$line: no line number $line:
too many arguments
$undef: missing name
$undef: too many arguments
circular include
explicit $error
extraneous arguments on
$else/$endif filename: cannot open
invalid preprocessing directive
unexpected $else

unexpected $endif
unterminated $if
value redefined

SYNTAX ERRORS

There are many possible syntax errors. As mentioned in Chapter 16, the actual source of an error may precede the place where an erroneous construction is detected. The messages for syntax errors are:

end of file expected
global, record, or procedure declaration
expected invalid argument list
invalid by clause
invalid case clause
invalid case control expression
invalid create expression
invalid declaration
invalid default clause
invalid do clause
invalid else clause
invalid every control expression
invalid field name
invalid global declaration
invalid if control expression
invalid initial expression
invalid keyword construction
invalid local declaration
invalid argument
invalid argument for unary operator
invalid argument in alternation invalid
argument in assignment
invalid argument in augmented assignment
invalid repeat expression
invalid section
invalid then clause
invalid to clause
invalid until control expression
invalid   while   control
expression link list expected
missing colon
missing colon or ampersand
missing end
missing field list in record
declaration missing identifier
missing left brace
missing link file name
missing of
missing parameter list in procedure declaration
missing procedure name
missing record name
missing right brace
missing right brace or semicolon

missing right bracket
missing right bracket or ampersand
missing right parenthesis
missing semicolon
missing semicolon or
operator missing then
syntax error

If any of these errors occurs in a program, no ucode files are produced and the program is not linked.

LINKING ERROR

There is one error that can occur during linking:

inconsistent redeclaration

If this error occurs, no icode file is produced.

RUN-TIME ERRORS

Run-time error messages are numbered and divided into categories, depending on the nature of the error.

Category 1: Invalid Type or Form

101 integer expected or out of range
102 numeric expected
103 string expected
104 cset expected
105 file expected
106 procedure or integer expected
107 record expected
108 list expected
109 string or file expected
110 string or list expected
111 variable expected
112 invalid type to size operation
113 invalid type to random operation
114 invalid type to subscript operation
115 structure expected
116 invalid type to element generator
117 missing main procedure
118 co-expression expected
119 set expected
120 two csets or two sets expected
121 function not supported
122 set or table expected
123 invalid type
124 table expected

125 list, record, or set expected
126 list or record expected

Category 2: Invalid Value or Computation

201 division by zero
202 remaindering by zero
203 integer overflow
204 real overflow, underflow, or division by zero
205 invalid value
206 negative first argument to real exponentiation
207 invalid field name
208 second and third arguments to map of unequal length
209 invalid second argument to open
210 non-ascending arguments to detab/entab
211 by value equal to zero
212 attempt to read file not open for reading
213 attempt to write file not open for writing
214 input/output error
215 attempt to refresh &main
216 external function not found

Category 3: Capacity Exceeded

301 evaluation stack overflow
302 memory violation
303 inadequate space for evaluation stack
304 inadequate space in qualifier list
305 inadequate space for static allocation
306 inadequate space in string region
307 inadequate space in block region
308 system stack overflow in co-expression
316 interpreter stack too large
318 co–expression stack too large

Category 4: Feature Not Implemented

401 co–expressions not implemented

Category 5: Programmer-Specified Error

500 program malfunction

H

Platform-Specific Differences

Implementations of Icon are available for many platforms, ranging from personal computers to mainframes. In some cases, Icon is implemented for different operat-ing systems on the same computer, and in some cases there are several different implementations for the same operating system and computer.

All of these implementations are based on a generic implementation devel-oped at The University of Arizona. Consequently, all implementations are the same in most respects, and most programs written on one platform run on other platforms with little or no change.

Different computer architectures and operating systems, however, vary some-what in the environments they provide. This may affect some features of Icon. In addition, the generic implementation of Icon is written in C. Different C compilers themselves differ in the features they support. Some implementations of Icon also contain additional platform-dependent features.

While differences in Icon due to different computer architectures, operating systems, and C compilers are relatively minor and only affect portions of Icon, persons who write Icon programs for use on a variety of platforms should be aware of possible problems.

Icon user manuals for specific platforms of Icon contain information about features that are not supported or that differ from the standard implementation, as well as information about platform-dependent extensions.

The following sections list areas where differences are likely to be encountered.

CHARACTER SETS

Most computers use the ASCII character set. The notable exceptions are IBM 370 mainframes, which use the EBCDIC character set.

Both ASCII and EBCDIC have 256 characters. The difference between the two character sets lies in the correspondence between character codes and glyphs. See Appendix B for a listing of both character sets.

Since Icon operates internally on characters without regard for their associated glyphs, differences in character sets do not affect most programs. For example, although the letter A is assigned to character code 65 in ASCII but to character code 193 in EBCDIC, most operations that use the letter A do not depend on its specific character code.

The places where differences in character sets are most apparent is in sorting and lexical comparison, which are based on character codes. For example, in ASCII the uppercase letters have smaller codes than the lowercase ones, but the converse is true for EBCDIC. Consequently,

```
"A" << "a"
```

succeeds for ASCII implementations of Icon but fails for EBCDIC implementations of Icon. Sorting produces correspondingly different results in ASCII and EBCDIC platforms.

It is worth noting that different implementations of Icon on EBCDIC platforms treat this matter differently. Some map EBCDIC to ASCII on input and vice-versa on output, thus obtaining the ASCII correspondence between character codes and graphics internally.

The cset &ascii presents a different problem. On ASCII implementations of Icon, it consists of characters with codes 0 through 127 — the first half of the entire character set. Different EBCDIC implementations of Icon treat &ascii differently. Some assign the same character codes to it as on ASCII platforms, so that the corresponding graphics are different from those on ASCII platforms. Other EBCDIC implementations assign character codes to &ascii so that the graphics are the same as on ASCII implementations. Similarly, the interpretation of ASCII control charac-ters given in \^ escape sequences in literals varies for EBCDIC implementations.

Since most EBCDIC consoles do not support brackets, the combination $< and $> can be used in place of [and] in program text. Similarly, $(and $) are equivalent to { and } . These multi-character equivalents also are available on ASCII implemen-tations of Icon, allowing programs that use them to run on both ASCII and EBCDIC platforms.

LANGUAGE FEATURES

The following features are not supported on all platforms.

Co-Expressions

Co-expressions require a platform-specific context switch. If co-expressions are not implemented, features related to them are not available, but the rest of Icon is unaffected.

Large-Integer Arithmetic

Large-integer arithmetic may not be supported on platforms with small amounts of memory. If large-integer arithmetic is not supported, integer overflow results in error termination.

Executing Commands

The system() function is supported on most, but not all, implementations of Icon that run in command-line environments. It is not supported (and has no meaning) for platforms that use visual interfaces unless the platform also provides command-line facilities. In any event, the use of system() is highly specific to the platform on which Icon runs.

Pipes

Pipes and the "p" option for the open() function generally are supported only on UNIX platforms. Some other options for open() also are platform-dependent.

Keyboard Functions

The keyboard functions kbhit(), getch(), and getche() are useful on personal-computer platforms where program operation can be controlled by user-typed characters, independently of standard input. Not all platforms support these keyboard functions.

Environment Variables

On platforms on which environment variables do not exist *per se*, the imple-mentation of Icon may provide an equivalent feature that supports getenv(). If environment variables are not supported, getenv() fails.

The syntax for the IPATH and LPATH environment variables depends on the platform.

Dynamic Loading

Dynamic loading requires an operating system facility that is not available on all platforms. If dynamic loading is not supported, loadfunc() is not defined.

Graphics Facilities

Not all platforms support Icon's graphic facilities. For platforms that do, there may be minor differences and a few features that are not supported.

Determining Features

The presence or absence of features of a particular implementation of Icon can be checked during program execution. The keyword &features generates strings listing the features available in an implementation. The first value is the name of the platform for the implementation, and the second value is the character set, followed by specific features. For example,

```
every write(&features)
```

might produce

```
UNIX
ASCII co-
expressions dynamic
loading environment
variables large
integers
pipes
system function
```

Some implementations support additional features.

Supported language features are of particular interest for programs that are to be run on platforms that are different from those on which they are developed. For example, a program that uses co-expressions can check for their presence as follows:

```
if not(&features == "co-expressions") then
    stop("*** co-expressions not supported")
```

Determining Functions

The function function() generates the names of the (built-in) functions.

OTHER ISSUES

Real Numbers

The precision and range of real numbers varies considerably from platform to platform. In addition, the string representation for real numbers may vary.

Changing Directories

Whether the change in directory produced by chdir() persists after program execution depends on the operating system.

Input and Output

As noted in Chapter 11, random-access input and output may behave strangely on text files in translated mode for platforms that use multi-character line termina-tors.

Some platforms support special file names for input and output to devices, such as the console, printer, and auxiliary ports.

Some platforms, notably VAX/VMS and IBM mainframes, use different notions of file naming than are used in examples in this book.

Exit Codes

On most operating systems, the exit code for the normal termination of a program is 0 and the exit code for error termination is 1. Some platforms, however, use other values.

Command-Line Option

The –x option to icont for launching an icode file automatically is not supported on some platforms and may malfunction on other platforms if the amount of available memory is inadequate. Since this option is only a shortcut, the lack of support for –x is only an inconvenience. On most platforms it is easy to provide a script that accomplishes the same thing.

I

Sample Programs

This appendix contains several sample programs that illustrate Icon programming techniques in the context of somewhat larger problems than those given in the body of the book.

These programs were written by several different programmers. Conse-quently, they have somewhat different programming styles and layouts than those used elsewhere in this book. Some programs have been modified slightly for presentation here.

All of these programs can be found in the Icon program library.

COMMAND-LINE OPTIONS

The procedure options() was mentioned in Chapter 15 as being particularly useful for programs that run in command-line environments. The code for this procedure follows.

In the initialization section, notice the use of tests for the null value to provide defaults for omitted arguments.

```
# Author: Robert J. Alexander with additions by Gregg M. Townsend

procedure options(arg, optstring, errproc)
    local f, fList, fileArg, fn, ignore, ptname, opttable, opttype, p, x, option
```

```
# Initialize.
#
/optstring := string(&letters)
/errproc := stop
option := table()
fList := [] opttable
:= table()

# Scan the option specification string.
#
optstring ? {
  while optname := move(1) do
    { if optname == " " then next
      if optname == "–" then
      optname := tab(many(&letters)) | move(1) | break
      opttype := tab(any('!:+.')) | "!"
      opttable[optname] := opttype
      }
  }

# Iterate over program invocation argument words.
#
while x := get(arg) do {
  if /x then ignore := &null   # if end of args from file, stop ignoring
  else x ? {
    if ="–" & not pos(0) & /ignore then {
      if ="–" & pos(0) then ignore := 1        # ignore following args if – –
    else {
      tab(0) ? until pos(0) do {
      if opttype := \opttable[
      optname := ((pos(1), tab(0)) | move(1))] then {
      option[optname] :=
        if any(':+.', opttype) then {
          p := "" ~== tab(0) | get(arg) |
            return errproc("No parameter following –" ||
          optname) case opttype of {
            ":":  p
            "+": integer(p) | return errproc("–" || optname ||
                  " needs numeric parameter")
            ".": real(p) | return errproc("–" || optname ||
                  " needs numeric parameter")
          }
        }
      else 1
      }
    else return errproc("Unrecognized option: –" || optname)
    }
```

```
        }
      }
    #  If the argument begins with the character "@", fetch option
    #  words from lines of a text file.
    #
    else if ="@" & not pos(0) & /ignore then {
      f := open(fn := tab(0)) | return errproc("Can't open " || fn)
      fileArg := []
        while put(fileArg,
        read(f)) close(f)
        push(arg) # push null to signal end of args from file while
        push(arg, pull(fileArg))
        }
      else put(fList, x)
      }

    while push(arg, pull(fList))

    return option

  end
```

STRUCTURE IMAGES

The procedures ximage() and xdump(x), also discussed in Chapter 15, illustrate how values of any type can be handled. These procedure are worth study; they contain many sophisticated programming techniques.

```
    # Author: Robert J. Alexander

    procedure ximage(x, indent, done)
      local i, s, ss, state, t, xtag, tp, sn, sz
      static tr

      # If this is the outer invocation, do some initialization.
      #
      if /(state := done) then {
        tr := &trace ; &trace := 0 # postpone tracing while in here indent
        := ""
        done := table()
        }

      # Determine the type and process accordingly.
      #
      indent := (if indent == "" then "\n" else "") || indent || " "
      ss := ""
```

```
tp := type(x)
s := if xtag := \done[x] then xtag else case tp of {

  # Unstructured types just return their image().
  #
  "null" | "string" | "integer" | "real" | "cset" | "co-expression" |
    "file" | "procedure" | "window": image(x)
  "list": {                          # list
    image(x) ? {
      tab(6)
      sn := tab(find("("))
      sz := tab(0)
      }
    done[x] := xtag := "L" || sn

    # Figure out if there is a predominance of any object in the
    # list. If so, make it the default object.
    #
    t := table(0)

    every t[!x] +:= 1

    s := [, 0]

    every t := !sort(t) do if s[2] < t[2] then s := t

    if s[2] > *x / 3 & s[2] > 2 then
      { s := s[1]
      t := ximage(s, indent || "  ", done)
      if t ? (not any('\"') & ss := tab(find(" :=")))
        then t := "{" || t || indent || " " || ss || "}"
      }
    else s := t := &null

    # Output the non-defaulted elements of the list.
    #
    ss := ""

    every i := 1 to *x do if x[i] ~=== s then {
      ss ||:= indent || xtag || "[" || i || "] := " ||
        ximage(x[i], indent, done)
      }

    s := tp || sz s[-1:-1]
    := ", " || \t xtag || " :=
    " || s || ss
    }
```

```
"set": {                            # set
  image(x) ? {
    tab(5)
    sn := tab(find("("))
    }

  done[x] := xtag := "S" || sn

  every i := !sort(x) do {
    t := ximage(i, indent || "  ", done)
    if t ? (not any('\"") & s := tab(find(" :="))) then
      t := "{" || t || indent || "  " || s || "}"
    ss ||:= indent || "insert(" || xtag || ", " || t || ")"
    }

  xtag || " := " || "set()" || ss
  }
"table": {                          # table
  image(x) ? {
    tab(7)
    sn := tab(find("("))
    }

  done[x] := xtag := "T" || sn

  #  Output the table elements. This is a bit tricky, since
  #  the subscripts might be structured, too.
  #
  every i := !sort(x) do {
    t := ximage(i[1], indent || "  ", done)
    if t ? (not any('\"") & s := tab(find(" :=")))
      then t := "{" || t || indent || " " || s || "}"
    ss ||:= indent || xtag || "[" ||
      t || "] := " || ximage(i[2], indent, done)
    }

  #  Output the table, including its default value (which might
  #  also be structured.
  #
  t := ximage(x[[]], indent || "  ", done)

  if t ? (not any('\"") & s := tab(find(" :="))) then
    t := "{" || t || indent || " " || s || "}"

  xtag || " := " || "table(" || t || ")" || ss
  }
```

```
      default: {                    # record
        image(x) ? {
          move(7)
          t := ""
          while t ||:= tab(find("_")) || move(1)
          t[-1] := ""
          sn := tab(find("("))
          }
        done[x] := xtag := "R_" || t || "_" || sn
        every i := 1 to *x do {
          name(x[i]) ? (tab(find(".")), sn := tab(0))
          ss ||:= indent || xtag || sn || " := " || ximage(\x[i], indent, done)
          }
        xtag || " := " || t || "()" || ss
        }
      }

   # If this is the outer invocation, clean up before returning.
   #
   if /state then {
      &trace := tr                 # restore &trace
      }

   return

s end

# Write ximages of x1, x1, ..., xn.

procedure xdump(x[ ])

   every write(&errout, ximage(!x))

   return x[-1] | &null

end
```

CONCORDANCES

This program produces a simple concordance, a listing of all words in the input and the numbers of the lines in which they appear. Words less than three characters long are ignored. If a word occurs more than once on a line, the number of occurrences is given in parentheses after the line number.

There are two options:

     −l *n*   set maximum line length to *n* (default 72); wraps
     −w *n*   set maximum width for word to *n* (default 15); truncates

Note that the program is organized to make it easy, via item(), to handle other kinds of tabulations.

```
# Author: Ralph E. Griswold

link options

$define ColMax      72
$define MinLength    3
$define NameWidth  15

global uses, colmax, namewidth, lineno

procedure main(args)
  local opts, uselist, name, line, pad, i, j, fill

  opts := options(args, "l+w+")                      # process options
  colmax := \opts["l"] | ColMax
  namewidth := \opts["w"] | NameWidth

  pad := repl(" ", namewidth)
  uses := table()
  lineno := 0

  every tabulate(item(), lineno)                     # tabulate all citations

  uselist := sort(uses, 3)                           # sort by uses

  while fill := left(get(uselist), namewidth) do {
    line := format(get(uselist))                     # line numbers
    while (*line + namewidth) > colmax do {          # handle long lines
      line ?:= {
        i := j := 0
        every i := upto(' ') do {
          if i > (colmax − namewidth) then break
          else j := i
          }
        write(fill, tab(j))
        move(1)
        fill := pad
        tab(0)                                       # new value of line
        }
      }
    if *line > 0 then write(fill, trim(line))
    }
end

# Add to count of line number to citations for name.
#
```

```
procedure tabulate(name, lineno)

  /uses[name] := table(0)
  uses[name][lineno] +:= 1

  return

end

# Format the line numbers, breaking long lines as necessary.
#
procedure format(linenos)
  local i, line

  linenos := sort(linenos,
  3) line := ""

  while line ||:= get(linenos) do
    line ||:= ("(" || (1 < get(linenos)) || ") ") | " "

  return line

end

#  Get an item. Different kinds of concordances can be obtained by
#  modifying this procedure.
#
procedure item()
  local i, word, line

  while line := read() do {
    lineno +:= 1
    write(right(lineno, 6), " ", line)
    line := map(line)                          # fold to lowercase
    i := 1
    line ? {
      while tab(upto(&letters)) do {
        word := tab(many(&letters))
        if *word >= MinLength then             # skip short words
          suspend word
        }
      }
    }

end
```

ANIMAL GAME

This is the familiar "animal game", written in Icon. The program asks its human opponent a series of questions in an attempt to guess the animal about which the human opponent is thinking. It is an "expert system" that starts out with limited knowledge, knowing only one question, but gets smarter as it plays and learns from its opponents. At the conclusion of a session, the program asks permission to remember what it learned for future sessions. The saved file is a text file that can be edited, so typographical errors entered during the heat of battle can be corrected.

The game is not limited to guessing about animals. Simply by modifying the first two lines of the main procedure, the user can create a program that builds a knowledge base in other categories. An example is:

```
GameObject := "president"
Tree := Question("Did he write the Gettysburg address", "Reagan",
  "Lincoln")
```

Typing list at any yes/no prompt shows an inventory of animals known, and there are some other commands too (see the procedure Confirm()).

```
# Author: Robert J. Alexander

global GameObject, Tree, Learn

record Question(question, yes, no)

procedure main()

   GameObject := "animal"
   Tree := Question("Does it live in water", "goldfish", "canary")

   Get()                    # Recall prior knowledge

   Game()                   # Play a game

   return

end

# Game() — Conducts a game.
#
procedure Game()

   while Confirm("Are you thinking of ", Article(GameObject), "
     ", GameObject) do Ask(Tree)

   write("Thanks for a great game.")

   if \Learn &Confirm("Want to save knowledge learned this session")
   then Save()

   return

end
```

```
# Confirm() — Handles yes/no questions and answers.
#
procedure Confirm(q[])
  local answer, s static
  ok

  initial {
    ok := table()
    every ok["y" | "yes" | "yeah" | "uh huh"] := "yes"
    every ok["n" | "no" | "nope" | "uh uh" ] := "no"
    }

  while /answer do {
    every   writes(!q)
    write("?")
    case s := read() | exit(1) of {
      # Commands recognized at a yes/no prompt.
      #
      "save":    Save()
      "get":     Get()
      "list": List() "dump":
      Output(Tree) default: {

        (answer := \ok[map(s, &ucase, &lcase)]) |
          write("This is a \"yes\" or \"no\" question.")
        }
      }
    }

  return answer == "yes"

end

#  Ask() — Navigates through the barrage of questions leading to a
#  guess.
#
procedure Ask(node)
  local guess, question

  case type(node) of
    { "string": {
      if not Confirm("It must be ", Article(node), " ", node, ", right") then
        { Learn := "yes"
        write("What were you thinking of?")
        guess := read() | exit(1)
        write("What question would distinguish ", Article(guess), "
          ", guess, " from ", Article(node), " ", node, "?")
```

```
            question := read() | exit(1)
            if question[-1] == "?" then question[-1] := ""
            question[1] := map(question[1], &lcase, &ucase)
            if Confirm("For ", Article(guess), " ", guess, ",
               what would the answer be")
            then return Question(question, guess, node)
          else return Question(question, node, guess)

          }
       }

       "Question": {
         if Confirm(node.question) then node.yes := Ask(node.yes)
         else node.no := Ask(node.no)
          }
       }

   end

   # Article() — Come up with the appropriate indefinite article.
   #
   procedure Article(word)

      return if any('aeiouAEIOU', word) then "an" else "a"

   end

   # Save() — Store our acquired knowledge in a disk file name
   # based on the GameObject.
   #
   procedure Save()
      local f

      f := open(GameObject || "s", "w")

      Output(Tree, f)

      close(f)

      return

   end

   # Output() — Recursive procedure used to output the knowledge tree.
   #
   procedure Output(node, f, sense)
      static indent

      initial indent := 0

      /f := &output
      /sense := " "

      case type(node) of {
```

```
      "string": write(f, repl(" ", indent), sense, "A: ", node)
      "Question": {
        write(f, repl(" ", indent), sense, "Q: ", node.question)
        indent +:= 1
        Output(node.yes, f, "y")
        Output(node.no, f, "n")
        indent -:= 1
        }
      }

  return

end

# Get() — Read in a knowledge base from a file.
#
procedure Get()
  local f

  f := open(GameObject || "s", "r") | fail

  Tree := Input(f)

  close(f)

  return

end

# Input() — Recursive procedure used to input the knowledge tree.
#
procedure Input(f)
  local nodetype, s

  read(f) ? (tab(upto(~' \t')) & =("y" | "n" | "") &
        nodetype := move(1) & move(2) & s := tab(0))

  return if nodetype == "Q" then Question(s, Input(f), Input(f)) else s

end

# List() — Lists the objects in the knowledge base.
#

$define Length        78

procedure List()
  local lst, line, item

  lst := Show(Tree, [
  ]) line := ""

  every item := !sort(lst) do {
    if *line + *item > Length then {
```

```
            write(trim(line))
            line := ""
            }
         line ||:= item || ", "
         }
      write(line[1:-2])

   return

end

#
# Show() — Recursive procedure used to navigate the knowledge tree.
#
procedure Show(node, lst)

   if type(node) == "Question" then {
     lst := Show(node.yes, lst)
     lst := Show(node.no, lst)
     }
   else put(lst, node)

   return lst

end
```

RANDOMLY GENERATED SENTENCES

This program generates randomly selected strings ("sentences") from a grammar specified by the user. Grammars are basically context-free and resemble BNF in form, although there are a number of extensions.

The program works interactively, allowing the user to build, test, modify, and save grammars. Input to the program consists of various kinds of specifications, which can be intermixed. The two main kinds of specifications are:

- Productions that define nonterminal symbols in a syntax similar to the rewrit-ing rules of BNF, with alternatives being represented by the concatenation of nonterminal and terminal symbols.

- Generation specifications that cause the generation of a specified number of sentences from the language defined by a given nonterminal symbol.

An example of a grammar is:

```
<rule1>::=<qual> <noun> <tverb> <object>;
<rule2>::=<noun> <iverb>, <clause> ...
<rule3>::=<qual> <noun> <iverb>.
<poem>::=<rule1><nl><rule2><nl><rule3><nl><nl> <noun>::=he|she|the
shadowy figure|the boy|a child|a ghost|a black cat
```

```
<tverb>::=outlines|stares at|captures|damns|destroys|raises|throws
<iverb>::=alights|hesitates|turns away|kneels|stares|hurries
<clause>::=and <iverb>|but <iverb>|and <iverb>|while <ger> <adj>
<adj>::=silently|darkly|with fear|expectantly|fearfully|quietly|hauntingly
<ger>::=waiting|pointing|breathing|reclining|disappearing
<object>::=<article> <onoun>
<article>::=a|the
<onoun>::=sky|void|abyss|star|darkness|lake|moon|cloud|sun|mountain
<qual>::=while|as|momentarily|frozen,
```

A generation specification consists of a nonterminal symbol followed by a nonnegative integer. For example, <poem>4 specifies the generation of four <poem>s.

Typical output is:

```
as the boy throws a darkness;
a child turns away, but hesitates ...
momentarily the shadowy figure alights.

as the shadowy figure outlines the
darkness; a child returns, but hurries ...
momentarily she stares.

frozen, the boy captures a star;
a black cat kneels, and alights ...
as the boy hesitates.

momentarily a ghost destroys the sun;
the boy turns away, but stares ...
as a child alights.
```

The program has many other features as shown in the listing that follows.

```
# Author: Ralph E. Griswold

link options
link random

global defs, ifile, in, limit, prompt, tswitch

record nonterm(name)
record charset(chars)

$define Limit        1000

procedure main(args)
   local line, plist, s, opts

   # procedures to try on input lines
   #
```

```
    plist := [define, generate, grammar, source, comment, prompter, error]

    defs := table()                           # table of definitions
    defs["lb"] := [["<"]]                      # built-in definitions
    defs["rb"] := [[">"]]
    defs["vb"] := [["|"]]
    defs["nl"] := [["\n"]]
    defs[""] := [[""]]
    defs["&lcase"] := [[charset(&lcase)]]
    defs["&ucase"] := [[charset(&ucase)]]
    defs["&digit"] := [[charset(&digits)]]

    opts := options(args,
    "tl+s+r") limit := \opts["l"] |
    Limit tswitch := \opts["t"]
    &random := \opts["s"]
    if /opts["s"] & /opts["r"] then randomize()

    ifile := [&input]                          # stack of input files
    prompt := ""

    while in := pop(ifile) do {                # process all files
      repeat {
        if *prompt ~= 0 then writes(prompt)
        line := read(in) | break
        while line[-1] == "\\" do line := line[1:-1] || read(in) |
        break (!plist)(line)
        }
      close(in)
      }
end

# Process alternatives.
#
procedure alts(defn)
  local alist

  alist := []

  defn ? while put(alist, syms(tab(upto('|') | 0))) do move(1) | break

  return alist

end

# Look for comment.
#
procedure comment(line)

  if line[1] == "#" then return else fail

end
```

```
# Look for definition.
#
procedure define(line)

   return line ? defs[(="<", tab(find(">::=")))] := (move(4), alts(tab(0)))

end

# Define nonterminal.
#
procedure defnon(sym)
  local chars, name
  if sym ?
    { ="""" &
    chars := cset(tab(-1))
    & =""""
    }
  then return charset(chars) else return nonterm(sym)

end

# Note erroneous input line.
#
procedure error(line)

   write("*** erroneous line: ", line)

   return

end

# Generate sentences.
#
procedure gener(goal)
  local pending, symbol

  pending := [nonterm(goal)]

  while symbol := get(pending) do {
    if \tswitch then write(&errout, symimage(symbol),
    listimage(pending)) case type(symbol) of {
      "string": writes(symbol) "charset":
      writes(?symbol.chars) "nonterm": {

        pending := ?\defs[symbol.name] ||| pending | {
          write(&errout, "*** undefined nonterminal: <",
            symbol.name,
          ">") break
```

```
                     }
                 if *pending > \limit then {
                     write(&errout, "*** excessive symbols
                     remaining") break
                     }
                 }
             }
         }

     write()

 end

 # Look for generation specification.
 #
 procedure generate(line)
   local goal, count

     if line ? {
         ="<" &
         goal := tab(upto('>')) \ 1
         & move(1) &
         count := (pos(0) & 1) | integer(tab(0))
         }
     then {
         every 1 to count do
             gener(goal)
         return
         }

     else fail

 end

 # Get right hand side of production.
 #
 procedure getrhs(a)
   local rhs

     rhs := ""

     every rhs ||:= listimage(!a) || "|"

     return rhs[1:-1]

 end

 # Look for request to write out grammar.
 #
 procedure grammar(line)
   local file, out, name

     if line ? {
```

```
        name := tab(find("–>"))
        & move(2) &
        file := tab(0) &
        out := if *file = 0 then &output else {
          open(file, "w") | {
            write(&errout, "*** cannot open ", file)
            fail
            }
          }
        }
     then {
        (*name = 0) | (name[1] == "<" & name[–1] == ">") |
        fail pwrite(name, out)
        if *file ~= 0 then
        close(out) return
        }
   else fail

end

# Produce image of list of grammar symbols.
#
procedure listimage(a)
   local s, x

   s := ""

   every x := !a do
     s ||:= symimage(x)

   return s

end

# Look for new prompt symbol.
#
procedure prompter(line)

   if line[1] == "=" then
     {    prompt      :=
     line[2:0] return
     }

end

# Write out grammar.
#
procedure pwrite(name, ofile)
   local nt, a
   static builtin
```

```
         initial builtin := ["lb", "rb", "vb", "nl", "", "&lcase", "&ucase", "&digit"]

      if *name = 0 then {
        a := sort(defs, 3)
        while nt := get(a) do {
          if nt == !builtin then {
            get(a)
            next
            }
          write(ofile, "<", nt, ">::=", getrhs(get(a)))
          }
        }
      else write(ofile, name, "::=", getrhs(\defs[name[2:-1]]))
        | write("*** undefined nonterminal: ", name)

   end

   # Look for file with input.
   #
   procedure source(line)
      local file, new

      return line ? { if
        ="@" then {
          new := open(file := tab(0)) | {
            write(&errout, "*** cannot open ", file)
            fail
            }
          push(ifile, in)
          & in := new
          return
          }
        }

   end

   # Produce string image of grammar symbol.
   #
   procedure symimage(x)

      return case type(x) of
        { "string": x
        "nonterm": "<" || x.name || ">"
        "charset": "<'" || x.chars || "'>"
        }

   end

   # Process the symbols in an alternative.
   #
   procedure syms(alt)
```

```
          local slist static
          nonbrack
          initial nonbrack := ~'<'

          slist := []

          alt ? while put(slist, tab(many(nonbrack))) |
             defnon(2(="<", tab(upto('>')), move(1))))

          return slist

       end
```

N QUEENS

This program displays all the solutions for *n* non-attacking queens on an *n×n* chessboard. It is a generalization of the techniques described in Chapter 17.

The solutions are written showing the positions of the queens on the chess-board. The following solution for 8 queens is typical:

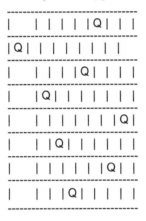

```
# Author: Steven B. Wampler

link options

global n, solution

$define Queens        8

procedure main(args)
   local i, opts

   opts := options(args, "n+")
   n := \opts["n"] | Queens
   if n <= 0 then stop("-n needs a positive numeric parameter")

   solution := list(n)              # list of column solutions
```

```
      write(n, "–Queens:")
      every q(1)  # start by placing queen in first column
   end

   # Place a queen in column c.
   #
   procedure q(c)
     local r
     static up, down, rows

     initial {
        up := list(2 * n – 1, 0)
        down := list(2 * n – 1,
        0) rows := list(n, 0)
        }

      every 0 = rows[r := 1 to n] = up[n + r – c] = down[r + c – 1]
        & rows[r] <– up[n + r – c] <– down[r + c – 1] <– 1 do {
          solution[c] := r              # record placement
          if c = n then show()
          else q(c + 1)                 # try to place next queen
          }
   end


   # Show the solution on a chess board.
   #
   procedure show()
     static count, line, border

     initial {
        count := 0
        line := repl("| ", n) || "|" border :=
        repl("– – – –", n) || "–"

        }

      write("solution: ", count +:= 1)
      write(" ", border)

      every line[4 * (!solution – 1) + 3] <– "Q" do
        { write(" ", line)
        write(" ", border)
        }

      write()
   end
```

N QUEENS DISPLAYED GRAPHICALLY

This version of the *n*-queens program displays the solutions in a window. The display is animated so that the queens "move" from solution to solution.

This program uses graphics features that are not described in Chapter 12, but it should be clear what is being done.

An example from the display for 8 queens is shown below. Compare it to the textual version shown in the preceding section.

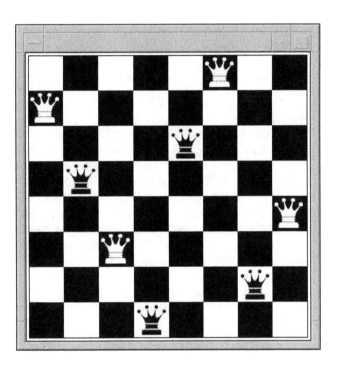

```
#  Author: Ralph E. Griswold, based on a program by
#  Stephen B. Wampler

link options
link wopen

global solution
global black_queen, white_queen

$define Edge        4
$define Offset      40
$define Queens      8
$define Size        44
```

```
global queens

procedure main(args)
  local i, opts, wsize, bqueen, wqueen

  opts := options(args, "n+")
  queens := \opts["n"] | Queens
  if queens <= 0 then stop("-n needs a positive numeric parameter")

  wsize := queens * Size + 2 * Offset

  WOpen("size=" || wsize || ", " || wsize, "label=" || queens
    || "-queens") | stop("*** cannot open window")
  black_queen := WOpen("canvas=hidden", "size=41, 41")
    | stop("*** cannot open window for black queen")
  white_queen := WOpen("canvas=hidden", "size=41, 41")
    | stop("*** cannot open window for white queen")

  DrawImage(black_queen, 0, 0,
    "41, c1, _
    66666666666666666666666666666666666666666_
    66666666666666666666666666666666666666666_
    66666666666666666666666666666666666666666_
    66666666666666400366666666630046666666666_
    66666666666665000046666664000056666666666_
    66666666666664000036666663000046666666666_
    66666666666666000056666665000066666666666_
    66666666666665224666666664225666666666666_
    66663346666666446666666644666666666433666_
    66620004666666631666666661366666664000266_
    66600002666666640666666666046666666662000066_
    66600003666666650466666664056666666663000066_
    66640026666666660166666610666666666200466_
    66666651666666660046666400666666661566666_
    66666662266666660026666200666666622666666_
    66666666036666660004663000666666306666666_
    66666666403666664000022000466663046666666_
    66666666620266620000000000266620266666666_
    66666666650002100000000000012000566666666_
    66666666663000000000000000000003666666666_
    66666666666000000000000000000006666666666_
    66666666666300000000000000000036666666666_
    66666666666500000000000000000056666666666_
    66666666666100000000000000000166666666666_
    66666666666300000000000000000366666666666_
    66666666666522222222222222256666666666_
    66666666666644444444444444466666666666_
    66666666666640000000000000000046666666666_
    66666666666651000000000000001566666666666_
```

```
           6666666666666400000000000000004666666666666_
           6666666666666510000000000000001566666666666_
           6666666666666400000000000000000466666666666_
           6666666666666644444444444444444666666666666_
           6666666665322222222222222222223566666666666_
           6666666660000000000000000000000066666666666_
           6666666640000000000000000000000046666666_
           6666666630000000000000000000000036666666_
           6666666630000000000000000000000036666666_
           6666666630000000000000000000000036666666_
           6666666630000000000000000000000036666666_
           6666666666666666666666666666666666666666"
           )

DrawImage(white_queen, 0, 0,
    "41, c1, _
    00000000000000000000000000000000000000000000_
    00000000000000000000000000000000000000000000_
    00000000000026630000000036620000000000000_
    00000000000016666200000026666100000000000_
    00000000000026666300000036666200000000000_
    00000000000066661000000166660000000000000_
    00000000000014420000000024410000000000000_
    00033200000000220000000022000000002330000_
    00466620000000350000000053000000026664000_
    00666640000000260000000062000000046666000_
    00666630000000162000000261000000036666000_
    00266400000000065000000560000000004662000_
    00000150000000006620002660000000051000000_
    00000044000000006640004660000000440000000_
    00000006300000006662003666000000036000000_
    00000002630000266664466662000036200000000_
    00000000464000466666666664000464000000000_
    00000000166645666666666665466610000000000_
    00000000036666666666666666666630000000000_
    00000000006666666666666666666600000000000_
    00000000003666666666666666666630000000000_
    00000000001666666666666666661000000000000_
    00000000000566666666666666650000000000000_
    00000000000366666666666666630000000000000_
    00000000000144444444444444410000000000000_
    00000000000022222222222222220000000000000_
    00000000000026666666666666662000000000000_
    00000000000015666666666666651000000000000_
    00000000000026666666666666662000000000000_
    00000000000015666666666666651000000000000_
    00000000000026666666666666662000000000000_
```

```
                00000000000002222222222222220000000000000_
                00000000134444444444444444444431000000000_
                00000000666666666666666666666666000000000_
                00000002666666666666666666666666200000000_
                00000003666666666666666666666666300000000_
                00000003666666666666666666666666300000000_
                00000003666666666666666666666666300000000_
                00000003666666666666666666666666300000000_
                00000000000000000000000000000000000000000_
                0000000000000000000000000000000000000000"
              )

        DrawBoard()

        solution := list(queens)              # list of column solutions

        every q(1)                            # start with queen in first column

        until WQuit()                         # wait for user to dismiss

   end

   # Place a queen in column c.
   #
   procedure q(c)
     local r
     static up, down, rows

     initial {
       up := list(2 * queens – 1, 0)
       down := list(2 * queens – 1,
       0) rows := list(queens, 0)
       }

     every 0 = rows[r := 1 to queens] = up[queens + r – c]
       = down[r + c – 1] & rows[r] <– up[queens + r – c] <–
         down[r + c – 1] <– 1 do {
           solution[c] := r                   # record placement
           if c = queens then show()
     else q(c + 1)                            # try to place next queen
         }
   end

   # Show the solution on a chess board.
   #
   procedure show()
     local i, j, queen

     every i := 1 to *solution do
       { j := solution[i]
```

```
            queen := if (i + j) % 2 = 0 then black_queen else white_queen
            CopyArea(queen, &window, , , , , Offset + (i – 1) * Size + 1,
               Offset + (j – 1) * Size + 1)
            }

         WDelay(500)                         # pause to avoid blurred motion

         while *Pending() > 0 do
            { case Event() of {
               "q": exit()
               "p": until Event() === "c"
               }
            }

         every i := 1 to *solution do
            { j := solution[i]
            if (i + j) % 2 = 1 then Fg("black") else Fg("white")
            FillRectangle(Offset + (i – 1) * Size, Offset + (j – 1) * Size,
               Size, Size)
            }

      return

   end

   procedure
      DrawBoard() local i, j

      every i := 0 to queens – 1 do
         every j := 0 to queens – 1 do
            if (i + j) % 2 = 1 then
               FillRectangle(Offset + i * Size, Offset + j *
                  Size, Size, Size)

      DrawRectangle(Offset – 1, Offset – 1, queens * Size +
         1, queens * Size + 1)

      DrawRectangle(Offset – Edge – 1, Offset – Edge – 1,
         queens * Size + 2 * Edge + 1, queens * Size + 2 * Edge + 1)

      return

   end
```

J

Icon Resources

Icon evolved through a series of versions. The current version is 9, which presently is available for the Acorn Archimedes, the Amiga, Macintosh/MPW, Microsoft Windows, MS-DOS, many UNIX platforms, VAX/VMS, and Windows NT. There also are earlier versions for several other platforms. Icon's graphics facilities presently are supported for Microsoft Windows, UNIX, VAX/VMS, and Windows NT. All implementations of Icon are in the public domain.

Documentation on Icon is extensive. In addition to this book, there is a book on the implementation of Icon (Griswold and Griswold, 1986), and one on graphics programming (Griswold, Jeffery, and Townsend, forthcoming). There are two newsletters (Griswold, Griswold, and Townsend, 1978- and 1990-), many technical reports, and user manuals for various platforms.

Implementations of Icon, the Icon program library, documentation, and other materials are available via the Internet. On the World Wide Web, the Icon home page is located at

http://www.cs.arizona.edu/icon/

From there, there are links to general information about Icon, reference material, the current status of Icon, the Icon program library, documentation, technical support, and so on.

The address for anonymous FTP is

ftp.cs.arizona.edu

From there, cd /icon and get README.

The newsgroup comp.lang.icon handles news related to Icon. There also is a mailing list connected to the newsgroup via a gateway. To subscribe, send mail to

icon-group-request@cs.arizona.edu

Information about Icon also is available from

Icon Project
Department of Computer Science
The University of Arizona
P.O. Box 210077
Tucson, Arizona   85721-0077
U.S.A.

voice: (520) 621-6613 fax:
(520) 621-4246

e-mail: icon-project@cs.arizona.edu

Glossary

Documentation about Icon uses some terms in a technical way. This glossary explains such terms. Icon terminology developed over time, and some terms have been used differently in different documents. What follows reflects current usage.

This glossary assumes familiarity with computer terminology.

activation: evaluation of a co-expression.

allocation: the process of providing space in memory for values created during program execution. See also garbage collection.

alternation: a control structure that generates the results of its first operand followed by the results of its second operand. See also disjunction.

argument: an expression that provides a value for a function or procedure call; sometimes used to mean operand.

argument list: a list of expressions that provide values for parameters in a procedure call.

assignment: association of a value with a variable.

associativity: the order in which like operators are evaluated in the absence of parentheses. Associativity can be left-to-right, in which case the first (left-most) operator is evaluated first or right-to-left, in which case the last (right-most) operator is evaluated first.

attribute: in the context of graphics, a value that affects the window, drawing, and text written to the window.

augmented assignment: assignment combined with a binary operation. The binary operation is performed on the value of the left-operand variable and the value of the right operand, and then the result is assigned to the left-operand variable.

backtracking: control backtracking or data backtracking; usually used as a syn-onym for the former.

binary operator: an operator with two operands. See also infix operator.

bounded expression: an expression that is limited to at most one result because of the syntactic context in which it appears. See also limitation.

built-in: a feature that is part of the Icon programming language, as opposed to a feature written in Icon.

call: see invocation.

case expression: a control structure in which the expression to evaluate is selected by a value.

co-expression: an expression coupled with an environment for its execution. If the expression is a generator, its results can be obtained one at a time by activation.

character: the elementary unit from which strings and csets are composed. Charac-ters are used to represent letters, digits, punctuation marks, and so forth. Characters are represented internally by small nonnegative integers (typically 8 bits). Some characters have associated glyphs. Icon has no character data type.

coercion: implicit type conversion.

collating sequence: the sorting order for strings imposed by the internal represen-tation of characters.

command-line argument: a string given after the program name when Icon is invoked from a command line. Command-line arguments are passed to the main procedure as a list of strings in its first argument.

comparison operation: a binary operation that compares two values according to a specified criterion. A comparison operation succeeds and returns the value of its right operand if the criterion is satisfied. Otherwise it fails. See also numerical comparison, lexical comparison, and value comparison.

compilation: the process of converting Icon source code to code for a virtual machine. The result of compiling a source code file is a pair of ucode files for the virtual machine.

conditional code: source code that is included or not included in a program as the result of preprocessing.

conditional compilation: the inclusion or exclusion of source code as the result of conditional directives.

conditional directive: a preprocessor directive that includes or excludes source code depending on whether or not a preprocessor symbol is defined.

conjunction: a binary operation that evaluates its operands but performs no computation on them; used to test if two expressions both succeed. Conjunction has the effect of logical *and*. See also: mutual evaluation and disjunction.

control backtracking: returning control to previously evaluated but suspended generators. Control backtracking is the underlying mechanism for accomplish-ing goal-directed evaluation.

control character: a character that has special interpretation in an input/output context. Examples are backspace and newline.

control structure: an expression whose evaluation may alter the otherwise sequen-tial order of evaluation of expressions.

conversion: see type conversion.

cset: an unordered collection of characters.

cursor: the position in string scanning.

data backtracking: restoring previous values to variables during control backtrack-ing. Data backtracking occurs only for a few specific operations.

data structure: a collection of values. Different kinds of data structures are orga-nized and accessed in different ways. Icon structures are records, lists, sets, and tables.

data type: a designation that identifies values that share common properties and operations. Icon has 12 data types: co-expression, cset, file, integer, list, null, procedure, real, set, string, table, and window. In addition, each record decla-ration defines a data type. The term data type often is shortened to type.

declaration: a component of a program that specifies its properties and structure. There are seven kinds of declarations: global, invocable, link, local, procedure, record, and static.

default case clause: a component of a case expression that contains an expression that is evaluated if no other expression is selected in a case expression. A default case clause is indicated by the reserved word default.

default value: a value that is provided in place of an omitted or null-valued argument of a function.

default table value: a value specified when a table is created to serve as the value corresponding to keys that are not in the table.

define directive: a preprocessor directive that associates a preprocessor symbol with some text so that the text is substituted for subsequent uses of the symbol in the program.

deque: a "double-ended queue" that allows both addition and removal at each end. Icon lists are deques.

dereferencing: producing the value of a variable. Dereferencing is done automati-cally when the value of a variable is needed in a computation. Dereferencing also can be done explicitly using the dereferencing operator.

dialog: in the context of graphics, a temporary window that provides information and in which the user can enter text, make a choice, and so on.

directive: a preprocessor command.

disjunction: logical *or*; used to describe the effect of alternation. See also conjunc-tion.

dump: see termination dump.

element: a value in a record, list, or set; or a key/value pair in a table.

environment variable: a named attribute of the system environment under which a program runs. Environment variables can be used to specify the size of Icon's memory regions, the locations of libraries, and so forth.

error: a condition or situation that is invalid. Errors may occur during compilation, linking, or execution. An error in compilation prevents linking. An error in linking prevents the production of an icode file. An error that occurs during execution is called a run-time error. See also error conversion.

error conversion: changing run-time errors to expression failure rather than pro-gram termination. This is accomplished by setting the keyword &error.

error directive: a preprocessor directive that forces an error in compilation.

escape sequence: a sequence of characters in a string or cset literal that encodes a single character. Escape sequences usually are used for characters that cannot be given literally.

evaluation: execution of an expression to produce its outcome.

event: in the context of graphics, a user action such as a mouse click or typed character that a program can detect.

execution: the process of running an Icon program resulting from compilation and linking.

expression: a component of a program that performs a computation. See also statement.

failure: the lack of a result; expression evaluation that does not produce a result. Failure is the opposite of success. Failure is not an error.

field: an element of a record.

file: stored data, usually on magnetic media such as disk; also an Icon data type that references such a file.

first-class data type: a data type whose values can be used without restriction: passed as arguments to procedures, assigned to variables, and returned by procedures. All data types in Icon are first class.

floating point: an approximate representation of real numbers in computer hard-ware.

font: the size and general appearance of text written in a window.

function: a built-in procedure.

garbage collection: the process of reclaiming space in memory that has been allocated but is no longer needed. Garbage collection occurs automatically when insufficient space remains for allocation. Garbage collection can be forced by calling collect().

generation: the production of more than one result in sequence.

generator: an expression that is capable of producing more than one result.

generic procedure: a procedure that accepts arguments of any type and/or returns a value of any type.

GIF: a format used for storing image data in a file.

global declaration: a scope declaration that makes a variable accessible throughout an entire program.

global variable: a variable whose value is accessible throughout the entire program and from the beginning of execution to the end.

glyph: a graphic symbol such as a letter, digit, or punctuation mark.

goal-directed evaluation: the attempt to produce a successful outcome by resuming suspended generators to get alternative values when an expression otherwise would fail. Goal-directed evaluation is implicit in expression evaluation. See also iteration and control backtracking.

graphics: drawing, text, and images in a window.

heterogeneous structure: a structure whose elements have different types.

homogeneous structure: a structure all of whose elements have the same type.

icode: the result of linking ucode files to produce executable code for the Icon virtual machine. Icode files are in a binary format that depends to some extent on the architecture of a specific computer.

identifier: a string of characters that names a variable.

image: see string image.

implicit conversion: type conversion that occurs automatically as needed; also called coercion.

include directive: a preprocessor directive that copies a file into a program.

include file: a file that is copied into a program as a consequence of an include directive.

infix operator: an operator that appears between operands. See also binary opera-tor.

initial clause: an optional component of a procedure that contains expressions to be evaluated only on the first invocation of the procedure.

integer: a whole number, such as 137, 0, and –15; a data type.

invocable declaration: a declaration that specifies procedures that are to be in-cluded when a program is linked, even if there is no explicit reference to them in the program. Such procedures may be called using string invocation.

invocation: the evaluation of a procedure or function. Invocation and call are sometimes used synonymously.

iteration: production of all the results of a generator. Iteration can be accomplished by a control structure or by conjunction with an expression that always fails. See also goal-directed evaluation.

key: a value used to identify an entry in a table.

keyword: An ampersand (&) followed by a string of letters that has a special meaning. Some keywords are variables. Contrast with reserved word.

lexical comparison: comparison of strings "alphabetically" according to the nu-merical values used to represent characters. Also called string comparison. See also collating sequence.

lexical scoping: A method of scoping that depends on the text of a program rather than on the program state during execution. Icon uses lexical scoping.

library module: a file consisting of one or more procedures or other declarations that have been compiled into ucode so that they may be incorporated in a program by linking.

limitation: restricting the number of times a generator is resumed. Limitation can be specified by a control structure or occur because of the syntactic context in which the generator appears. See also bounded expression.

line directive: a preprocessor directive that sets the source-program line number and file name for diagnostic purposes.

line terminator: a character or pair of characters that is used by convention to mark the end of a line of text in a file. In UNIX, the line terminator is a linefeed character; on the Macintosh, it is the return character; in DOS, it is a linefeed character followed by a return character. Other platforms generally use one of these conventions. See also: newline character.

link declaration: a declaration that causes a library module to be included in a program during linking.

linker: the program that converts ucode to icode. Linking may combine ucode files from several compilations to produce a single icode file.

linking: the process of converting one or more pairs of ucode files into an icode file suitable for execution.

list: a data structure that consists of a sequence of values called elements. Lists can be accessed by position (subscripted) and as stacks and queues. Positional accesses produce variables.

literal: a sequence of characters in a source program that directly represents a value, such as the integer 1 and the string "hello".

local variable: a variable that is accessible only to the procedure in which it is declared and during a single invocation of the procedure. Local variables are created when a procedure is invoked and are destroyed when a procedure returns or fails, but not when a procedure suspends. See also: global variable and static variable.

matching function: a function that returns a portion of the subject in string scanning. The term sometimes is extended to include matching procedures.

member: a value in a set; also called element.

memory: the space in which a program and the objects it creates are stored. Memory is implemented in RAM. Also called storage.

memory region: a portion of memory used for storing Icon values. There are separate memory regions for strings and for other objects. Also called storage region.

mixed-mode arithmetic: arithmetic performed on a combination of integers and real numbers. The result is a real number.

module: see library module.

mutual evaluation: an expression consisting of an argument list but with no function or procedure. A mutual evaluation expression succeeds only if all the expressions in the argument list succeed. The result of a specific argument can be selected by an integer preceding the argument list.

newline character: the single character used to represent a line terminator in Icon regardless of the actual representation used in the underlying system.

null value: the single value of the null type. Icon identifiers have the null value initially.

object: in the most general sense, any value. More specifically, a value that is represented by a pointer to memory. These are strings, csets, real numbers, large integers, co-expressions, files, procedures, windows, and data structures. Some-times the term object is used for just data structures.

operand: an expression that provides a value for an operation. See also argument.

operation: an expression that is part of the built-in computational repertoire of Icon and cast in the form of an operator and operands. Sometimes used in a broader sense to include function and procedure calls to distinguish expressions that perform computation from control structures.

operator: a symbol consisting of one or more characters that designates an opera-tion.

outcome: a result or failure as a consequence of evaluating an expression.

palette: a specification of a list of colors that can be used for drawing an image in a window.

parameter: an identifier in a procedure declaration that specifies a variable to which a value is passed when the procedure is called. Parameters are local variables.

passing arguments: the assignment of argument values in a procedure call to the parameters of the procedure.

path: a specification for the location of a file. Paths are used for locating library modules and include files.

pointer semantics: the representation of structures by references to their locations in memory, allowing multiple variables to refer to the same structure.

polymorphous operation: an operation that applies to more than one data type. The size operation, $*X$, is an example.

precedence: the order in which unlike binary operators in an unparenthesized expression are evaluated. The operator with the highest precedence is evaluated first.

predefined symbol: a preprocessor name for which there is a built-in definition. See also define directive.

prefix operator: an operator that stands before its operand. All prefix operators in Icon are unary operators.

preprocessing: a step prior to compilation in which directives can be used to define constants, include files, and include or exclude code conditionally.

preprocessor symbol: a name associated with some replacement text in the prepro-cessor. Preprocessor symbols may be predefined or defined by define direc-tives.

procedure: a computational unit whose definition is cast in the form of an identifier, which names the procedure, followed by a list of parameters to be used in the computation. The term procedure includes both built-in procedures (also called functions) and declared procedures, but sometimes it is used in the more restricted sense of the latter.

procedure return: irrevocably leaving the invocation of a procedure. When a procedure returns, it may produce a result or it may fail.

programmer-defined control structure: a control structure that is implemented by a procedure whose arguments are co-expressions and whose call has braces instead of parentheses around the argument list. Also called programmer-defined control operation.

program state: a global condition that affects an aspect of program execution. For example, tracing is a global state.

queue: a sequence of values in which values are added at one end and removed from the other. Icon lists can be used as queues. Queue access is called first-in, first-out (FIFO). See also: stacks and deques.

radix literal: an integer literal that is expressed as a value given to a specified base (radix).

range specification: a specification for consecutive characters in a string or values in a list.

real: a data type that approximates real numbers. Reals are represented in floating point format.

record: a data structure consisting of a fixed number of values that are referenced by field names. The fields of a record are variables.

record constructor: a function that creates an instance of a record. A record constructor is provided automatically for every record declaration.

record declaration: a declaration that defines a record.

reference: a value that identifies a structure. There may be several references to the same structure.

reserved word: a string of letters that has syntactic meaning and cannot be used as an identifier. Contrast with keyword.

result: a value or a variable produced by evaluating an expression. See also outcome.

result sequence: the sequence of results that a generator is *capable* of producing. This is an abstract concept used for characterizing generators, not a program con-struct.

return: see procedure return.

run-time: the time during program execution.

run-time error: an error that occurs during program execution. Run-time errors cause program termination unless error conversion is enabled.

resumption: continuing the evaluation of a suspended generator. See also suspen-sion.

run-time system: a collection of routines used during program execution.

scanning: see string scanning.

scope: the extent in time and location in which a variable is accessible. There are three kinds of scope: global, local, and static.

section: a list formed from consecutive values in another list. A section is a list separate from the list from which it is derived.

serial number: a number that uniquely identifies a structure or window. Each type of structure has its own sequence of serial numbers that starts with 1 for the first structure of that type and increases by one for each newly created structure of that type. Each record type has its own sequence of serial numbers.

set: a data structure consisting of distinct values upon which set operations can be performed. A value in a set is called a member and sometimes by the more general term element.

stack: a sequence of values in which values are added and removed at only one end. Icon lists can be used as stacks. Stack access is called last-in, first-out (LIFO). See also: queues and deques.

standard input: the file from which information is read by default. &input is the standard input file.

standard error output: the file to which error messages and tracing information is written by default. &errout is the standard error output file.

standard output: the file to which information is written by default. &output is the standard output file.

statement: a component of a program that determines how computations are done but performs no computation of its own. Icon has no statements. See also expression.

static declaration: a scope declaration that makes a variable accessible to all invocations of the procedure in which the declaration appears but nowhere else.

static variable: a variable with static scope.

storage: see memory.

string image: a string that describes a value.

string: a sequence of characters. Strings in Icon are values in their own right, not arrays of characters.

string invocation: the invocation of a function, procedure, or operator by its string name.

string name: a string that identifies a function, procedure, or operator. The string name for a function or procedure is just the name by which it is used. The string name for an operator resembles the symbols that designate the operator.

string scanning: high-level string analysis using the concepts of a subject string and movement of a cursor position in it.

structure: see data structure.

subject: the string on which string scanning operates.

subscript: a value used as an index to select an element of a structure or a substring of a string. Tables can be subscripted by a value of any type; all other subscripts are integers.

substring: a string within a string.

success: evaluation of an expression that produces a result; the opposite of failure.

suspension: interruption of the evaluation of a generator when a result is produced. See also resumption.

syntax error: a grammatical error in a program. Syntax errors are detected during compilation.

table: a data structure composed of key/value pairs, in which keys are distinct. Tables can be subscripted by keys to assign or access corresponding values. Table subscripting produces variables.

table lookup: referencing a table by a key to produce the corresponding value. If the table does not contain the key, the default table value is produced.

termination: the end of execution.

termination dump: a listing of information upon program termination.

thrashing: a situation in which garbage collection occurs frequently because the amount of available memory is small.

traceback: a listing of procedure calls leading to the evaluation of the current expression. A traceback is provided when a program terminates with a run-time error, or in any event if termination dumping is enabled.

tracing: diagnostic information about procedure calls and co-expression activation that is written to standard error output. Tracing is a program state enabled when the value of &trace is nonzero.

transmission: passing a value to a co-expression when it is activated.

translated mode: a mode of input/output in which line terminators in files are automatically translated into newlines on reading and newlines are automati-cally translated to line terminators on writing. See also untranslated mode.

type: see data type.

type conversion: converting a value from one data type to another. Type conversion occurs automatically when a value is not of the expected data type; this is called implicit type conversion or coercion. Type conversion can be performed explic-itly by using type-conversion functions. If implicit type conversion cannot be done, a run-time error occurs. If explicit type conversion cannot be done, the type-conversion function fails.

ucode: the result of compiling Icon source code into code for Icon's virtual machine. Ucode files are readable text.

unary operator: an operator with one operand. See also prefix operator.

undefine directive: a preprocessor directive that removes a preprocessor definition. See also define directive.

untranslated mode: a mode of input/output in which line terminators in files are not automatically translated on reading and writing. See also translated mode.

value comparison: the comparison of values of any type.

variable: a reference to a value and to which assignment can be made. There are several kinds of variables, including identifiers, elements of records, lists and tables, subscripted string-valued variables, and some keywords. See also dereferencing.

virtual machine: a computer that exists in concept only and is used as a basis for an implementation that is not specific to any real computer.

visual interface: a mechanism whereby a program and a user can communicate through a window.

window: a rectangular area of the screen in which drawing can be done and in which user events can be accepted; also an Icon data type.

References

American National Standards Institute. 1986. *American National Standard Code for Information Interchange, ANSI X3.4-1986.*

Berk, Toby; Brownston, Lee; and Kaufman, Arie. A New Color-Naming System for Graphics Languages. *IEEE Computer Graphics and Applications.* May, 1982, 37-44.

Bird, R. S. Tabulation Techniques for Recursive Programs, *Computing Surveys,* December, 1980, 403-417.

The Bright Forest Company. *The ProIcon Programming Language for Apple Macintosh Computers.* 1989. Tucson, Arizona.

Dahl, O.-J., Dijkstra, E. W., and Hoare, C.A.R. 1972. *Structured Programming.* New York: Academic Press.

Gimpel, James F. 1976. *Algorithms in SNOBOL4.* New York: John Wiley & Sons.

Griswold, Ralph E. *Version 9 of the Icon Compiler.* 1996. Technical Report IPD237. Tucson, Arizona: Department of Computer Science, The University of Arizona.

Griswold, Ralph E. and Griswold, Madge T. 1986. *The Implementation of the Icon Programming Language*, Princeton, New Jersey: Princeton University Press.

Griswold, Ralph E.; Griswold, Madge T.; and Townsend, Gregg M. eds. 1978-. *The Icon Newsletter*. Tucson, Arizona: Department of Computer Science, The Univer-sity of Arizona and The Bright Forest Company.

Griswold, Ralph E.; Griswold, Madge T.; and Townsend, Gregg M. eds. 1990-. *The Icon Analyst*. Tucson, Arizona: Department of Computer Science, The Univer-sity of Arizona and The Bright Forest Company.

Griswold, Ralph E.; Griswold, Madge T.; and Townsend, Gregg M. eds. June, 1996. *The Icon Analyst*. Tucson, Arizona: Department of Computer Science, The University of Arizona and The Bright Forest Company.

Griswold, Ralph E.; Jeffery, Clinton L.; and Townsend, Gregg M. 1996. Version *9.3 of the Icon Programming Language.* Technical Report IPD278. Tucson, Arizona: Department of Computer Science, The University of Arizona.

Griswold, Ralph E.; Jeffery, Clinton L.; and Townsend, Gregg M. *Graphics Programming in Icon.* Forthcoming.

Griswold, Ralph E. and Townsend, Gregg M. 1995. *Calling C Functions from Version 9 of Icon.* Technical Report IPD240. Tucson, Arizona: Department of Computer Science, The University of Arizona.

Griswold, Ralph E. and Townsend, Gregg M. 1996. *The Icon Program Library, Version 9.3.* Technical Report IPD279. Tucson, Arizona: Department of Computer Science, The University of Arizona.

Hofstadter, Douglas R. 1979. *Gödel, Escher, Bach: An Eternal Golden Braid.* New York: Basic Books.

International Standards Organization. 1987. *ISO Standard 8859-1: Information Processing — 8-Bit single-Byte Coded Graphic Character Sets — Part 1: Latin alphabet No. 1.*

Knuth, Donald E. 1968. *The Art of Computer Programming, Volume I.* Reading, Massachusetts: Addison-Wesley Publishing Company, Inc.

Manna, Zohar. 1974. *Mathematical Theory of Computation.* New York: McGraw-Hill Book Company.

Marlin, Christopher D. 1980. *Coroutines: A Programming Methodology, a Language Design, and an Implementation*, New York: Springer-Verlag.

Microsoft Corporation. 1991. *MS-DOS User's Guide and Reference*. p. 631.

Murray, James D. and vanRyper, William. 1994. *Encyclopedia of Graphics File Formats*. Sebastopol, California: O'Reilly Associates.

Ralston, Anthony and Reilly, Edwin D. eds. 1993. *Encyclopedia of Computer Science, Third Edition*. New York: Van Nostrand Reinhold. p. 489-490.

Townsend, Gregg M. and Cameron, Mary. 1996. VIB: A Visual Interface Builder for Icon; Version 3. Technical Report IPD265. Tucson, Arizona: Department of Computer Science, The University of Arizona.

Walker, Kenneth. *The Implementation of An Optimizing Compiler for Icon*. Doctoral Dissertation. 1991. Tucson, Arizona: Department of Computer Science, The University of Arizona.

Index

www.ingramcontent.com/pod-product-compliance
Lightning Source LLC
LaVergne TN
LVHW060134070326
832902LV00018B/2786